Mindfulness

MW00794913

W0006522

HBR Emotional Intelligence Series

How to be human at work

The HBR Emotional Intelligence Series features smart, essential reading on the human side of professional life from the pages of *Harvard Business Review*.

Empathy

Happiness

Mindfulness

Resilience

Other books on emotional intelligence from *Harvard Business Review*:

HBR's 10 Must Reads on Emotional Intelligence

HBR Guide to Emotional Intelligence

Mindfulness

HBR EMOTIONAL INTELLIGENCE SERIES

Harvard Business Review Press

Boston, Massachusetts

Copyright 2017
Harvard Business School Publishing Corporation
All rights reserved
Printed in the United States of America

10 9 8

The web addresses referenced in this book were live and correct at the time of the book's publication but may be subject to change.

Library of Congress Cataloging-in-Publication Data

Title: Mindfulness.
Other titles: HBR emotional intelligence series.
Description: Boston, Massachusetts : Harvard Business Review Press, [2017] | Series: HBR emotional intelligence series
Identifiers: LCCN 2016056277 | ISBN 9781633693197 (pbk. : alk. paper)
Subjects: LCSH: Mindfulness (Psychology) | Mindfulness-based cognitive therapy.
Classification: LCC BF637.M56 M56 2017 | DDC 152.4—dc23 LC record available at https://lccn.loc.gov/2016056277

ISBN: 978-1-63369-319-7
eISBN: 978-1-63369-320-3

The paper used in this publication meets the requirements of the American National Standard for Permanence of Paper for Publications and Documents in Libraries and Archives Z39.48-1992.

Contents

Contents

Mindfulness

HBR EMOTIONAL INTELLIGENCE SERIES

1

Mindfulness in the Age of Complexity

An interview with Ellen Langer by Alison Beard

Over nearly four decades, Ellen Langer's research on mindfulness has greatly influenced thinking across a range of fields, from behavioral economics to positive psychology. It reveals that by paying attention to what's going on around us, instead of operating on autopilot, we can reduce stress, unlock creativity, and boost performance. Her "counterclockwise" experiments, for example, demonstrated that elderly men could improve their health by simply acting as if it were 20 years earlier. In this interview with senior editor Alison Beard, Langer applies her thinking to leadership and management in an age of increasing chaos.

HBR: *Let's start with the basics. What, exactly, is mindfulness? How do you define it?*

Langer: Mindfulness is the process of actively noticing new things. When you do that, it puts you in the present. It makes you more sensitive to context and perspective. It's the essence of engagement. And it's energy-begetting, not energy-consuming. The mistake most people make is to assume it's stressful and exhausting—all this thinking. But what's stressful is all the mindless negative evaluations we make and the worry that we'll find problems and not be able to solve them.

We all seek stability. We want to hold things still, thinking that if we do, we can control them. But since everything is always changing, that doesn't work. Actually, it causes you to lose control.

Take work processes. When people say, "This is the way to do it," that's not true. There are always many ways, and the way you choose should depend on the current context. You can't solve to-day's problems with yesterday's solutions. So when someone says, "Learn this so it's second nature," let a bell go off in your head, because that means mindlessness. The rules you were given were the rules that worked for the person who created them, and the more different you are from that person, the worse they're going to work for you. When you're mindful, rules, routines, and goals guide you; they don't govern you.

What are some of the specific benefits of being more mindful, according to your research?

Better performance, for one. We did a study with symphony musicians, who, it turns out, are bored to death. They're playing the same pieces over and over again, and yet it's a high-status job that they can't easily walk away from. So we had groups of them perform. Some were told to replicate a previous performance they'd liked—that is, to play pretty mindlessly. Others were told to make their individual performance new in subtle ways—to play mindfully. Remember: This wasn't jazz, so the changes were very subtle indeed. But when we played recordings of the symphonies for people who knew nothing about the study, they overwhelmingly preferred the mindfully played pieces. So here we had a group performance where everybody was doing their own thing, and it was better. There's this view that if you let everyone do their own thing, chaos will reign. When people are doing their own thing in a rebellious way, yes, it might. But if everyone is working in the same context and is fully present, there's no reason why you shouldn't get a superior coordinated performance.

There are many other advantages to mindfulness. It's easier to pay attention. You remember more of what you've done. You're more creative. You're able to take advantage of opportunities when they present themselves. You avert the danger not yet arisen. You like people better, and people like you better, because you're less evaluative. You're more charismatic.

The idea of procrastination and regret can go away, because if you know why you're doing something, you don't take yourself to task for not doing something else. If you're fully present when you decide to prioritize this task or work at this firm or create this product or pursue this strategy, why would you regret it?

I've been studying this for nearly 40 years, and for almost any measure, we find that mindfulness generates a more positive result. That makes sense when you realize it's a superordinate variable. No matter what you're doing—eating a sandwich, doing an interview, working on some gizmo, writing a report—you're doing it mindfully or mindlessly. When it's the former, it leaves an imprint on what you do. At the very highest levels of any field—

Fortune 50 CEOs, the most impressive artists and musicians, the top athletes, the best teachers and mechanics—you'll find mindful people, because that's the only way to get there.

How have you shown a link between mindfulness and innovation?

With Gabriel Hammond, a graduate student, I ran a study where we asked participants to come up with new uses for products that had failed. We primed one group for mindlessness by telling them how the product had fallen short of its original intended use—to cite a famous example from 3M, a failed glue. We primed the other for mindfulness by simply describing the product's properties— a substance that adheres for only a short amount of time. Of course, the most creative ideas for new uses came from the second group.

I'm an artist as well as a researcher, writer, and consultant—each activity informs the others for me—and I got the idea to study mindfulness and mistakes when I was painting. I looked up and saw I was using ocher when I'd meant to use magenta, so I started trying to fix it. But then I realized I'd made the decision to use magenta only seconds before. People do this all the time. You start with uncertainty, you make a decision, and if you make a mistake, it's a calamity. But the path you were following was just a decision. You can change it at any time, and maybe an alternative will turn out better. When you're mindful, mistakes become friends.

How does being mindful make someone more charismatic?

We've shown this in a few studies. An early one was with magazine salespeople: The mindful ones sold more and were rated as more likable by buyers. More recently, we've looked at the bind that women executives face: If they act in strong, stereotypically masculine ways, they're seen as bitchy, but if they act feminine, they're seen as weak and not leadership material. So we asked two groups of women to give persuasive speeches. One group was told to act masculine, the other to act feminine. Then half of each group was instructed to give their speech mindfully, and we found that audiences preferred the mindful speakers, regardless of what gender role they were playing out.

And mindfulness also makes you less judgmental about others?

Yes. We all have a tendency to mindlessly pigeonhole people: He's rigid. She's impulsive. But when you freeze someone in that way, you don't get the chance to enjoy a relationship with them or use their talents. Mindfulness helps you to appreciate why people behave the way they do. It makes sense to them at the time, or else they wouldn't do it.

We did a study in which we asked people to rate their own character traits—the things they would most like to change and the things they most valued about themselves—and we found a big irony. The traits that people valued tended to be positive versions of the ones they wanted to change. So the reason I personally can't stop being impulsive is that I value being spontaneous. That means if you want to change my behavior, you'll have to persuade me not to like spontaneity. But chances are that when you see me from this proper perspective— spontaneous rather than impulsive—you won't want to change me.

Mindful management

What else can managers do to be more mindful?

One tactic is to imagine that your thoughts are totally transparent. If they were, you wouldn't think awful things about other people. You'd find a way to understand their perspective.

And when you're upset about something—maybe someone turned in an assignment late or didn't do it the way you wanted—ask yourself, "Is it a tragedy or an inconvenience?" It's probably the latter. Most of the things that get us upset are.

I also tell people to think about work/life *integration*, not balance. "Balance" suggests that the two are opposite and have nothing in common. But that's not true. They're both mostly about people. There are stresses in both. There are schedules to be met. If you keep them separate, you don't learn to transfer what you do successfully in one domain to the other. When we're mindful, we realize that categories are person constructed and don't limit us.

Remember, too, that stress is not a function of events; it's a function of the view you take of events. You think a particular thing is going to happen and that when it does, it's going to be awful. But prediction is an illusion. We can't know what's going to happen. So give yourself five reasons you won't lose the job. Then think of five reasons why, if you did, it would be an advantage—new opportunities, more time with family, et cetera. Now you've gone from thinking it's definitely going to happen to thinking maybe it will and even if it does, you'll be OK.

If you feel overwhelmed by your responsibilities, use the same approach. Question the belief that you're the only one who can do it, that there's only one way to do it, and that the company will collapse if you don't do it. When you open your views to be mindful, the stress just dissipates.

Mindfulness helps you realize that there are no positive or negative outcomes. There's A, B, C, D, and more, each with its challenges and opportunities.

Give me some scenarios, and I'll explain how mindfulness helps.

I'm the leader of a team in dissent. People are arguing vehemently for different strategies, and I have to decide on one.

There's an old story about two people coming before a judge. One guy tells his side of the story, and the judge says, "That's right." The other guy tells his side of the story, and the judge says, "That's right." They say, "We can't both be right." And the judge says, "That's right." We have this mindless notion to settle disputes with a choice between this way or that way, or a compromise. But win-win solutions can almost always be sought. Instead of letting people lock into their positions, go back and open it up. Have opponents play the debate from the other side so that they realize there are good arguments either way. Then find a way for both of them to be right.

I'm an executive with lots of commitments who's facing a personal crisis.

If I couldn't do this interview because I was having a problem at home, I would say, "Alison, I hope you'll forgive me, but my mind is elsewhere right now because I'm having this crisis." And you might say, "Oh, no, I had a crisis last week. It's OK. I understand." And then, when the crisis was over, we could come back to what we were doing, but with a whole new relationship, which would set us up for all sorts of good things in the future.

I'm a boss giving a review to an underperforming employee.

Make clear that the evaluation is *your* perspective, not a universal one, which opens up the dialogue. Let's say a student or a worker adds one and one and gets one. The teacher or employer can just say "Wrong," or he can try to figure out how the person got to one. Then the worker says, "If you add one wad of chewing gum to another wad, one plus one equals one." Now the boss has learned something.

As a leader, you can walk around as if you're God and get everybody to quiver. But then you're not going to learn anything, because they're not going to tell you, and you're going to be lonely and unhappy. It doesn't have to be lonely at the top. You can be there and be open.

How do you create a more mindful organization?

When I'm doing consulting work with companies, I usually start by showing everyone how mindless they are and what they're missing as a result. You can be mindless only if two conditions are met: You've found the very best way of doing things, and nothing changes. Of course, those conditions can't be met. So if you're going to work, you should be there and notice things. Then I explain that there are alternative ways of getting anywhere, and in fact, you can't even be sure that the destination you've chosen is ultimately where you'll want to be. Everything looks different from different perspectives.

I tell leaders they should make not knowing OK—I don't know, you don't know, nobody knows—rather than acting like they know, so everyone else pretends *they* know, which leads to all sorts of discomfort and anxiety. Eliminate zero-accident policies. If you have a zero-accident policy, you're going to have a maximum-lying policy. Get people to ask, "Why? What are the benefits of doing it this way versus another way?" When you do that, everyone relaxes a little, and you're all better able to see and take advantage of opportunities.

I was working with a nursing home years ago, and a nurse walked in, complaining that one of the residents didn't want to go to the dining room. She wanted to stay in her room and eat peanut butter. So I butted in and said, "What's wrong with that?" Her answer was "What if everybody wants to do it?" And I said, "Well, if everybody did it, you'd save a lot of money on food. But, more seriously, it would tell you something about how the food is being prepared or served. If it's only one person occasionally, what's the big deal? If it happens all the time, there's an opportunity here."

I imagine you don't like checklists?

The first time you go through a checklist, it's fine. But after that, most people tend to do it mindlessly. So in aviation you have flaps up, throttle open, anti-ice off. But if snow is coming and the anti-ice is off, the plane crashes.

Checklists aren't bad if they require qualitative information to be obtained in that moment. For example, "Please note the weather conditions. Based on these conditions, should the anti-ice be on or off?" or "How is the patient's skin color different from yesterday?" If you ask questions that encourage mindfulness, you bring people into the present and you're more likely to avoid an accident.

Mindful, qualitative comments help in interpersonal relationships, too, by the way. If you're giving a compliment, "You look great" is not nearly as effective as something like "Your eyes are sparkling today." To say that, you have to be there, and people will recognize and appreciate it.

Mindfulness and focus

The business environment has changed a lot since you began studying mindfulness. It's more complex and uncertain. We have new data and analysis coming at us all the time. So mindfulness becomes more important for navigating the chaos—but the chaos makes it a lot harder to be mindful.

I think chaos is a perception. People say that there's too much information, and I would say that there's no more information now than there was before. The difference is that people believe they have to know it—that the more information they have, the better the product is going to be and the more money the company is going to make. I don't think it depends as much on the amount of information someone has as on the way it's taken in. And that needs to be mindfully.

How has technology changed our ability to be mindful? Is it a help or a hindrance?

Again, one can bring mindfulness to anything. We've studied multitasking and found that if you're open and keep the boundaries loose, it can be an advantage. The information from one thing can help you with another. I think what we should do is learn from the way technology is fun and compelling and build that into our work.

HBR recently published an article on the importance of focus in which the author, Daniel Goleman, talks about the need for both exploration and exploitation. How do you balance mindfulness—constantly

*looking for the new—with the ability to buckle down
and get things done?*

Vigilance, or very focused attention, is probably
mindless. If I'm racing through the woods on
horseback, watching the branches so that I don't
get hit in the face, I might miss the boulder on the
ground, so then my horse stumbles and I'm thrown
off. But I don't think that's what Dan means
by focus. What you want is a soft openness—to
be attentive to the things you're doing but not
single-minded, because then you're missing other
opportunities.

*We hear the management community talking more
about mindfulness now. When did you realize that
the ideas you've been studying for decades had become mainstream?*

I was at a party, and two different people came up
to me and said, "Your mindfulness is everywhere."

Of course, I just saw a new film that starts with someone going around Harvard Square asking people what mindfulness is, and nobody knows. So there's still a lot of work to do.

What are you working on next?

The Langer Mindfulness Institute works in three arenas: health, aging, and the workplace. In health we want to see just how far we can push the mind-body notion. Years ago we did studies on chambermaids (who lost weight after being told their work was exercise) and vision (where people did better on eye tests that had them work up from large letters at the bottom to small ones at the top, creating the expectation that they would be able to read them). Now we're trying a mindfulness cure on many diseases that people think are uncontrollable to see if we can at least ameliorate the symptoms. We're also doing counterclockwise retreats around the world, starting in San Miguel de Allende, Mexico, using research-proven techniques to help people live boldly. And we're doing conferences and consulting on work/life integration, mindful leadership and strategy processes, stress reduction, and innovation, with companies such as Thorlo and Santander and NGOs such as CARE and Vermont's Energy Action Network.

I'm told that I drive my students crazy because I'm always coming up with new ideas. I'm thinking about maybe a mindfulness camp for children. One exercise might be to take a group of 20 kids and keep dividing them into subsets—male/female, younger/older, dark hair/light hair, wearing black/not wearing black—until they realize that everyone is unique. As I've said for 30 years, the best way to decrease prejudice is to increase discrimination. We would also play games and midway through mix up the teams. Or maybe we'd give each child a chance to rewrite the rules of the game, so it becomes clear that performance is only a reflection of one's ability under certain circumstances.

You know, if they allowed three serves in tennis, I would be a much better player.

What's the one thing about mindfulness you'd like every executive to remember?

It's going to sound corny, but I believe it fully: Life consists only of moments, nothing more than that. So if you make the moment matter, it all matters. You can be mindful, you can be mindless. You can win, you can lose. The worst case is to be mindless and lose. So when you're doing anything, be mindful, notice new things, make it meaningful to you, and you'll prosper.

ELLEN LANGER, PHD, is a professor of psychology at Harvard University and founder of the Langer Mindfulness Institute. **ALISON BEARD** is a senior editor at *Harvard Business Review*.

Reprinted from *Harvard Business Review*, March 2014 (product #R1403D).

2

Mindfulness Can Literally Change Your Brain

By Christina Congleton, Britta K. Hölzel,
and Sara W. Lazar

The business world is abuzz with mindfulness. But perhaps you haven't heard that the hype is backed by hard science. Recent research provides strong evidence that practicing nonjudgmental, present-moment awareness (aka mindfulness) changes the brain, and it does so in ways that anyone working in today's complex business environment—and certainly every leader—should know about.[1]

We contributed to this research in 2011 with a study on participants who completed an eight-week mindfulness program.[2] We observed significant increases in the density of their gray matter. In the years since, neuroscience laboratories from around the world have also investigated ways in which meditation, one key way to practice mindfulness, changes the brain. This year, a team of scientists from the University of British Columbia and the Chemnitz University of Technology were able to pool data from more than 20 studies to determine which areas of the brain are consistently affected.[3] They identified at least eight different regions. Here we will focus on two that we believe to be of particular interest to business professionals.

The first is the anterior cingulate cortex (ACC), a structure located deep inside the forehead, behind the brain's frontal lobe. The ACC is associated with self-regulation, meaning the ability to purposefully direct attention and behavior, suppress inappropriate knee-jerk responses, and switch strategies flexibly.[4] People with damage to the ACC show impulsivity and unchecked aggression, and those with impaired connections between this and other brain regions perform poorly on tests of mental flexibility:

They hold onto ineffective problem-solving strategies rather than adapting their behavior.[5] Meditators, on the other hand, demonstrate superior performance on tests of self-regulation, resisting distractions and making correct answers more often than non-meditators.[6] They also show more activity in the ACC than nonmeditators.[7] In addition to self-regulation, the ACC is associated with learning from past experience to support optimal decision making.[8] Scientists point out that the ACC may be particularly important in the face of uncertain and fast-changing conditions.

The second brain region we want to highlight is the hippocampus, a region that showed increased amounts of gray matter in the brains of our 2011 mindfulness program participants. This seahorse-shaped area is buried inside the temple on each side of the brain and is part of the limbic system, a set of inner structures associated with emotion and memory. It is covered in receptors for the stress hormone cortisol, and studies have shown that it can be damaged by chronic stress, contributing to a harmful spiral in the body.[9] Indeed, people with stress-related disorders like depression and PTSD tend to have a smaller hippocampus.[10] All of this points to the importance of this brain area in resilience—another key skill in the current high-demand business world.

These findings are just the beginning of the story. Neuroscientists have also shown that practicing mindfulness affects brain areas related to perception, body awareness, pain tolerance, emotion regulation, introspection, complex thinking, and sense of self. While more research is needed to document these changes over time and to understand underlying mechanisms, the converging evidence is compelling.

Mindfulness should no longer be considered a "nice to have" for executives. It's a "must have": a way to keep our brains healthy, to support self-regulation and effective decision-making capabilities, and to protect ourselves from toxic stress. It can be integrated into one's religious or spiritual life or practiced as a form of secular mental training. When we take a seat, take a breath, and commit to being mindful—particularly when we gather with others who are doing the same—we have the potential to be changed.

CHRISTINA CONGLETON is a leadership and change consultant at Axon Leadership and has researched stress and the brain at Massachusetts General Hospital and the University of Denver. She holds a master's in human development and psychology from Harvard University. BRITTA K. HÖLZEL conducts MRI research to investigate the neural mechanisms of mindfulness practice. Previously a research fellow at Massachusetts General Hospital and Harvard Medical School, she currently works at the Technical University Munich. She holds a doctorate in psychology from Giessen University in Germany. SARA W. LAZAR is an associate researcher in the psychiatry department at Massachusetts General Hospital and an assistant professor in psychology at Harvard Medical School. The focus of her research is to elucidate the neural mechanisms underlying the beneficial effects of yoga and meditation, both in clinical settings and in healthy individuals.

Notes

1. S. N. Banhoo, "How Meditation May Change the Brain," *New York Times*, January 28, 2011.

2. B. K. Hölzel et al., "Mindfulness Practice Leads to Increases in Regional Brain Gray Matter Density," *Psychiatry Research* 191, no. 1 (January 30, 2011): 36–43.

3. K. C. Fox et al., "Is Meditation Associated with Altered Brain Structure? A Systematic Review and Meta-Analysis of Morphometric Neuroimaging in Meditation Practitioners," *Neuroscience and Biobehavioral Reviews* 43 (June 2014): 48–73.

4. M. Posner et al., "The Anterior Cingulate Gyrus and the Mechanism of Self-Regulation," *Cognitive, Affective, & Behavioral Neuroscience* 7, no. 4 (December 2007): 391–395.

5. O. Devinsky et al., "Contributions of Anterior Cingulate Cortex to Behavior," *Brain* 118, part 1 (February 1995): 279–306; and A. M. Hogan et al., "Impact of Frontal White Matter Lesions on Performance Monitoring: ERP Evidence for Cortical Disconnection," *Brain* 129, part 8 (August 2006): 2177–2188.

6. P. A. van den Hurk et al., "Greater Efficiency in Attentional Processing Related to Mindfulness Meditation," *Quarterly Journal of Experimental Psychology* 63, no. 6 (June 2010): 1168–1180.

7. B. K. Hölzel et al., "Differential Engagement of Anterior Cingulate and Adjacent Medial Frontal Cortex in Adept Meditators and Non-meditators," *Neuroscience Letters* 421, no. 1 (June 21): 16–21.

8. S. W. Kennerley et al., "Optimal Decision Making and the Anterior Cingulate Cortex," *Nature Neuroscience* 9 (June 18, 2006): 940–947.

9. B. S. McEwen and P. J. Gianaros. "Stress- and Allostasis-Induced Brain Plasticity," *Annual Review of Medicine* 62 (February 2011): 431–445.
10. Y. I. Sheline, "Neuroimaging Studies of Mood Disorder Effects on the Brain." *Biological Psychiatry* 54, no. 3 (August 1, 2003): 338–352; and T. V. Gurvits et al., "Magnetic Resonance Imaging Study of Hippocampal Volume in Chronic, Combat-Related Posttraumatic Stress Disorder," *Biological Psychiatry* 40, no. 11 (December 1, 1996): 1091–1099.

Adapted from content posted on hbr.org on
January 8, 2015 (#H01T5A).

3

How to Practice Mindfulness Throughout Your Work Day

By Rasmus Hougaard and Jacqueline Carter

You probably know the feeling all too well: You arrive at the office with a clear plan for the day, and then, in what feels like just a moment, you find yourself on your way back home. Nine or ten hours have passed but you've accomplished only a few of your priorities. And, most likely, you can't even remember exactly what you did all day. If this sounds familiar, don't worry: You're not alone. Research shows that people spend nearly 47% of their waking hours thinking about something other than what they're doing.[1] In other words, many of us operate on autopilot.

Add to this that we have entered what many people are calling the "attention economy." In the attention economy, the ability to maintain focus and concentration is every bit as important as technical or management skills. And because leaders must be able to absorb and synthesize a growing flood of information in order to make good decisions, they're hit particularly hard by this emerging trend.

The good news is you can train your brain to focus better by incorporating mindfulness exercises throughout your day. Based on our experience with thousands of leaders in more than 250 organizations, here are some guidelines for becoming a more focused and mindful leader.

First, start off your day right. Researchers have found that we release the most stress hormones within minutes after waking.[2] Why? Because thinking of the day ahead triggers our fight-or-flight instinct and releases cortisol into our blood. Instead, try this: When you wake up, spend two minutes in your bed simply noticing your breath. As thoughts about the day pop into your mind, let them go and return to your breath.

Next, when you get to the office, take 10 minutes at your desk or in your car to boost your brain with the following short mindfulness practice before you dive into activity. Close your eyes, relax, and sit upright. Place your full focus on your breath. Simply maintain an ongoing flow of attention on the experience of your breathing: Inhale, exhale; inhale, exhale. To help your focus stay on your breathing, count silently at each exhalation. Any time you find your mind distracted, simply release the distraction by returning your focus to your breath. Most important, allow yourself to enjoy these minutes. Throughout the rest of the day, other people and competing urgencies will fight for your attention. But for these 10 minutes, your attention is all your own.

Once you finish this practice and get ready to start working, mindfulness can help increase your effectiveness. Two skills define a mindful mind: *focus* and *awareness*. Focus is the ability to concentrate on what you're doing in the moment, while awareness is the ability to recognize and release unnecessary distractions as they arise. Understand that mindfulness is not just a sedentary practice; it is about developing a sharp, clear mind. And mindfulness in action is a great alternative to the illusory practice of multitasking. Mindful working means applying focus and awareness to everything you do from the moment you enter the office. Focus on the task at hand, and recognize and release internal and external distractions as they arise. In this way, mindfulness helps increase effectiveness, decrease mistakes, and even enhance creativity.

To better understand the power of focus and awareness, consider an affliction that touches nearly all of us: email addiction. Emails have a way of seducing our attention and redirecting it to lower-priority tasks because completing small, quickly accomplished tasks releases dopamine, a pleasurable hormone, in our brains. This release makes us addicted to email and compromises our concentration. Instead, apply mindfulness when opening your inbox. *Focus* on what is important and maintain *awareness* of what is merely noise. To get a better start to your day, avoid checking your email first thing in the morning. Doing so will help you sidestep an onslaught of distractions and short-term problems during a time of day that holds the potential for exceptional focus and creativity.

As the day moves on and the inevitable back-to-back meetings start, mindfulness can help you lead shorter, more effective meetings. To avoid entering a meeting with a wandering mind, take two minutes to practice mindfulness, which you can do en route. Even better, let the first two minutes of the meeting be silent, allowing everybody to arrive both physically and mentally. Then, if possible, end the meeting five minutes before the hour to allow all participants a mindful transition to their next appointment.

As the day progresses and your brain starts to tire, mindfulness can help you stay sharp and avoid poor decisions. After lunch, set a timer on your phone to ring every hour. When the timer rings, cease your current activity and do one minute of mindfulness practice. These mindful performance breaks will help keep you from resorting to autopilot and lapsing into action addiction.

Finally, as the day comes to an end and you start your commute home, apply mindfulness. For at least 10 minutes of the commute, turn off your phone, shut off the radio, and simply be. Let go of any thoughts that arise. Attend to your breath. Doing so will allow you to let go of the stresses of the day so you can return home and be fully present with your family.

Mindfulness is not about living life in slow motion. It's about enhancing focus and awareness both in work and in life. It's about stripping away distractions and staying on track with both individual and organizational, goals. Take control of your own mindfulness: Test these tips for 14 days, and see what they do for you.

RASMUS HOUGAARD is the founder and managing director of The Potential Project, a leading global provider of corporate-based mindfulness solutions. He is a coauthor with Jacqueline Carter of *One Second Ahead: Enhance Your Performance at Work with Mindfulness*. JACQUELINE CARTER is a partner with The Potential Project and has worked with leaders around the globe, including executives from Sony, American Express, RBC, and KPMG.

Notes

1. S. Bradt, "Wandering Mind Not a Happy Mind," *Harvard Gazette*, November 11, 2010.
2. J. C. Pruessner et al., "Free Cortisol Levels After Awakening: A Reliable Biological Marker for the Assessment of Adrenocortical Activity," *Life Sciences* 61, no. 26 (November 1997): 2539–2549.

Adapted from content posted on hbr.org on
March 4, 2016 (#H02OTU).

4

Resilience for the Rest of Us

By Daniel Goleman

There are two ways to become more resilient: one by talking to yourself, the other by retraining your brain.

If you've suffered a major failure, take the sage advice given by psychologist Martin Seligman in the HBR article "Building Resilience" (April 2011). Talk to yourself. Give yourself a cognitive intervention, and counter defeatist thinking with an optimistic attitude. Challenge your downbeat thinking, and replace it with a positive outlook.

Fortunately, major failures come along rarely in life.

But what about bouncing back from the more frequent annoying screwups, minor setbacks, and irritating upsets that are routine in any leader's life? Resilience is, again, the answer—but with a different flavor. You need to retrain your brain.

The brain has a very different mechanism for bouncing back from the cumulative toll of daily hassles. And with a little effort, you can upgrade its ability to snap back from life's downers.

Whenever we get so upset that we say or do something we later regret (and who doesn't now and then?), that's a sure sign that our amygdala—the brain's radar for danger and the trigger for the fight-or-flight response—has hijacked the brain's executive centers in the prefrontal cortex. The neural key to resilience lies in how quickly we recover from that hijacked state.

The circuitry that brings us back to full energy and focus after an amygdala hijack concentrates in the left side of our prefrontal area, says Richard Davidson, a neuroscientist at the University of Wisconsin. He's also found that when we're distressed, there's heightened activity on the right side of the prefrontal area. Each of us has a characteristic level of left/right activity that predicts our daily mood range—if we're tilted to the right, more upsets; if to the left, we're quicker to recover from distress of all kinds.

To tackle this in the workplace, Davidson teamed with the CEO of a high-pressure, 24/7, biotech startup and meditation expert Jon Kabat-Zinn of the University of Massachusetts Medical School. Kabat-Zinn offered the employees at the biotech outfit instruction in mindfulness, an attention-training method that teaches the brain to register anything happening in the present moment with full focus— but without reacting.

The instructions are simple:

1. Find a quiet, private place where you can be undistracted for a few minutes. For instance, close your office door and mute your phone.

2. Sit comfortably, with your back straight but relaxed.

3. Focus your awareness on your breath, staying attentive to the sensations of the inhalation and exhalation, and start again on the next breath.

4. Do not judge your breathing or try to change it in any way.

5. See anything else that comes to mind as a distraction—thoughts, sounds, whatever. Let them go and return your attention to your breath.

After eight weeks and an average of 30 minutes a day practicing mindfulness, the employees had shifted their ratio from tilted toward the stressed-out right side to leaning toward the resilient left side. What's more, they said they remembered what they loved about their work: They got in touch with what had brought them energy in the first place.

To get the full benefit of mindfulness, a daily practice of 20 to 30 minutes works best. Think of it like a mental exercise routine. It can be very helpful to have guided instructions, but the key is to find a slot for the practice in your daily routine. (There are even instructions for using a long drive as your practice session.)

Mindfulness has steadily been gaining credence among hard-nosed executives. There are centers where mindfulness instruction has been tailored to businesspeople, from tony resorts like Miraval Resort in Arizona to programs in mindful leadership at the University of Massachusetts Medical School. Google University has been offering a course in mindfulness to employees for years.

Might you benefit from tuning up your brain's resilience circuitry by learning to practice mindfulness? Among high-performing executives, the effects of stress can be subtle. My colleagues Richard Boyatzis and Annie McKee suggest as a rough diagnostic of leadership stress asking yourself, "Do I have a vague sense of unease, restlessness, or the feeling that life

is not great (a higher standard than 'good enough')?"
A bit of mindfulness might put your mind at ease.

DANIEL GOLEMAN is a codirector of the Consortium for Research on Emotional Intelligence in Organizations at Rutgers University, coauthor of *Primal Leadership: Leading with Emotional Intelligence* (Harvard Business Review Press, 2013), and author of *The Brain and Emotional Intelligence: New Insights.*

Adapted from content posted on hbr.org on
March 4, 2016.

5

Emotional Agility

*How Effective Leaders Manage
Their Thoughts and Feelings*

By Susan David and Christina Congleton

Sixteen thousand—that's how many words we speak, on average, each day. So imagine how many unspoken ones course through our minds. Most of them are not facts but evaluations and judgments entwined with emotions—some positive and helpful (*I've worked hard and I can ace this presentation; This issue is worth speaking up about; The new VP seems approachable*), others negative and less so (*He's purposely ignoring me; I'm going to make a fool of myself; I'm a fake*).

The prevailing wisdom says that difficult thoughts and feelings have no place at the office: Executives, and particularly leaders, should be either stoic or cheerful; they must project confidence and damp down any negativity bubbling up inside them. But that goes against basic biology. All healthy human beings have an inner stream of thoughts and feelings that include criticism, doubt, and fear. That's just our minds doing the job they were designed to do: trying to anticipate and solve problems and avoid potential pitfalls.

In our people-strategy consulting practice advising companies around the world, we see leaders stumble not because they *have* undesirable thoughts and feelings—that's inevitable—but because they get *hooked* by them, like fish caught on a line. This happens in one of two ways. They buy into the thoughts, treating them like facts (*It was the same in my last job . . . I've been a failure my whole career*), and avoid situations that evoke them (*I'm not going to take on that new challenge*). Or, usually at the behest of their supporters, they challenge the existence of the thoughts and try to rationalize them away (*I shouldn't have thoughts like this . . . I know I'm not a total failure*), and perhaps force themselves into similar situations, even when those go against their core values and goals (*Take on that new assignment—you've got to get over this*). In either case, they are paying too much attention to their internal chatter and allowing it to sap important cognitive resources that could be put to better use.

This is a common problem, often perpetuated by popular self-management strategies. We regularly see executives with recurring emotional challenges at work—anxiety about priorities, jealousy of others' success, fear of rejection, distress over perceived slights—who have devised techniques to "fix" them: positive affirmations, prioritized to-do lists, immersion in certain tasks. But when we ask how long the challenges have persisted, the answer might be 10 years, 20 years, or since childhood.

Clearly, those techniques don't work—in fact, ample research shows that attempting to minimize or ignore thoughts and emotions serves only to amplify them. In a famous study led by the late Daniel Wegner, a Harvard professor, participants who were told to avoid thinking about white bears had trouble doing so; later, when the ban was lifted, they thought about white bears much more than the control group did. Anyone who has dreamed of chocolate cake and french fries while following a strict diet understands this phenomenon.

Effective leaders don't buy into *or* try to suppress their inner experiences. Instead they approach them in a mindful, values-driven, and productive way— developing what we call *emotional agility.* In our complex, fast-changing knowledge economy, this ability to manage one's thoughts and feelings is essential to business success. Numerous studies, from the University of London professor Frank Bond and others, show that emotional agility can help people alleviate stress, reduce errors, become more innovative, and improve job performance.

We've worked with leaders in various industries to build this critical skill, and here we offer four practices—adapted from Acceptance and Commitment Therapy (ACT), originally developed by the University of Nevada psychologist Steven C. Hayes—that are designed to help you do the same: Recognize your patterns; label your thoughts and emotions; accept them; and act on your values.

Fish on a line

Let's start with two case studies. Cynthia is a senior corporate lawyer with two young children. She used to feel intense guilt about missed opportunities—both at the office, where her peers worked 80 hours a week while she worked 50, and at home, where she was often too distracted or tired to fully engage with her husband and children. One nagging voice in her head told her she'd have to be a better employee or risk career failure; another told her to be a better mother or risk neglecting her family. Cynthia wished that at least one of the voices would shut up. But neither would, and in response she failed to put up her hand for exciting new prospects at the office and compulsively checked messages on her phone during family dinners.

Jeffrey, a rising-star executive at a leading consumer goods company, had a different problem. Intelligent, talented, and ambitious, he was often angry— at bosses who disregarded his views, subordinates who didn't follow orders, or colleagues who didn't pull their weight. He had lost his temper several times at work and been warned to get it under control. But when he tried, he felt that he was shutting off a core part of his personality, and he became even angrier and more upset.

These smart, successful leaders were hooked by their negative thoughts and emotions. Cynthia was absorbed by guilt; Jeffrey was exploding with anger.

Cynthia told the voices to go away; Jeffrey bottled his frustration. Both were trying to avoid the discomfort they felt. They were being controlled by their inner experience, attempting to control it, or switching between the two.

Getting unhooked

Fortunately, both Cynthia and Jeffrey realized that they couldn't go on—at least not successfully and happily—without more-effective inner strategies. We coached them to adopt the four practices:

Recognize your patterns

The first step in developing emotional agility is to notice when you've been hooked by your thoughts and feelings. That's hard to do, but there are certain telltale signs. One is that your thinking becomes rigid and repetitive. For example, Cynthia began to see that her self-recriminations played like a broken record, repeating the same messages over and over again. Another is that the story your mind is telling seems old, like a rerun of some past experience. Jeffrey noticed that his attitude toward certain colleagues (*He's incompetent; There's no way I'm letting anyone speak to me like that*) was quite familiar. In fact, he had experienced something similar in his previous job—and in the one before that. The source of trouble was not just Jeffrey's environment but his own patterns of thought and feeling. You have to realize that you're stuck before you can initiate change.

Label your thoughts and emotions

When you're hooked, the attention you give your thoughts and feelings crowds your mind; there's no room to examine them. One strategy that may help you consider your situation more objectively is the simple act of labeling. Just as you call a spade a spade, call a thought a thought and an emotion an emotion. *I'm not doing enough at work or at home* becomes *I'm having the thought that I'm not doing enough at work or at home.* Similarly, *My coworker is wrong—he makes me so angry* becomes *I'm having the thought that my coworker is wrong, and I'm feeling anger.* Labeling allows you to see your thoughts and feelings for what they are: transient sources of data that may or may not prove helpful. Humans are psychologically able to take this helicopter view of private experiences, and mounting scientific evidence shows that simple, straightforward mindfulness practice like this not only improves behavior and well-being but also promotes beneficial biological changes in the brain and at the cellular level. As Cynthia started to slow down and label her thoughts, the criticisms that had once pressed in on her like a dense fog became more like clouds passing through a blue sky.

Accept them

The opposite of control is acceptance: not acting on every thought or resigning yourself to negativity but responding to your ideas and emotions with an open attitude, paying attention to them and letting yourself experience them. Take 10 deep breaths, and notice what's happening in the moment. This can bring relief, but it won't necessarily make you feel good. In fact, you may realize just how upset you really are. The important thing is to show yourself (and others) some compassion and examine the reality of the situation. What's going on—both internally and externally? When Jeffrey acknowledged and made room for his feelings of frustration and anger rather than rejecting them, quashing them, or taking them out on others, he began to notice their energetic quality. They were a signal that something important was at stake and that he needed to take productive action. Instead of yelling at people, he could make a clear request of a colleague or move swiftly on a pressing issue. The more Jeffrey accepted his anger and brought his curiosity to it, the more it seemed to support rather than undermine his leadership.

Act on your values

When you unhook yourself from your difficult thoughts and emotions, you expand your choices. You can decide to act in a way that aligns with your values. We encourage leaders to focus on the concept of *workability*: Is your response going to serve you and your organization in the long term as well as the short term? Will it help you steer others in a direction that furthers your collective purpose? Are you taking a step toward being the leader you most want to be and living the life you most want to live? The mind's thought stream flows endlessly, and emotions change like the weather, but values can be called on at any time, in any situation.

WHAT ARE YOUR VALUES?

This list is drawn from the Personal Values Card Sort (2001), developed by W. R. Miller, J. C'de Baca, D. B. Matthews, and P. L. Wilbourne, of the University of New Mexico. You can use it to quickly identify the values you hold that might inform a challenging situation at work. When you next make a decision, ask yourself whether it is consistent with these values.

Accuracy	Duty	Justice	Realism
Achievement	Family	Knowledge	Responsibility
Authority	Forgiveness	Leisure	Risk
Autonomy	Friendship	Mastery	Safety
Caring	Fun	Moderation	Self-knowledge
Challenge	Generosity	Nonconformity	Service
Comfort	Genuineness	Openness	Simplicity
Compassion	Growth	Order	Stability
Contribution	Health	Passion	Tolerance
Cooperation	Helpfulness	Popularity	Tradition
Courtesy	Honesty	Power	Wealth
Creativity	Humility	Purpose	
Dependability	Humor	Rationality	

When Cynthia considered her values, she recognized how deeply committed she was to both her family and her work. She loved being with her children, but she also cared passionately about the pursuit of justice. Unhooked from her distracting and discouraging feelings of guilt, she resolved to be guided by her principles. She recognized how important it was to get home for dinner with her family every evening and to resist work interruptions during that time. But she also undertook to make a number of important business trips, some of which coincided with school events that she would have preferred to attend. Confident that her values—not solely her emotions—were guiding her, Cynthia finally found peace and fulfillment.

It's impossible to block out difficult thoughts and emotions. Effective leaders are mindful of their inner experiences but not caught in them. They know how to free up their internal resources and commit to actions that align with their values. Developing emotional agility is no quick fix. Even those who, like Cynthia and Jeffrey, regularly practice the steps we've outlined here will often find themselves hooked. But over time, leaders who become increasingly adept at it are the ones most likely to thrive.

SUSAN DAVID is the CEO of Evidence Based Psychology, a cofounder of the Institute of Coaching, and an instructor in psychology at Harvard University. CHRISTINA CONGLETON is a leadership and change consultant at Axon Leadership and has researched stress and the brain at Massachusetts General Hospital and the University of Denver. She holds a master's in human development and psychology from Harvard University.

Reprinted from *Harvard Business Review*,
November 2013 (product #R1311L).

6

Don't Let Power Corrupt You

By Dacher Keltner

n the behavioral research I've conducted over the past 20 years, I've uncovered a disturbing pattern: While people usually gain power through traits and actions that advance the interests of others, such as empathy, collaboration, openness, fairness, and sharing, when they start to feel powerful or enjoy a position of privilege, those qualities begin to fade. The powerful are more likely than other people to engage in rude, selfish, and unethical behavior. The 19th-century historian and politician Lord Acton got it right: Power *does* tend to corrupt.

I call this phenomenon "the power paradox," and I've studied it in numerous settings: colleges, the U.S.

Senate, pro sports teams, and a variety of other professional workplaces. In each I've observed that people rise on the basis of their good qualities, but their behavior grows increasingly worse as they move up the ladder. This shift can happen surprisingly quickly. In one of my experiments, known as "the cookie monster" study, I brought people into a lab in groups of three, randomly assigned one to a position of leadership, and then gave them a group writing task. A half hour into their work, I placed a plate of freshly baked cookies—one for each team member, plus an extra—in front of everyone. In all groups each person took one and, out of politeness, left the extra cookie. The question was: Who would take a second treat, knowing that it would deprive others of the same? It was nearly always the person who'd been named the leader. In addition, the leaders were more likely to eat with their mouths open, lips smacking, and crumbs falling onto their clothes.

Studies show that wealth and credentials can have a similar effect. In another experiment, Paul Piff of UC Irvine and I found that whereas drivers of the least expensive vehicles—Dodge Colts, Plymouth Satellites—*always* ceded the right-of-way to pedestrians in a crosswalk, people driving luxury cars such as BMWs and Mercedes yielded only 54% of the time; nearly half the time they ignored the pedestrian and the law. Surveys of employees in 27 countries have revealed that wealthy individuals are more likely to say it's acceptable to engage in unethical behavior, such as taking bribes or cheating on taxes. And recent research led by Danny Miller at HEC Montréal demonstrated that CEOs with MBAs are more likely than those without MBAs to engage in self-serving behavior that increases their personal compensation but causes their companies' value to decline.

These findings suggest that iconic abuses of power —Jeffrey Skilling's fraudulent accounting at Enron,

Tyco CEO Dennis Kozlowski's illegal bonuses, Silvio Berlusconi's bunga bunga parties, Leona Helmsley's tax evasion—are extreme examples of the kinds of misbehavior to which all leaders, at any level, are susceptible. Studies show that people in positions of corporate power are three times as likely as those at the lower rungs of the ladder to interrupt coworkers, multitask during meetings, raise their voices, and say insulting things at the office. And people who've just moved into senior roles are particularly vulnerable to losing their virtues, my research and other studies indicate.

The consequences can be far-reaching. The abuse of power ultimately tarnishes the reputations of executives, undermining their opportunities for influence. It also creates stress and anxiety among their colleagues, diminishing rigor and creativity in the group and dragging down team members' engagement and performance. In a recent poll of 800 managers and employees in 17 industries, about half the respondents who reported being treated rudely at work said they deliberately decreased their effort or lowered the quality of their work in response.

So how can you avoid succumbing to the power paradox? Through awareness and action.

A need for reflection

A first step is developing greater self-awareness. When you take on a senior role, you need to be attentive to the feelings that accompany your newfound power and to any changes in your behavior. My research has shown that power puts us into something like a manic state, making us feel expansive, energized, omnipotent, hungry for rewards, and immune to risk—which opens us up to rash, rude, and unethical actions. But new studies in neuroscience find that simply by reflecting on those thoughts and emotions—"Hey, I'm feeling as if I should rule

77

the world right now"—we can engage regions of our frontal lobes that help us keep our worst impulses in check. When we recognize and label feelings of joy and confidence, we're less likely to make irrational decisions inspired by them. When we acknowledge feelings of frustration (perhaps because subordinates aren't behaving the way we want), we're less likely to respond in adversarial or confrontational ways.

You can build this kind of self-awareness through everyday mindfulness practices. One approach starts with sitting in a comfortable and quiet place, breathing deeply, and concentrating on the feeling of inhaling and exhaling, physical sensations, or sounds or sights in your environment. Studies show that spending just a few minutes a day on such exercises gives people greater focus and calm, and for that reason techniques for them are now taught in training programs at companies like Google, Facebook, Aetna, General Mills, Ford, and Goldman Sachs.

It's also important to reflect on your demeanor and actions. Are you interrupting people? Do you check your phone when others are talking? Have you told a joke or story that embarrassed or humiliated someone else? Do you swear at the office? Have you ever taken sole credit for a group effort? Do you forget colleagues' names? Are you spending a lot more money than in the past or taking unusual physical risks?

If you answered yes to at least a few of these questions, take it as an early warning sign that you're being tempted into problematic, arrogant displays of power. What may seem innocuous to you probably doesn't to your subordinates. Consider a story I recently heard about a needlessly hierarchical lunch delivery protocol on a cable television writing team. Each day when the team's sandwiches arrived, they were doled out to the writers in order of seniority. In failing to correct this behavior, the group's leaders were almost certainly diminishing its collaborative and creative potential. For a contrast, consider U.S. military mess halls, where the practice is the reverse, as the ethnographer and author Simon Sinek notes in the title of his most recent book, *Leaders Eat Last*. Officers adhere to the policy not to cede authority but to show respect for their troops.

Practicing graciousness

Whether you've already begun to succumb to the power paradox or not, you must work to remember and repeat the virtuous behaviors that helped you rise in the first place. When teaching executives and others in positions of power, I focus on three essential practices—empathy, gratitude, and generosity—that have been shown to sustain benevolent leadership, even in the most cutthroat environments.

For example, Leanne ten Brinke, Chris Liu, Sameer Srivastava, and I found that U.S. senators who used empathetic facial expressions and tones of voice when speaking to the floor got more bills passed than those who used domineering, threatening gestures and tones in their speeches. Research by Anita Woolley of Carnegie Mellon and Thomas Malone of MIT has likewise shown that when teammates subtly signal understanding, engagement, interest, and concern for one another, the team is more effective at tackling hard analytical problems.

Small expressions of gratitude also yield positive results. Studies show that romantic partners who acknowledge each other's value in casual conversation are less likely to break up, that students who receive a pat on the back from their teachers are more likely to take on difficult problems, and that people who express appreciation to others in a newly formed group feel stronger ties to the group months later. Adam Grant of Wharton has found that when managers take the time to thank their employees, those workers are more engaged and productive. And my own research on NBA teams with Michael Kraus of Yale University shows that players who physically display their appreciation—through head raps, bear hugs, and hip and chest bumps—inspire their teammates to play better and win nearly two more games per season (which is both statistically significant and often the difference between making the play-offs and not).

Simple acts of generosity can be equally powerful. Studies show that individuals who share with others in a group—for example, by contributing new ideas or directly assisting on projects not their own—are deemed more worthy of respect and influence and more suitable for leadership. Mike Norton at Harvard Business School has found that when organizations provide an opportunity to donate to charities at work, employees feel more satisfied and productive.

It might seem difficult to constantly follow the ethics of "good power" when you're the boss and responsible for making sure things get done. Not so. Your capacity for empathy, gratitude, and generosity can be cultivated by engaging in simple social behaviors whenever the opportunity presents itself: a team meeting, a client pitch or negotiation, a 360-degree feedback session. Here are a few suggestions.

To practice empathy:

- Ask a great question or two in every interaction, and paraphrase important points that others make.

- Listen with gusto. Orient your body and eyes toward the person speaking, and convey interest and engagement vocally.

- When someone comes to you with a problem, signal concern with phrases such as "I'm sorry" and "That's really tough." Avoid rushing to judgment and advice.

- Before meetings, take a moment to think about the person you'll be with and what is happening in his or her life.

Arturo Bejar, Facebook's director of engineering, is one executive I've seen make empathy a priority as he guides his teams of designers, coders, data specialists, and writers. Watching him at work, I've noticed that his meetings all tend to be structured around a cascade of open-ended questions and that he never fails to listen thoughtfully. He leans toward whoever is speaking and carefully writes down everyone's ideas on a notepad. These small expressions of empathy signal to his team that he understands their concerns and wants them to succeed together.

To practice gratitude:

- Make thoughtful thank-yous a part of how you communicate with others.

- Send colleagues specific and timely emails or notes of appreciation for jobs done well.

- Publicly acknowledge the value that each person contributes to your team, including the support staff.

- Use the right kind of touch—pats on the back, fist bumps, or high fives—to celebrate successes.

When Douglas Conant was CEO of the Campbell Soup Company, he emphasized a culture of gratitude across the organization. Each day he and his executive assistants would spend up to an hour scanning his email and the company intranet for news of employees who were "making a difference." Conant would then personally thank them—everyone from senior executives to maintenance people—for their contributions, usually with handwritten notes. He estimates that he wrote at least 10 a day, for a total of about 30,000 during his decade-long tenure, and says he would often find them pinned up in employees' workspaces. Leaders I've taught have shared other tactics: giving small gifts to employees, taking them out to nice lunches or dinners, hosting employee-of-the-month celebrations, and setting up real or virtual "gratitude walls," on which coworkers can thank one another for specific contributions.

To practice generosity:

- Seek opportunities to spend a little one-on-one time with the people you lead.

- Delegate some important and high-profile responsibilities.

- Give praise generously.

- Share the limelight. Give credit to all who contribute to the success of your team and your organization.

Pixar director Pete Docter is a master of this last practice. When I first started working with him on the movie *Inside Out*, I was curious about a cinematic marvel he'd created five years before: the montage at the start of the film *Up*, which shows the protagonist, Carl, meeting and falling in love with a girl, Ellie; enjoying a long married life with her; and then watching her succumb to illness. When I asked how he'd accomplished it, his answer was an exhaustive list of the 250 writers, animators, actors, story artists, designers, sculptors, editors, programmers, and computer modelers who had worked on it with him. When people ask about the box-office success of *Inside Out*, he gives a similar response. Another Facebook executive I've worked with, product manager Kelly Winters, shares credit in a similar way. When she does PowerPoint presentations or talks to reporters about the success of her Compassion team, she always lists or talks about the data analysts, engineers, and content specialists who made it happen.

You can outsmart the power paradox by practicing the ethics of empathy, gratitude, and generosity. It will bring out the best work and collaborative spirit of those around you. And you, too, will benefit, with a burnished reputation, long-lasting leadership, and the dopamine-rich delights of advancing the interests of others.

DACHER KELTNER is a professor of psychology at the University of California, Berkeley, and the faculty director of the Greater Good Science Center.

Reprinted from *Harvard Business Review*, October 2016 (product #R1610K).

7

Mindfulness for People Who Are Too Busy to Meditate

By Maria Gonzalez

Mindfulness has become almost a buzzword. But what is it, really? Quite simply, mindfulness is being present and aware, moment by moment, regardless of circumstances.

For instance, researchers have found that practicing mindfulness can reprogram the brain to be more rational and less emotional. When faced with a decision, meditators who practiced mindfulness showed increased activity in the posterior insula of the brain, an area linked to rational decision making. This allowed them to make decisions based more on fact than emotion. This is good news since other research has found that reasoning is actually suffused with emotion—the two are inseparable. What's more, our positive and negative feelings about people, things, and ideas arise much more rapidly than our conscious thoughts—in a matter of milliseconds. We push threatening information away and hold friendly information close. We apply fight-or-flight reflexes not only to predators, but also to data itself.

There are specific techniques that you can practice to help you reap the benefits of mindfulness. You may have heard about a mindfulness-enhancing technique where you meditate for a period of time before going about the rest of your day. This is definitely valuable. But I prefer practicing mindfulness all day, in every circumstance. In essence, you start living all of life mindfully, and over time there is no distinction between your formal mindfulness practice and making a presentation, negotiating a deal, driving your car, working out, or playing a round of golf.

Try a technique I call "micro meditations." These are meditations that can be done several times a day for one to three minutes at a time. Periodically throughout the day, become aware of your breath. It could be when you feel yourself getting stressed or overwhelmed, with too much to do and too little time, or perhaps when you notice yourself becoming increasingly distracted and agitated.

First, notice the quality of your breathing. Is it shallow or deep? Are you holding your breath and in so doing perhaps also holding your stomach? Are you hunching your shoulders?

Next, start breathing so that you are bringing the breath into the belly. Do not strain. If this feels too unnatural, then try bringing the breath down into the lower chest. If the mind wanders, gently come back to the breath—without judging yourself for momentarily losing focus.

You will notice that by regularly practicing this micro meditation you will become more aware and calmer. You'll find yourself to be increasingly mindful, calm, and focused. It's helpful to create reminders for yourself to practice these meditations throughout the day. You can do them two to four times a day, every hour, before you go to a meeting, or whenever you feel like multitasking is eroding your concentration—whatever is feasible and feels right to you. Micro meditations can put you back on track and help you develop your mindfulness muscle.

A second technique I use is one I call "mindfulness in action." Instead of adding a new routine to your day, just experience your day a little differently by paying attention in a particular way, for seconds at a time.

For instance, if you've ever been in a meeting and suddenly noticed that you missed what was just said because you were "somewhere else" for the last few minutes, chances are you weren't being mindful. Maybe you were thinking about your next meeting, everything on your to do list, or an incoming text. Or perhaps you just zoned out. This is incredibly common. Unfortunately, not being present in this way can cause misunderstandings, missed opportunities, and wasted time.

The next time you're in a meeting, try to do nothing but *listen* for seconds at a time. This is harder than it sounds, but with practice you will be able to listen continuously, without a break in concentration. Whenever you notice that your mind has wandered, come right back to listening to the voice of the person who is speaking. You may have to redirect your attention dozens of times in a single meeting—it's extremely common. Always bring yourself back gently and with patience. You are training the mind to be right here, right now.

These techniques can, as I've said, rewire the brain. As a result, three critical things happen. First, your ability to concentrate increases. Second, you see things with increasing clarity, which improves your judgment. And third, you develop equanimity. Equanimity enables you to reduce your physiological and emotional stress and enhances the likelihood that you will be able to find creative solutions to problems.

Practicing mindfulness—and reaping its benefits— doesn't have to be a big time commitment or require special training. You can start right now—in this moment.

MARIA GONZALEZ is the founder and president of Argonauta Consulting. Her most recent book is *Mindful Leadership: The 9 Ways to Self-Awareness, Transforming Yourself, and Inspiring Others.* She has recently launched the Mindful Leadership app.

Adapted from content posted on hbr.org on
March 31, 2014 (product #H00QLQ).

8

Is Something Lost When We Use Mindfulness as a Productivity Tool?

By Charlotte Lieberman

I came to mindfulness as a healing practice after overcoming an addiction to the drug Adderall during my junior year of college. I found myself in this situation because I thought that using Adderall to help me focus was no big deal—an attitude shared by 81% of students nationwide.[1]

Adderall simply seemed like an innocuous shortcut to getting things done efficiently and effortlessly. I still remember the rush I felt my first night on Adderall: I completed every page of assigned Faulkner reading (not easy), started and finished a paper several weeks before the due date (because why not?), Swiffered my room (twice), and answered all of my unread emails (even the irrelevant ones). It's also worth noting that I had forgotten to eat all night and somehow found myself still awake at 4 a.m., my jaw clenched and my stomach rumbling. Sleep was nowhere in sight.

What I saw initially as a shortcut to more focus and productivity ultimately turned out instead to be a long detour toward self-destruction. Rather than thinking of focus as the by-product of my own power and capability, I looked outside of myself, thinking that a pill would solve my problems.

Long story short, I eventually came to grips with my problem, got off the drug, and found an antidote to my crippling self-doubt: meditation—particularly, mindfulness (or Vipassana) meditation.

So to me, it's somewhat ironic that mindfulness has taken the media by storm precisely because of its scientifically proven benefits for focus and productivity.[2]

And it's not just because I came to mindfulness as a way of healing from the fallout of the amount of pressure I put on myself to be productive. While mindfulness is not a little blue pill, it's starting to be thought of as a kind of shortcut to focus and productivity, not unlike a morning coffee. A wisdom tradition associated with personal growth and insight is now being absorbed by our culture as a tool for career development and efficiency. But should mindfulness really be used to attain a particular goal? Is it OK to think of a practice that's all about "being" as just another tool for "doing"?

Companies seem to think so. Given the mindfulness buzz, it's no surprise that corporate mindfulness programs are proliferating across the country. Google offers "Search Inside Yourself" classes that teach mindfulness meditation at work. As celebrated in the recent book *Mindful Work* by David Gelles, corporations like Goldman Sachs, HBO, Deutsche Bank, Target, and Bank of America tout the productivity-related benefits of meditation to their employees.

The world of professional athletics—most recently the NFL—too has drawn attention to the achievement-oriented underpinnings of the main-stream mindfulness movement. The 2015 *Wall Street Journal* article that explored the Seattle Seahawks' success in the 2014 Super Bowl explained that the team's secret weapon was its willingness to work with a sports psychologist who teaches mindfulness. Sea-hawks assistant head coach Tom Cable went so far as to describe the team as "incredibly mindful."

This article was written in January, a month before the Seahawks lost the 2015 Super Bowl. In the wake of their defeat, I heard several conversations among acquaintances and family members (all of whom were sports fans and were nonmeditating but aware of meditation) in which they expressed skepticism about the power of meditation for focus and success. I mean, how much can we embrace mindfulness as a tool for success if a team famous for meditating lost the Super Bowl?

Still a lot, I think. And I'm fine stopping here to admit (if you haven't already concluded yourself) that the commodification of mindfulness as a productivity tool leaves me with a strange taste in my mouth. Above all, I am resistant to the teleological attitude toward meditation: that it's a "tool" designed for a particular purpose, contingent on "results."

And yet asserting this skepticism brings me back to a conversation I had with my vegan cousin a few years ago. He is a PhD student in biological anthropology, an animal activist, and a longtime vegan. When I asked him if he was irked by all the celebrities going vegan to lose weight, he shook his head vigorously. "I'd rather have people do the right thing for the wrong reason than not do the right thing at all," he explained (the "right" thing here being veganism).

This philosophy seems applicable to the mindfulness craze (aka "McMindfulness") too. I'm happy more people are getting the myriad benefits of meditation. I am glad that you're no longer thought of as a patchouli-scented hippie if you're an avid meditator. If corporate mindfulness programs mean that employee self-care is more valued in the workplace, then so be it.

But I also think there's room to consider an alternative way of talking about meditation, especially when it comes to how we relate to our work.

Looking at mindfulness as a tool for accomplishing what we need to get done keeps us trapped in a future-oriented mindset, rather than encouraging us to dilate the present moment. Of course, this doesn't invalidate the neuroscience; mindfulness helps us get more stuff done. But what about allowing mindfulness to just be? To have the effects it is going to have, without attaching a marketing pitch to this ancient practice?

Psychologist Kristin Neff is renowned for coining the term "self-compassion." In particular, Neff has asserted that the first component of self-compassion is kindness, the ability to shrug off those times when we "let ourselves down," when we don't get to check off everything from our to do lists. The other two components of self-compassion are awareness and mindfulness. The goal is not to get more done but to understand that we are enough—and that our worth is not contingent on what we get done. (Although studies have shown that self-forgiveness actually helps us procrastinate less.[3])

I'm not an idealist. I'm not saying everyone should start "Om-ing," devoting themselves solely to self-compassion, and forgetting all about their to do lists. But I am saying that compassion, and self-compassion, ought to move into the foreground as we talk about mindfulness—even in corporate mindfulness programs.

There's no shame in wanting to be productive at work. But there's also no shame in being able to cut yourself some slack, to extend yourself some love during those times at work when things don't feel so great.

CHARLOTTE LIEBERMAN is a New York–based writer and editor.

Notes

1. A. D. DeSantis and A. C. Hane, "'Adderall Is Definitely Not a Drug': Justifications for the Illegal Use of ADHD Stimulants," *Substance Use and Misuse* 45, no. 1–2 (2010): 31–46.
2. D. M. Levy et al., "The Effects of Mindfulness Meditation Training on Multitasking in a High-Stress Information Environment," Graphics Interface Conference, 2012.
3. M. J. A. Wohl et al., "I Forgive Myself, Now I Can Study: How Self-Forgiveness for Procrastinating Can Reduce Future Procrastination," *Personality and Individual Differences* 48 (2010): 803–808.

Adapted from content posted on hbr.org on
August 25, 2015 (product #H02AJ1).

9

There Are Risks to Mindfulness at Work

By David Brendel

Mindfulness is close to taking on cult status in the business world. But as with any rapidly growing movement—regardless of its potential benefits—there is good reason here for caution.

Championed for many years by pioneering researchers such as Ellen Langer and Jon Kabat-Zinn, mindfulness is a mental orientation and set of strategies for focusing one's mind on here-and-now experiences, such as abdominal muscle movements during respiration or the chirping of birds outside one's window. It is rooted in ancient Eastern philosophies, such as Taoism and Buddhism. Contemporary empirical research demonstrates its benefits for reducing anxiety and mental stress.[1] A recent study suggested that it might cut the risk of stroke and heart attack as well.

Mindful meditation and related practices are now widely accepted. For example, the *New Republic* published an article entitled "How 2014 Became the Year of Mindfulness." Mindfulness has also recently been featured on CBS's *60 Minutes* and been lauded by the *Huffington Post*. Dan Harris, a well-known ABC News correspondent, has published a best-selling book called *Ten Percent Happier*, which describes his journey to discovering mindful meditation as an optimal way to manage his very publicly shared anxiety disorder. There is increasing interest in how mindfulness can be applied in clinical medicine and psychology, and some large insurance companies are even beginning to consider providing coverage for mindfulness strategies for certain patients.

As an executive coach and physician, I often sing the praises of mindfulness practices and recommend them to clients to manage stress, avoid burnout, enhance leadership capacity, and steady the mind when in the midst of making important business decisions, career transitions, and personal life changes. Drawing on concepts from Eastern philosophies and research evidence from contemporary neuroscience, I help some clients employ controlled breathing and similar strategies in our sessions and in their everyday lives.[2] I also refer clients to trusted colleagues who teach yoga and mindful meditation in greater depth than I can provide in my coaching sessions.

But my growing knowledge of (and enthusiasm for) mindfulness is now tempered by a concern about its potential excesses and the risk that it may be crowding out other equally important models and strategies for managing stress, achieving peak performance, and reaching professional and personal fulfillment. At times, it appears that we are witnessing the development of a "cult of mindfulness" that, if not appropriately recognized and moderated, may result in an unfortunate backlash against it. Here are a couple of my concerns.

The avoidance risk

Some people use mindfulness strategies to avoid critical thinking tasks. I've worked with clients who, instead of rationally thinking through a career challenge or ethical dilemma, prefer to disconnect from their challenges and retreat into a meditative mindset. The issue here is that some problems require more thinking, not less. Sometimes stress is a signal that we need to consider our circumstances through greater self-reflective thought, not a "mindful" retreat to focused breathing or other immediate sensory experiences. Mindfulness strategies can prime the mind for sounder rational thinking—but the former clearly should not displace the latter. One of my clients spent so much time meditating and "mindfully" accepting her life "on its own terms" that she failed to confront underperforming workers (and discipline or fire the worst offenders) in her company. After periods of meditating, she struggled to return to focused, task-oriented thinking. She required significant reminders and reassurance from me that embracing Buddhist meditation does not entail tolerating substandard performance from her employees. Mindful meditation should always be used in the service of enhancing, not displacing, people's rational and analytical thought processes about their careers and personal lives.

The groupthink risk

As mindfulness practices enter mainstream American life, some organizations and companies are admirably encouraging their people to make use of them in the workplace.[3] But I'm aware of situations where this new orientation has gone too far. In one case, the director of a business unit in a financial services corporation required his direct reports to participate several times per week in a 10- to 15-minute mindfulness session that involved controlled breathing and guided imagery. Many participants came to dread the exercise. Some of them felt extremely awkward and uncomfortable, believing that mindfulness practices should be done in private. The very exercise that was supposed to reduce their work-related stress actually had increased it. The practice continued for weeks until several members of the group finally gathered the courage to tell the group leader that they would strongly prefer the daily exercises be optional, with impunity for nonparticipants. Mindfulness is rooted in a philosophy and psychology of self-efficacy and proactive self-care. Imposing it on people in a top-down manner degrades the practice and the people who might benefit from using it of their own volition.

That mindfulness has emerged as a major cultural phenomenon on the contemporary American scene and in the business world in particular can be good news for people dealing with stress, burnout, and other realities of the modern workplace. But mindfulness practices need to be incorporated as one among many self-chosen strategies for people aiming to cope with stress, think effectively, make sound decisions, and achieve fulfillment. Mindfulness practices should be used to enhance our rational and ethical thinking processes, not limit or displace them. And mindfulness practices should never be imposed on people, especially in the workplace. At its very core, mindfulness will be a huge step forward for Western culture if it stays focused on creating opportunities for individuals to discover their own personalized strategies for taming anxieties, managing stress, optimizing work performance, and reaching happiness and fulfillment.

DAVID BRENDEL is an executive coach, leadership development specialist, and psychiatrist based in Boston. He is founder and director of Leading Minds Executive Coaching and a cofounder of Strategy of Mind, a leadership development and coaching company.

Notes

1. J. Corliss, "Mindfulness Meditation May Ease Anxiety, Mental Stress," *Harvard Health Blog*, January 8, 2014.
2. M. Baime, "This Is Your Brain on Mindfulness," *Shambhala Sun*, July 2011, 44–84; and "Relaxation Techniques: Breath Control Helps Quell Errant Stress Response," *Harvard Health Publications*, January 2015.
3. A. Huffington, "Mindfulness, Meditation, Wellness and Their Connection to Corporate America's Bottom Line," *Huffington Post*, March 18, 2013.

Adapted from content posted on hbr.org on
February 11, 2015 (product #H01VIF).

Index

How to be human at work.

HBR's Emotional Intelligence Series features smart, essential reading on the human side of professional life from the pages of *Harvard Business Review*. Each book in the series offers uplifting stories, practical advice, and research from leading experts on how to tend to our emotional well-being at work.

Harvard Business Review Emotional Intelligence Series

Available in paperback or ebook format. The specially priced six-volume set includes:

- Mindfulness
- Resilience
- Influence and Persuasion
- Authentic Leadership
- Happiness
- Empathy

The most important management ideas all in one place.

We hope you enjoyed this book from *Harvard Business Review*. For the best ideas HBR has to offer turn to HBR's 10 Must Reads Boxed Set. From books on leadership and strategy to managing yourself and others, this 6-book collection delivers articles on the most essential business topics to help you succeed.

HBR's 10 Must Reads Series

The definitive collection of ideas and best practices on our most sought-after topics from the best minds in business.

- Change Management
- Collaboration
- Communication
- Emotional Intelligence
- Innovation
- Leadership
- Making Smart Decisions
- Managing Across Cultures
- Managing People
- Managing Yourself
- Strategic Marketing
- Strategy
- Teams
- The Essentials

hbr.org/mustreads

Empathy

HBR Emotional Intelligence Series

How to be human at work

The HBR Emotional Intelligence Series features smart, essential reading on the human side of professional life from the pages of *Harvard Business Review*.

Empathy

Happiness

Mindfulness

Resilience

Other books on emotional intelligence from *Harvard Business Review*:

HBR's 10 Must Reads on Emotional Intelligence

HBR Guide to Emotional Intelligence

Empathy

HBR EMOTIONAL INTELLIGENCE SERIES

Harvard Business Review Press

Boston, Massachusetts

Library of Congress Cataloging-in-Publication Data

Title: Empathy.
Other titles: HBR emotional intelligence series.
Description: Boston, Massachusetts : Harvard Business Review Press, [2017] | Series: HBR emotional intelligence series
Identifiers: LCCN 2016056297 | ISBN 9781633693258 (pbk.)
Subjects: LCSH: Empathy. | Management.
Classification: LCC BF575.E55 E45 2017 | DDC 152.4/1—dc23 LC record available at https://lccn.loc.gov/2016056297

ISBN: 978-1-63369-325-8
eISBN: 978-1-63369-326-5

Contents

Contents

Contents

Empathy

1

What Is Empathy?

By Daniel Goleman

The word "attention" comes from the Latin *attendere*, meaning "to reach toward." This is a perfect definition of focus on others, which is the foundation of empathy and of an ability to build social relationships—the second and third pillars of emotional intelligence (the first is self-awareness).

Executives who can effectively focus on others are easy to recognize. They are the ones who find common ground, whose opinions carry the most weight, and with whom other people want to work. They emerge as natural leaders regardless of organizational or social rank.

The Empathy Triad

We talk about empathy most commonly as a single attribute. But a close look at where leaders are focusing when they exhibit it reveals three distinct kinds of empathy, each important for leadership effectiveness:

- *Cognitive empathy*: the ability to understand another person's perspective

- *Emotional empathy*: the ability to feel what someone else feels

- *Empathic concern*: the ability to sense what another person needs from you

Cognitive empathy enables leaders to explain themselves in meaningful ways—a skill essential to getting the best performance from their direct reports. Contrary to what you might expect, exercising cognitive empathy requires leaders to think about feelings rather than to feel them directly.

4

An inquisitive nature feeds cognitive empathy. As one successful executive with this trait puts it, "I've always just wanted to learn everything, to understand anybody that I was around—why they thought what they did, why they did what they did, what worked for them and what didn't work." But cognitive empathy is also an outgrowth of self-awareness. The executive circuits that allow us to think about our own thoughts and to monitor the feelings that flow from them let us apply the same reasoning to other people's minds when we choose to direct our attention that way.

Emotional empathy is important for effective mentoring, managing clients, and reading group dynamics. It springs from ancient parts of the brain beneath the cortex—the amygdala, the hypothalamus, the hippocampus, and the orbitofrontal cortex—that allow us to feel fast without thinking deeply. They tune us in by arousing in our bodies the emotional states of others: I literally feel your pain. My brain patterns match up with yours when I listen to you tell a gripping story. As Tania Singer, the director of the social neuroscience department at the Max Planck Institute for Human Cognitive and Brain Sciences, in Leipzig, Germany, says, "You need to understand your own feelings to understand the feelings of others." Accessing your capacity for emotional empathy depends on combining two kinds of attention: a deliberate focus on your own echoes of someone else's feelings and an open awareness of that person's face, voice, and other external signs of emotion. (See the sidebar "When Empathy Needs to Be Learned.")

WHEN EMPATHY NEEDS TO BE LEARNED

Emotional empathy can be developed. That's the conclusion suggested by research conducted with physicians by Helen Riess, the director of the Empathy and Relational Science Program at Boston's Massachusetts General Hospital. To help the physicians monitor

(Continued)

themselves, Riess set up a program in which they learned to focus using deep, diaphragmatic breathing and to cultivate a certain detachment—to watch an interaction from the ceiling, as it were, rather than being lost in their own thoughts and feelings. "Suspending your own involvement to observe what's going on gives you a mindful awareness of the interaction without being completely reactive," says Riess. "You can see if your own physiology is charged up or balanced. You can notice what's transpiring in the situation." If a doctor realizes that she's feeling irritated, for instance, that may be a signal that the patient is bothered too.

Those who are utterly at a loss may be able to prime emotional empathy essentially by faking it until they make it, Riess adds. If you act in a caring way—looking people in the eye and paying attention to their expressions, even when you don't particularly want to—you may start to feel more engaged.

Empathic concern, which is closely related to emotional empathy, enables you to sense not just how people feel but what they need from you. It's what you want in your doctor, your spouse—and your boss. Empathic concern has its roots in the circuitry that compels parents' attention to their children. Watch where people's eyes go when someone brings an adorable baby into a room, and you'll see this mammalian brain center leaping into action.

Research suggests that as people rise through the ranks, their ability to maintain personal connections suffers.

One neural theory holds that the response is triggered in the amygdala by the brain's radar for sensing danger and in the prefrontal cortex by the release of oxytocin, the chemical for caring. This implies that empathic concern is a double-edged feeling. We intuitively experience the distress of another as our own. But in deciding whether we will meet that person's needs, we deliberately weigh how much we value his or her well-being.

Getting this intuition-deliberation mix right has great implications. Those whose sympathetic feelings become too strong may themselves suffer. In the helping professions, this can lead to compassion fatigue; in executives, it can create distracting feelings of anxiety about people and circumstances that are beyond anyone's control. But those who protect themselves by deadening their feelings may lose touch with empathy. Empathic concern requires us to manage our personal distress without numbing ourselves to the pain of others. (See the sidebar "When Empathy Needs to Be Controlled.")

DANIEL GOLEMAN is a codirector of the Consortium for Research on Emotional Intelligence in Organizations at Rutgers University, coauthor of *Primal Leadership: Leading with Emotional Intelligence* (Harvard Business Review Press, 2013), and author of *The Brain and Emotional Intelligence: New Insights* and *Leadership: Selected Writings* (More Than Sound, 2011). His latest book is *A Force For Good: The Dalai Lama's Vision for Our World* (Bantam, 2015).

Excerpted from "The Focused Leader," adapted from *Harvard Business Review*, December 2013 (product #R1312B).

WHEN EMPATHY NEEDS TO BE CONTROLLED

Getting a grip on our impulse to empathize with other people's feelings can help us make better decisions when someone's emotional flood threatens to over-whelm us.

Ordinarily, when we see someone pricked with a pin, our brains emit a signal indicating that our own pain centers are echoing that distress. But physicians learn in medical school to block even such automatic responses. Their attentional anesthetic seems to be deployed by the temporal-parietal junction and re-gions of the prefrontal cortex, a circuit that boosts concentration by tuning out emotions. That's what is happening in your brain when you distance yourself from others in order to stay calm and help them. The same neural network kicks in when we see a problem in an emotionally overheated environment and need to focus on looking for a solution. If you're talking with someone who is upset, this system helps you understand the person's perspective intellectually by shifting from the heart-to-heart of emotional empathy to the head-to-heart of cognitive empathy.

What's more, some lab research suggests that the appropriate application of empathic concern is critical to making moral judgments. Brain scans have revealed that when volunteers listened to tales of people being subjected to physical pain, their own brain centers for experiencing such pain lit up instantly. But if the story was about psychological suffering, the higher brain centers involved in empathic concern and compassion took longer to activate. Some time is needed to grasp the psychological and moral dimensions of a situation. The more distracted we are, the less we can cultivate the subtler forms of empathy and compassion.

2

Why Compassion Is a Better Managerial Tactic Than Toughness

By Emma Seppala

Stanford University neurosurgeon James Doty tells the story of performing surgery on a little boy's brain tumor. In the middle of the procedure, the resident who is assisting him gets distracted and accidentally pierces a vein. With blood shedding everywhere, Doty is no longer able to see the delicate brain area he is working on. The boy's life is at stake. Doty is left with no other choice than to blindly reach into the affected area in the hopes of locating and clamping the vein. Fortunately, he is successful.

Most of us are not brain surgeons, but we certainly are all confronted with situations in which an employee makes a grave mistake, potentially ruining a critical project. The question is: How should we react when an employee is not performing well or makes a mistake?

Frustration is of course the natural response—and one we all can identify with. Especially if the mistake hurts an important project or reflects badly on us.

The traditional approach is to reprimand the employee in some way. The hope is that some form of punishment will be beneficial: It will teach the employee a lesson. Expressing our frustration also may relieve us of the stress and anger caused by the mistake. Finally, it may help the rest of the team stay on their toes to avoid making future errors.

Some managers, however, choose a different response when confronted by an underperforming employee: compassion and curiosity. Not that a part of them isn't frustrated or exasperated—maybe they still worry about how their employee's mistakes will reflect back on them—but they are somehow able to suspend judgment and may even be able to use the moment to do a bit of coaching.

What does research say is best? The more compassionate response will get you more powerful results.

First, compassion and curiosity increase employee loyalty and trust. Research has shown that feelings of warmth and positive relationships at work have a greater say over an employee's loyalty than the size of his or her paycheck.[1] In particular, a study by Jonathan Haidt of New York University shows that the more employees look up to their leaders and are moved by their compassion or kindness (a state he terms "elevation"), the more loyal they become to him or her.[2] So if you are more compassionate to your employee, not only will he or she be more loyal to you, but anyone else who has witnessed your behavior may also experience elevation and feel more devoted to you.

Conversely, responding with anger or frustration erodes loyalty. As Adam Grant, professor at the Wharton Business School and author of *Give and Take*, points out that, because of the law of reciprocity, if you embarrass or blame an employee too harshly, your reaction may end up coming around to haunt you. "Next time you need to rely on that employee, you may have lost some of the loyalty that was there before," he told me.

We are especially sensitive to signs of trustworthiness in our leaders, and compassion increases our willingness to trust.[3] Simply put, our brains respond more positively to bosses who have shown us empathy, as neuroimaging research confirms.[4] Employee trust *in turn* improves performance.[5]

Doty, who is also director of Stanford University's Center for Compassion and Altruism Research and Education, recalls his first experience in the operating room. He was so nervous that he perspired profusely. Soon enough, a drop of sweat fell into the operation site and contaminated it. The operation was a simple one, and the patients' life was in no way at stake. As for the operation site, it could have been easily irrigated. However, the operating surgeon—one of the biggest names in surgery at the time—was so angry that he kicked Doty out of the OR. Doty recalls returning home and crying tears of devastation.

Tellingly, Doty explains in an interview how, if the surgeon had acted differently, he would have gained Doty's undying loyalty. "If the surgeon, instead of raging, had said something like: 'Listen young man, look what just happened—you contaminated the field. I know you're nervous. You can't be nervous if you want to be a surgeon. Why don't you go outside and take a few minutes to collect yourself. Readjust your cap in such a way that the sweat doesn't pour down your face. Then come back and I'll show you something.' Well, then he would have been my hero forever."

Not only does an angry response erode loyalty and trust, it also inhibits creativity by jacking up the employee's stress level. As Doty explains, "Creating an environment where there is fear, anxiety, and lack of trust makes people shut down. If people have fear and anxiety, we know from neuroscience that their threat response is engaged, and their cognitive control is impacted. As a consequence, their productivity and creativity diminish." For instance, brain-imaging studies show that when we feel safe, our brain's stress response is lower.[6]

Grant also agrees that "when you respond in a frustrated, furious manner, the employee becomes less likely to take risks in the future because he or she worries about the negative consequences of making mistakes. In other words, you kill the culture of experimentation that is critical to learning and innovation." Grant refers to research by Fiona Lee at the University of Michigan that shows that promoting a culture of safety—rather than of fear of negative consequences—helps encourage the spirit of experimentation that is so critical for creativity.[7]

There is, of course, a reason we feel anger. Research shows that feelings of anger can have beneficial results. For example, they can give us the energy to stand up against injustice.[8] Moreover, they make us appear more powerful.[9] However, when as a leader you express negative emotions like anger, your employees actually view you as less effective.[10] Conversely, being likable and projecting warmth—not toughness—gives leaders a distinct advantage, as Amy Cuddy of Harvard Business School has shown.[11]

So how can you respond with more compassion the next time an employee makes a serious mistake?

1. Take a moment. Doty explains that the first thing to do is to get a handle on your own emotions—anger, frustration, or whatever the case may be. "You have to take a step back and control your own emotional response, because if you act out of emotional engagement, you are not thoughtful about your approach to the problem. By stepping back and taking a period of time to reflect, you enter a mental state that allows for a more thoughtful, reasonable, and discerned response." Practicing meditation can help improve your self-awareness and emotional control.[12]

You don't want to operate from a place where you are just pretending not to be angry. Research shows that this kind of pretense actually ends up raising heart rates for both you and your employee.[13] Instead, take some time to cool off so you can see the situation with more detachment.

2. Put yourself in your employee's shoes. Taking a step back will help give you the ability to empathize with your employee. Why was Doty, in the near-tragic moment in the operating room, able to respond productively rather than with anger? As a consequence of recalling his own first experience in the OR, he could identify and empathize with the resident. This allowed him to curb his frustration, avoid degrading the already horrified resident, and maintain the presence of mind to save a little boy's life.

The ability to perspective-take is a valuable one. Studies have shown that it helps you see aspects of the situation you may not have noticed and leads to better results in interactions and negotiations.[14] And because positions of power tend to lower our natural inclination for empathy, it is particularly important that managers have the self-awareness to make sure they practice seeing situations from their employee's perspective.[15]

3. Forgive. Empathy, of course, helps you forgive. Forgiveness not only strengthens your relationship with your employee by promoting loyalty, it turns out that it is also good for you. Whereas carrying a grudge is bad for your heart (blood pressure and heart rate both go up), forgiveness lowers both your blood pressure *and* that of the person you're forgiving.[16] Other studies show that forgiveness makes you happier and more satisfied with life, significantly reducing stress and negative emotions.[17]

When trust, loyalty, and creativity are high and stress is low, employees are happier and more productive, and turnover is lower.[18] Positive interactions even make employees healthier and require fewer sick days.[19] Other studies have shown how compassionate management leads to improvements in customer service and client outcomes and satisfaction.[20]

Doty told me he's never thrown anyone out of his OR. "It's not that I let them off the hook, but by choosing a compassionate response when they know they have made a mistake, they are not destroyed, they have learned a lesson, and they want to improve for you because you've been kind to them."

EMMA SEPPALA, PH.D., is the Science Director of Stanford University's Center for Compassion and Altruism Research and Education and author of *The Happiness Track*. She is also founder of Fulfillment Daily. Follow her on Twitter @emmaseppala or her website www.emmaseppala.com.

Notes

1. "Britain's Workers Value Companionship and Recognition Over a Big Salary, a Recent Report Revealed," AAT press release, July 15, 2014, https://www.aat.org.uk/about-aat/press-releases/britains-workers-value-companionship-recognition-over-big-salary.
2. T. Qiu et al., "The Effect of Interactional Fairness on the Performance of Cross-Functional Product Develop-

ment Teams: A Multilevel Mediated Model," *The Journal of Product Innovation Management* 26, no. 2 (March 2009): 173–187.

3. K. T. Dirks et al., "Trust in Leadership: Meta-Analytic Findings and Implications for Research and Practice," *Journal of Applied Psychology* 87, no 4 (August 2002): 611–628.

4. R. Boyatzis et al., "Examination of the Neural Substrates Activated in Memories of Experiences with Resonant and Dissonant Leaders," *The Leadership Quarterly* 23, no. 2 (April 2012): 259–272.

5. T. Bartram et al., "The Relationship between Leadership and Follower In-Role Performance and Satisfaction with the Leader: The Mediating Effects of Empowerment and Trust in the Leader," *Leadership & Organization Development Journal* 28, no. 1, (2007): 4–19.

6. L. Norman et al., "Attachment-Security Priming Attenuates Amygdala Activation to Social and Linguistic Threat," *Social Cognitive and Affective Neuroscience*, Advance Access, November 5, 2014, http://scan.oxfordjournals.org/content/early/2014/11/05/scan.nsu127.

7. F. Lee et al., "The Mixed Effects of Inconsistency on Experimentation in Organizations," *Organization Science* 15, no. 3 (2004): 310–326.

8. D. Lindebaum and P. J. Jordan, "When It Can Feel Good to Feel Bad and Bad to Feel Good: Exploring Asymmetries in Workplace Emotional Outcomes," *Human Relations*, August 27, 2014, http://hum.sagepub.com/content/early/2014/07/09/0018726714535824.full.

9. L. Z. Tiedens, "Anger and Advancement Versus Sadness and Subjugation: The Effect of Negative Emotion Expressions on Social Status Conferral," *Journal of Personality and Social Psychology* 80, no. 1 (January 2001): 86–94.

10. K. M. Lewis, "When Leaders Display Emotion: How Followers Respond to Negative Emotional Expression of Male and Female Leaders," *Journal of Organizational Behavior* 21, no. 1 (March 2000): 221–234.

11. E. Seppala, "The Hard Data on Being a Nice Boss," *Harvard Business Review*, November 24, 2014, https://hbr.org/2014/11/the-hard-data-on-being-a-nice-boss; and A. J. C. Cuddy et al., "Connect, Then Lead," *Harvard Business Review* (July–August 2013).

12. "Know Thyself: How Mindfulness Can Improve Self-Knowledge," Association for Psychological Science, March 14, 2013, http://www.psychologicalscience.org/index.php/news/releases/know-thyself-how-mindfulness-can-improve-self-knowledge.html.

13. E. Butler et al., "The Social Consequences of Expressive Suppression," *Emotion* 3, no. 1 (2013): 48–67.

14. A. Galinsky, et al., "Why It Pays to Get Inside the Head of Your Opponent: The Differential Effects of Perspective Taking and Empathy in Negotiations," *Psychological Science* 19, no. 4 (April 2008): 378–384.

15. L. Solomon, "Becoming Powerful Makes You Less Empathetic," *Harvard Business Review*, April 21, 2015, https://hbr.org/2015/04/becoming-powerful-makes-you-less-empathetic.

16. P. A. Hannon et al., "The Soothing Effects of Forgiveness on Victims' and Perpetrators' Blood Pressure," *Personal Relationships* 19, no. 2 (June 2012): 279–289.

17. G. Bono et al., "Forgiveness, Feeling Connected to Others, and Well-Being: Two Longitudinal Studies," *Personality and Social Psychology Bulletin* 34, no. 2 (February 2008): 182–195; and K. A. Lawler, "The Unique Effects of Forgiveness on Health: An Exploration of Pathways," *Journal of Behavioral Medicine* 28, no. 2 (April 2005): 157–167.

18. American Psychological Association, "By the Numbers: A Psychologically Healthy Workplace Fact Sheet," *Good Company Newsletter*, November 20, 2013, http://www.apaexcellence.org/resources/goodcompany/newsletter/article/487.

19. E. D. Heaphy and J. E. Dutton; "Positive Social Interactions and the Human Body at Work: Linking Organizations and Physiology," *Academy of Management Review* 33, no. 1 (2008): 137–162; and S. Azagba and M. Sharaf, "Psychosocial Working Conditions and the Utilization of Health Care Services," *BMC Public Health* 11, no. 642 (2011).

20. S. G. Barsdale and D. E. Gibson, "Why Does Affect Matter in Organizations?" *Academy of Management Perspectives* 21, no. 1 (February 2007): 36–59; and S. G. Barsdale and O. A. O'Neill, "What's Love Got to Do with It? A Longitudinal Study of the Culture of Companionate Love and Employee and Client Outcomes in the Long-Term

Care Setting," *Administrative Science Quarterly* 59, no. 4 (December 2014): 551–598.

Adapted from content posted on hbr.org
on May 7, 2015 (product #H021MP).

3

What Great Listeners Actually Do

By Jack Zenger and Joseph Folkman

Chances are you think you're a good listener. People's appraisal of their listening ability is much like their assessment of their driving skills, in that the great bulk of adults think they're above average.

In our experience, most people think good listening comes down to doing three things:

- Not talking when others are speaking

- Letting others know you're listening through facial expressions and verbal sounds ("Mm-hmm")

- Being able to repeat what others have said, practically word for word

In fact, much management advice on listening suggests that people should do these very things—encouraging listeners to remain quiet, nod and "mm-hmm" encouragingly, and then repeat back to the talker something like, "So, let me make sure I understand. What you're saying is . . ." However, recent research that we've conducted suggests that these behaviors fall far short of describing good listening skills.

We analyzed data that describes the behavior of 3,492 participants in a development program designed to help managers become better coaches. As part of this program, participants' coaching skills were evaluated through 360-degree assessments. We identified the individuals who were perceived as being the most effective listeners (the top 5%). We then compared the best listeners with the average of all other people in the data set and identified the 20 characteristics that seemed to set them apart. With those results in hand we identified the factors that differed between great and average listeners and analyzed the data to determine which characteristics their colleagues identified as the behaviors that made them outstanding listeners.

We found some surprising characteristics, along with some qualities we expected to hear. We grouped them into four main findings:

- *Good listening is much more than being silent while the other person talks.* To the contrary, people perceive the best listeners to be those who periodically ask questions that promote discovery and insight. These questions gently challenge old assumptions but do so in a constructive way. Sitting there silently nodding does not provide sure evidence that a person is listening, but asking a good question tells the speaker the listener has not only heard what was said but that they comprehended it well enough to want additional information. Good listening was consistently seen as a two-way dialogue, rather than a one-way "speaker versus hearer" interaction. The best conversations were active.

- *Good listening includes interactions that build up a person's self-esteem.* The best listeners make the conversation a positive experience for the other party, which doesn't happen when the listener is passive (or critical, for that matter). Good listeners make the other person feel supported and convey confidence in the speaker. Good listening is characterized by the creation of a safe environment in which issues and differences can be discussed openly.

- *Good listening is seen as a cooperative conversation.* In the interactions we studied, feedback flowed smoothly in both directions with neither party becoming defensive about comments the other made. By contrast, poor listeners were seen as competitive—as listening only to identify errors in reasoning or logic, using their silence as a chance to prepare their next response. That might make you an excellent debater, but it doesn't make you a good listener. Good listeners may challenge assumptions and disagree, but the person being listened to feels the listener is trying to help rather than trying to win an argument.

- *Good listeners tend to make suggestions.* In the study, good listening invariably included some feedback that was provided in a way others would accept and that opened up alternative paths to consider. This finding somewhat surprised us, since it's not uncommon to hear complaints that "So-and-so didn't listen, he just jumped in and tried to solve the problem." Perhaps what the data is telling us is that making suggestions is not itself the problem; it may be more about the skill with which those suggestions are made. Another possibility is that we're more likely to accept suggestions from people we already think are good listeners. (Someone who is silent for the whole conversation and then jumps in with a suggestion may not be seen as credible. Someone who seems combative or critical and then tries to give advice may not be seen as trustworthy.)

While many of us may think of being a good listener like being a sponge that accurately absorbs what the other person is saying, what these findings show is that instead, good listeners are like trampolines: You can bounce ideas off of them, and rather than absorbing your ideas and energy, they amplify, energize, and clarify your thinking. They make you feel better not by merely passively absorbing, but by actively supporting. This lets you gain energy and height, just like a trampoline.

Of course, there are different levels of listening. Not every conversation requires the highest levels of listening, but many conversations would benefit from greater focus and listening skill. Consider which level of listening you'd like to aim for.

> *Level 1*: The listener creates a safe environment in which difficult, complex, or emotional issues can be discussed.

> *Level 2*: The listener clears away distractions like phones and laptops, focusing attention on the other person and making appropriate eye contact. (This behavior not only affects how you are perceived as the listener; it immediately influences the listener's *own* attitudes and inner feelings. Acting the part changes how you feel inside. This in turn makes you a better listener.)

> *Level 3*: The listener seeks to understand the substance of what the other person is saying.

They capture ideas, ask questions, and restate issues to confirm that their understanding is correct.

Level 4: The listener observes nonverbal cues, such as facial expressions, perspiration, respiration rates, gestures, posture, and numerous other subtle body language signals. It is estimated that 80% of what we communicate comes from these signals. It sounds strange to some, but you listen with your eyes as well as your ears.

Level 5: The listener increasingly understands the other person's emotions and feelings about the topic at hand and identifies and acknowledges them. The listener empathizes with and validates those feelings in a supportive, nonjudgmental way.

Level 6: The listener asks questions that clarify assumptions the other person holds and helps the other person see the issue in a new light. This could include the listener injecting some thoughts and ideas about the topic that could be useful to the other person. However, good listeners never highjack the conversation so that they or their issues become the subject of the discussion.

Each of the levels builds on the others; thus, if you've been criticized for offering solutions rather than listening, it may mean you need to attend to some of the other levels (such as clearing away distractions or empathizing) before your proffered suggestions can be appreciated.

We suspect that in being a good listener, most of us are more likely to stop short rather than go too far. Our hope is that this research will help by providing a new perspective on listening. We hope those who labor under an illusion of superiority about their listening skills will see where they really stand. We also hope the common perception that good listening is mainly about acting like an absorbent sponge will wane. Finally, we hope all will see that the highest and best form of listening comes in playing the same role for the other person that a trampoline would play for a child: It gives energy, acceleration, height, and amplification. These are the hallmarks of great listening.

JACK ZENGER is the CEO and JOSEPH FOLKMAN is President of Zenger Folkman, a leadership development consultancy. They are coauthors of the October 2011 HBR article "Making Yourself Indispensable" and the book *How to Be Exceptional: Drive Leadership Success by Magnifying Your Strengths* (McGraw-Hill, 2012).

Adapted from content posted on hbr.org
on July 14, 2016 (product #H030DC).

4

Empathy Is Key to a Great Meeting

By Annie McKee

Yes, we all hate meetings. Yes, they are usually a waste of time. And yes, they're here to stay. So it's your responsibility as a leader to make them better. This doesn't mean just making them shorter, more efficient, and more organized. People need to enjoy them and, dare I say it, have fun.

Happiness matters a lot at work. How could it not, when many of us spend most of our waking hours there. The alternatives—chronic frustration, discontent, and outright hatred of our jobs—are simply not acceptable. Negative feelings interfere with creativity and innovation, not to mention collaboration.[1] And let's face it: Meetings are, for the most part, still where lots of collaboration, creativity, and innovation happen.[2] If meetings aren't working, then chances are we're not able to do what we need to do.

So how do we fix meetings so they are more enjoyable and produce more positive feelings? Sure, invite the right people, create better agendas, and be better prepared. Those are baseline fixes. But if you really want to improve how people work together at meetings, you'll need to rely on—and maybe develop—a couple of key emotional intelligence competencies: empathy and emotional self-management.

Why empathy? Empathy is a competency that allows you to read people. Who is supporting whom? Who is pissed off, and who is coasting? Where is the resistance? This isn't as easy as it seems. Sometimes, the smartest resisters often look like supporters, but they're not supportive at all. They're smart, sneaky idea killers.

Carefully reading people will also help you understand the major and often hidden conflicts in the group. Hint: These conflicts probably have nothing to do with the topics discussed or decisions being made at the meeting. They are far more likely to be linked to very human dynamics like who is allowed to influence whom (headquarters vs. the field, expats vs. local nationals) and power dynamics between genders and among people of various races.

Empathy lets you see and manage these power dynamics. Many of us would like to think that these sorts of concerns—and office politics in general—are beneath us, unimportant, or just for those Machiavellian folks we all dislike. Realistically, though, power is hugely important in groups because it is the real currency in most organizations. And it plays out in meetings. Learning to read how the flow of power is moving and shifting can help you lead the meeting—and everything else.

Keep in mind that employing empathy will help you understand how people are responding to *you*. As a leader you may be the most powerful person at the meeting. Some people, the dependent types, will defer at every turn. That feels good, for a minute. Carry on that way, and you're likely to create a dependent group—or one that is polarized between those who will do anything you want and those who will not.

This is where emotional self-management comes in, for a couple of reasons. First, take a look at the dependent folks in your meetings. Again, it can feel really good to have people admire you and agree with your every word. In fact, this can be a huge relief in our conflict-ridden organizations. But again, if you don't manage your response, you will make group dynamics worse. You will also look like a fool. Others are reading the group, too, and they will rightly read that you like it when people go along with you. They will see that you are falling prey to your own ego or to those who want to please or manipulate you.

Second, strong emotions set the tone for the entire group. We take our cue from one another about how to feel about what's going on around us. Are we in danger? Is there cause for celebration? Should we be fed up and cynical or hopeful and committed? Here's why this matters in meetings: If you, as a leader, effectively project out your more positive emotions, such as hope and enthusiasm, others will "mirror" these feelings and the general tone of the group will be marked by optimism and a sense of "we're in this together, and we can do it."[3] And there is a strong neurological link between feelings and cognition. We think more clearly and more creatively when our feelings are largely positive and when we are appropriately challenged.[4]

The other side of the coin is obvious. Your negative emotions are also contagious, and they are almost always destructive if unchecked and unmanaged. Express anger, contempt, or disrespect, and you will definitely push people into fight mode—individually and collectively. Express disdain, and you'll alienate people far beyond the end of the meeting. And it doesn't matter who you feel this way about. All it takes is for people to see it, and they will catch it— and worry that next time your target will be them.

This is not to say that all positive emotions are good all the time or that you should never express negative emotions. The point is that the leader's emotions are highly infectious. Know this and manage your feelings accordingly to create the kind of environment where people can work together to make decisions and get things done.

It may go without saying, but you can't do any of this with your phone on. As Daniel Goleman shares in his book *Focus: The Hidden Driver of Excellence*, we are not nearly as good at multitasking as we think we are. Actually we stink at it. So turn it off and pay attention to the people you are with today.

In the end, it's your job to make sure people leave your meeting feeling pretty good about what's happened, their contributions, and you as the leader. Empathy allows you to read what's going on, and self-management helps you move the group to a mood that supports getting things done—and happiness.

ANNIE MCKEE is a senior fellow at the University of Pennsylvania, director of the PennCLO Executive Doctoral Program, and the founder of the Teleos Leadership Institute. She is the coauthor, with Daniel Goleman and Richard Boyatzis, of *Pri-*

mal Leadership (Harvard Business Review Press, 2013) as well as a coauthor of *Resonant Leadership* (Harvard Business Review Press, 2005) and *Becoming a Resonant Leader* (Harvard Business Review Press, 2008). Her new book, *How to Be Happy at Work*, is forthcoming from Harvard Business Review Press.

Notes

1. D. Goleman et al., *Primal Leadership: Unleashing the Power of Emotional Intelligence* (rev. ed.) (Boston: Harvard Business Review Press, 2013).
2. K. D'Costa, "Why Do We Need to Have So Many Meetings?" *Scientific American*, November 17, 2014, https://blogs.scientificamerican.com/anthropology-in-practice/why-do-we-need-to-have-so-many-meetings/.
3. V. Ramachandran, "The Neurons That Shaped Civilization," TED talk, November 2009, https://www.ted.com/talks/vs_ramachandran_the_neurons_that_shaped_civilization?language=en.
4. M. Csikzsentmihalyi, *Creativity: Flow and the Psychology of Discovery and Invention* (New York: Harper Perennial, 1997).

Adapted from content posted on hbr.org
on March 23, 2015 (product #H01YDY).

5

It's Harder to Empathize with People If You've Been in Their Shoes

By Rachel Ruttan, Mary-Hunter McDonnell, and Loran Nordgren

Imagine that you have just become a new parent. Overwhelmed and exhausted, your performance at work is suffering. You desperately want to work from home part time to devote more attention to your family. One of your supervisors has had children while climbing the corporate ladder, while the other hasn't. Which supervisor is more likely to embrace your request?

Most people would recommend approaching the supervisor who has children, drawing on the intuition that shared experience breeds empathy. After all, she has "been there" and thus would seem best placed to understand your situation.

Our recent research suggests that this instinct is very often wrong.[1]

In a series of recent experiments, we found that people who have endured challenges in the past (like divorce or being skipped over for a promotion) were less likely to show compassion for someone facing the same struggle, compared with people with no experience in that particular situation.

In the first experiment, we surveyed people participating in a "polar plunge": a jump into a very icy Lake Michigan in March. All participants read a story about a man named Pat who intended to complete the plunge but chickened out and withdrew from the event at the last minute. Critically, participants read about Pat either before they had completed the plunge themselves or one week after. We found that polar plungers who had successfully completed the plunge were less compassionate and more contemptuous of Pat than were those who had not yet completed the plunge.

In another study, we looked at compassion toward an individual struggling with unemployment. More than 200 people read a story about a man who—despite his best efforts—is unable to find a job. Struggling to make ends meet, the man ultimately stoops to selling drugs in order to earn money. We found that people who had overcome a period of unemployment in the past were less compassionate and more judgmental of the man than people who were currently unemployed or had never been involuntarily unemployed.

A third study examined compassion toward a bullied teenager. Participants were told either that the teen was successfully coping with the bullying or that he failed to cope by lashing out violently. Compared with participants who had no experience with bullying, participants who reported having been bullied in the past themselves were more compassionate toward the teen who was appropriately coping with the experience. But, as in our earlier studies, participants who were bullied in the past were the *least* compassionate toward the teen who failed to successfully cope with the bullying.

Taken together, these results suggest that people who have endured a difficult experience are particularly likely to penalize those who struggle to cope with a similar ordeal.

But why does this occur? We suggest that this phenomenon is rooted in two psychological truths.

First, people generally have difficulty accurately recalling just how difficult a past aversive experience was. Though we may remember that a past experience was painful, stressful, or emotionally trying, we tend to underestimate just how painful that experience felt in the moment. This phenomenon is called an "empathy gap."[2]

Second, people who have previously overcome an aversive experience know that they were able to successfully overcome it, which makes them feel especially confident about their understanding of just how difficult the situation is. The combined experience of "I can't recall how difficult it was" and "I know that I got through it myself" creates the perception that the event can be readily conquered, reducing empathy toward others struggling with the event.

This finding seems to run counter to our intuitions. When we asked participants to predict who would show the most compassion for the bullied teenager, for instance—a teacher who'd endured bullying himself or one who never had—an overwhelming 99 out of the 112 people chose the teacher who had been bullied. This means that many people may be instinctively seeking compassion from the very people who are least likely to provide it.

This clearly has implications for peer-to-peer office communication (choose the person you vent to carefully). And mentorship programs, which often pair people from similar backgrounds or experiences, may need to be reexamined. But there are also important lessons for leaders. When approached by employees in distress, leaders may believe that their own emotional reaction to the issue should guide their response. For example, an executive who broke the glass ceiling may focus on her own success when considering an employee's concerns about discrimination. Similarly, managers in overworked industries such as consulting and banking may respond to employees' concerns about burnout and fatigue with comments such as, "I had to work those hours, so why are you complaining?" (And in fact, there is some evidence that this mechanism is at play when older workers push back on reforms designed to help cut down on overwork.)[3]

Simply put, leaders need to get outside of their own heads—to place *less* emphasis, not more, on their own past challenges. To bridge the empathy gap, leaders may be best served by focusing on how upset the other person seems to be or by reminding themselves that many others struggle with the same challenge. Returning to the opening example, the supervisor approached by an exhausted new parent could instead think about the countless other new parents who struggle to find work-life balance, many of whom are ultimately pushed out of the workplace.

When we're trying to encourage someone to be more empathetic, we often say something like, "walk a mile in his shoes." As it turns out, that may be exactly the wrong thing to say to people who have worn those shoes themselves.

RACHEL RUTTAN is a doctoral student at the Kellogg School of Management. MARY-HUNTER MCDONNELL is an assistant professor of management at the Wharton School. LORAN NORDGREN is an associate professor of management and organizations at the Kellogg School of Management.

Notes

1. R. L. Ruttan et al., "Having 'Been There' Doesn't Mean I Care: When Prior Experience Reduces Compassion for Emotional Distress," *Journal of Personality and Social Psychology* 108, no. 4 (April 2015): 610–622.

2. L. F. Nordgren et al., "Visceral Drives in Retrospect: Explanations About the Inaccessible Past," *Psychological Science* 17, no. 7 (July 2006): 635–640.

3. K. C. Kellogg, *Challenging Operations: Medical Reform and Resistance in Surgery* (Chicago: University of Chicago Press, 2011).

Adapted from content posted on hbr.org on
October 20, 2015 (product #H02FKN).

6

Becoming Powerful Makes You Less Empathetic

By Lou Solomon

Last year, I worked with a senior executive—let's call him Steve—who had received feedback from his boss that he was wearing the power of his new title in an off-putting way. Steve's boss told him that he had developed a subtle way of being right in meetings that sucked all the oxygen out of the room. No one wanted to offer ideas once Steve had declared the right answer. Since his promotion, Steve had become less of a team player and more of a superior who knew better than others. In short, he had lost his empathy.

Why does this sort of shift in behavior happen to so many people when they're promoted to the ranks of management? Research shows that personal power actually interferes with our ability to empathize. Dacher Keltner, an author and social psychologist at the University of California, Berkeley, has conducted empirical studies showing that people who have power suffer deficits in empathy, the ability to read emotions, and the ability to adapt behaviors to other people. In fact, power can actually change how the brain functions, according to research from Sukhvinder Obhi, a neuroscientist at Wilfrid Laurier University in Ontario, Canada.[1]

The most common leadership failures don't involve fraud, the embezzlement of funds, or sex scandals. It's more common to see leaders fail in the area of every day self-management—and the use of power in a way that is motivated by ego and self-interest.

How does it happen? Slowly, and then suddenly. It happens with bad mini choices, made perhaps on an unconscious level. It might show up as the subtle act of throwing one's weight around. Demands for special treatment, isolated decision making, and getting one's way. Leaders who are pulled over by the police for speeding or driving drunk become indignant and rail, "Do you know who I am?" Suddenly the story hits social media, and we change our minds about the once-revered personality.

This points to a bigger story about power and fame. How do people start out in pursuit of a dream and wind up aggrandizing themselves instead? They reach a choke point, where they cross over from being generous with their power to using their power for their own benefit.

Take the case of former Charlotte, North Carolina, mayor Patrick Cannon. Cannon came from nothing. He overcame poverty and the violent loss of his father at the age of 5. He earned a degree from North Carolina A&T State University and entered public service at the age of 26, becoming the youngest council member in Charlotte history. He was known for being completely committed to serving the public and generous with the time he spent as a role model for young people.

But in 2014, Cannon, then 47, pleaded guilty to accepting $50,000 in bribes while in office.[2] As he entered the city's federal courthouse, he tripped and fell. The media was there to capture the fall, which was symbolic of the much bigger fall of an elected leader and small business owner who once embodied the very essence of personal achievement against staggering odds. Cannon now has the distinction of being the first mayor in the city's history to be sent to prison. Insiders say he was a good man but all too human, and he seemed vulnerable as he became isolated in his decision making. And while a local minister argued that Cannon's one lapse in judgment should not define the man and his career of exceptional public service, he is now judged only by his weakness: his dramatic move from humility and generosity to corruption. And that image of Cannon tripping on his way into court is now the image that people associate with him.

What can leaders do if they fear that they might be crossing the line from power to abuse of power? First, you must invite other people in. You must be willing to risk vulnerability and ask for feedback. A good executive coach can help you return to a state of empathy and value-driven decisions. However, be sure to ask for feedback from a wide variety of people. Dispense with the softball questions (How am I doing?) and ask the tough ones (How does my style and focus affect my employees?).

Preventive maintenance begins with self-awareness and a daring self-inventory. Here are some important questions to ask yourself:

1. Do you have a support network of friends, family, and colleagues who care about you without the title and can help you stay down-to-earth?

2. Do you have an executive coach, mentor, or confidant?

3. What feedback have you gotten about not walking the talk?

4. Do you demand privileges?

5. Are you keeping the small, inconvenient promises that fall outside of the spotlight?

6. Do you invite others into the spotlight?

7. Do you isolate yourself in the decision-making process? Do the decisions you're making reflect what you truly value?

8. Do you admit your mistakes?

9. Are you the same person at work, at home, and in the spotlight?

10. Do you tell yourself there are exceptions or different rules for people like you?

If a leader earns our trust, we hold them to non-negotiable standards. Nothing will blow up more dramatically than a failure to walk the talk or the selfish abuse of power. We all want our leaders to be highly competent, visionary, take-charge people. However, empathy, authenticity, and generosity are what distinguish competence and greatness. The most self-aware leaders recognize the signals of abuse of power and correct course before it's too late.

LOU SOLOMON is the CEO of Interact, a communications consultancy. She is the author of *Say Something Real* and an adjunct faculty member at the McColl School of Business at Queens University of Charlotte.

Notes

1. J. Hogeveen et al., "Power Changes How the Brain Responds to Others," *Journal of Experimental Psychology* 143, no. 2 (April 2014): 755–762.
2. M. Gordon et al., "Patrick Cannon Pleads Guilty to Corruption Charge," *The Charlotte Observer*, June 3, 2014, www.charlotteobserver.com/news/local/article9127154 .html.

Adapted from content posted on hbr.org
on April 21, 2015 (product #H020S0).

7

A Process for Empathetic Product Design

By Jon Kolko

The discipline of product management is shifting from an external focus on the market, or an internal focus on technology, to an empathetic focus on people. While it's not too difficult to rally people around this general idea, it can be hard at first to understand how to translate it into tactics. So in this article, I'll walk through how we applied this approach to a particular product at a startup and how it led to large-scale adoption and, ultimately, the acquisition of the company.

I was previously VP of design at MyEdu, where we focused on helping students succeed in college, show their academic accomplishments, and gain employment. MyEdu started with a series of free academic planning tools, including a schedule planner. As we formalized a business model focused on college recruiting, we conducted behavioral, empathetic research with college students and recruiters. This type of qualitative research focuses on what people do, rather than what they say. We spent hours with students in their dorm rooms, watching them do their homework, watch TV, and register for classes. We watched them being college students, and our goal was not to identify workflow conflicts or utilitarian problems to solve; it was to build a set of intuitive feelings about what it means to be a college student. We conducted the same form of research with recruiters, watching them speak to candidates and work through their hiring process.

This form of research is misleadingly simple—you go and watch people. The challenge is in forging a disarming relationship with people in a very short period of time. Our goal is to form a master and apprentice relationship: We enter these research activities as a humble apprentice, expecting to learn from a master. It may sound a little funny, but college students are masters of being in academia, with all of the successes and failures this experience brings them.

As we complete our research, we transcribe the session in full. This time-consuming effort is critical, because it embeds the participants' collective voice in our heads. As we play, type, pause, and rewind our recordings, we begin to quite literally think from the perspective of the participant. I've found that I can repeat participant quotes and "channel" their voices years after a research session is over. We distribute the transcriptions into thousands of individual utterances, and then we post the utterances all over our war room.

The input of our behavioral research is a profile of the type of people we want to empathize with. The output of our research is a massive data set of verbatim utterances, exploded into individual, moveable parts.

Once we've generated a large quantity of data, our next step is to synthesize the contents into meaningful insights. This is an arduous, seemingly endless process—it will quite literally fill any amount of time you allot to it. We read individual notes, highlight salient points, and move the notes around. We build groups of notes in a bottom-up fashion, identifying similarities and anomalies. We invite the entire product team to participate: If they have 15 or 30 minutes, they are encouraged to pop in, read some notes, and shift them to places that make sense. Over time, the room begins to take shape. As groupings emerge, we give them action-oriented names. Rather than using pithy category labels like "Career Service" or "Employment," we write initial summary statements like "Students write résumés in order to find jobs."

When we've made substantial progress, we begin to provoke introspection on the categories by asking "why"-oriented questions. And the key to the whole process is that we answer these questions *even though we don't know the answer for sure.* We combine what we know about students with what we know about ourselves. We build on our own life experiences, and as we leverage our student-focused empathetic lens, we make inferential leaps. In this way, we drive innovation and simultaneously introduce risk. In this case, we asked the question, "Why do students develop résumés to find jobs?" and answered it, "Because they think employers want to see a résumé." This is what Roger Martin refers to as "abductive reasoning": a form of logical recombination to move past the expected and into the provocative world of innovation.[1]

Finally, when we've answered these "why" questions about each group, we create a series of insight statements, which are provocative statements of truth about human behavior. We'll build upon the why statement, abstracting our answer away from the students we spent time with and making a generalization about *all* students. We asked, "Why do students develop résumés to find jobs?" and we answered it, "Because they think employers want to see a résumé." Now we'll craft an insight statement: "Students think they have an idea of what employers want in a candidate, but they are often wrong." We've shifted from a passive statement to an active assertion. We've made a large inferential leap. And we've arrived at the scaffold for a new product, service, or idea.

We can create a similar provocative statement of truth about recruiters by learning from employers. Based on our research, we identified that recruiters spend very little time with each résumé but have very strong opinions about candidates. Our insight statement becomes "Recruiters make snap judgments, directly impacting a candidate's chances of success." (See table 1.)

The input of our synthesis process is the raw data from research, transcribed and distributed on a large wall. The output of our synthesis process is a series of insights: provocative statements of truth about human behavior.

TABLE 1

Student insight	Employer insight
Students think they have an idea of what employers want in a candidate, but they are often wrong.	**Recruiters make snap judgments, directly impacting a candidate's chances of success.**
"Your résumé is like your life: It is your golden ticket to the chocolate factory."—*Samantha, international business major*	"Don't apply to five of my jobs, because you aren't going to get any of them."—*Meg, recruiter*
• Emphasize bullets on a résumé rather than exhibit skills through artifacts (portfolio) • Think they should have a broad but shallow set of abilities rather than a depth of competency in one area • Typically apply for any and every job	• Form an opinion in seconds based on a single data point • Are looking for specific skills and evidence of competency in that skill • Create a mental narrative of what a candidate can do based on how the student presents herself

Now we can start to merge and compare insights in order to arrive at a value proposition. As we connect the two insights from students and employers and juxtapose them, we can narrow in on a "what-if" opportunity. What if we taught students new ways to think about finding a job? What if we showed students alternative paths to jobs? What if we helped students identify their skills and present them to employers in a credible way? (See table 2.)

If we subtly shift the language, we arrive at a capability value proposition: "MyEdu helps students identify their skills and present them to employers in a credible way."

This value proposition is a promise. We promise to students that if they use our products, we'll help them identify their skills and show those skills to employers. If we fail to deliver on that promise, students have a poor experience with our products—and leave. The same is true for any product or service company. If Comcast promises to deliver internet access to our

TABLE 2

Student insight	Employer Insight
Students think they have an idea of what employers want in a candidate, but they are often wrong.	**Recruiters make snap judgments, directly impacting a candidate's chances of success.**

What-if opportunity:
What if we helped students identify their skills and present them to employees in a credible way?

home but doesn't, we get frustrated. If they fail frequently enough, we dump them for a company with a similar or better value proposition.

Insights act as the input to this phase in the empathetic design process, and the output of this process is an emotionally charged value promise.

Armed with a value proposition, we have constraints around what we're building. In addition to providing an external statement of value, this statement also indicates how we can determine if the capabilities, features, and other details we brainstorm are appropriate to include in the offering. If we dream up a new feature and it doesn't help students identify their skills and present them to employers in a credible way, it's not appropriate for us to build. The value promise becomes the objective criteria in a subjective context, acting as a sieve through which we can pour our good ideas.

Now we tell stories—what we call "hero flows," or the main paths through our products that help people become happy or content. These stories paint a picture of how a person uses our product to receive the value promise. We write these, draw them as stick figures, and start to sketch the real product interfaces. And then, through a fairly standard product development process, we bring these stories to life with wireframes, visual comps, motion studies, and other traditional digital product assets.

Through this process, we developed the MyEdu Profile: a highly visual record that helps students highlight academic accomplishments and present them to employers in the context of recruiting.

During research, we heard from some college students that "LinkedIn makes me feel dumb." They don't have a lot of professional experiences, so asking them to highlight these accomplishments is a nonstarter. But as students use our academic planning tools, their behavior and activities translate to profile elements that highlight their academic accomplishments: We can deliver on our value proposition.

Our value proposition acts as the input to the core of product development. The output of this process is our products, which facilitate the iterative, incremental set of capabilities that shift behavior and help people achieve their wants, needs, and desires.

The LinkedIn example we highlighted illustrates what we call "empathetic research." We marinated in data and persevered through a rigorous process of sense making in order to arrive at insights. We leveraged these insights to provoke a value proposition, and then we built stories on top of the entire scaffold. And as a result of this process, we created a product with emotional resonance. The profile product attracted more than a million college students in about a year, and during a busy academic registration period, we saw growth of between 3,000 to 3,500 new student profiles a day. After we were acquired by education software company Blackboard and integrated this into the flagship learning management system, we saw growth of between 18,000 and 20,000 new student profiles a day.

The process described here is not hard, and it's not new—companies like Frog Design have been leveraging this approach for years, and I learned the fundamentals of empathetic design when I was an undergraduate at Carnegie Mellon. But for most companies, this process requires leaning on a different corporate ideology. It's a process informed by deep qualitative data rather than statistical market data. It celebrates people rather than technology. And it requires identifying and believing in behavioral insights, which are subjective and, in their ambiguity, full of risk.

JON KOLKO is the vice president of design at Blackboard, an education software company, the founder and director of Austin Center for Design, and the author of *Well-Designed: How to Use Empathy to Create Products People Love* (Harvard Business Review Press, 2014).

Note

1. R. Martin, *The Design of Business: Why Design Thinking Is the Next Competitive Advantage* (Boston: Harvard Business Review Press, 2009.)

Adapted from content posted on hbr.org
on April 23, 2015 (product #H0201E).

8

How Facebook Uses Empathy to Keep User Data Safe

By Melissa Luu-Van

Online security often focuses on technical details: software, hardware, vulnerabilities, and the like. But effective security is driven as much by people as it is by technology. After all, the point is to protect the consumers, employees, and partners who use our products.

The ways those people interact with technology and each other can completely change the effectiveness of your security strategy. So security products and tools must take into account the human context of the problems they're solving—and that requires empathy.

At Facebook, empathy helps us create solutions that work because they're designed around our users' experiences and well-being. Specifically, we see three ways to make security efforts more empathetic.

Consumer-driven goals that are actionable and specific. By researching the cultural and physical contexts in which people use the things you produce, you can define better, more precise goals for those products. Engaging with your users on a regular basis—through reporting tools built into your product, online surveys, or focus groups, for example—is a necessary step for understanding, rather than assuming you know, their challenges and needs.

For example, we recently asked several focus groups about their most important security concerns on Facebook. What are they worried about? What would help them feel safe? Overwhelmingly, people told us they wanted more control. Simply knowing that Facebook was working behind the scenes to protect their accounts wasn't enough. We learned that many Facebook users were unaware of all the security features we offer to add extra protection to their accounts. But once they learned about them, they were eager to use them. People also wanted to be able to control these features and to see how each tool protects their account. These findings told us two very important things about the security features. First, they needed to be easier to find. Second, they needed to be more visible and give people more control.

With that in mind, we created Security Checkup, a tool designed to make Facebook's security controls more visible and easier to use. During early testing and after our global launch, we asked people on Facebook about their experience using the new tool. They told us they found Security Checkup useful and helpful; the tool's completion rate quickly soared to over 90%. These results are validating—but not surprising, since we tailored Security Checkup to what we had learned about people's preferences and concerns.

Our primary goal has always been to protect the people who use Facebook, but through our research we've added the goal of helping people better protect themselves wherever they are on the web. The security lessons our users learn on Facebook could help them develop safer online habits—such as using unique passwords or checking app permissions—that can be used on other sites, too.

Collaborative, cross-functional teams. Security is often approached as an engineering-led effort in which cross-functional teams from research, design, or product are less important. However, we've found that disciplines besides engineering are just as critical to the thought process and product development, because diversity of thought is an important characteristic of empathy.

Cross-functional teams are particularly valuable for thinking through the various experiences people may have with a product. Car manufacturers have done this for years, adding seat belts and air bags to keep people safe even when a vehicle performs outside its intended purpose (that is, during a high-speed crash). The cars' designs were changed to make people's experiences safer by default. Similarly, Facebook's security tools are built with the belief that better product design leads to safer behavior. Many of our departments collaborate for this purpose, including research, security, user experience, marketing, product design, and communications.

Throughout various stages of the process, these teams convene to discuss potential engineering, design, or security challenges; identify solutions; and consider the impact any of these things might have on someone's overall experience using our products. We believe this collective expertise helps us avoid possible issues by addressing them early on in the development process. For example, during early iterations of Security Checkup we realized that simply drawing attention to our existing security features was interpreted by some people as a warning or alert that something was wrong. Because we had design and communication experts already working on the development team, we were able to create a security tool with a utilitarian tone to avoid making people feel unnecessarily concerned.

A focus on outcomes rather than inputs. Finally, and most important, empathy helps us keep people safe. If people don't have a safe experience, it doesn't matter how many security tools we make. That's why people's actual outcomes are always our highest priority. Empathy helps in a couple of ways.

First, having empathy for the people who use your products keeps you focused on helping them make small but useful tweaks (rather than major overhauls) to their online behavior. Because online security can be a daunting topic, many people shy away from being proactive about it. So encouraging people to start with small steps can go a long way. We've seen that even incremental progress helps people learn how to recognize risk and make safer choices. Simple behaviors like turning on extra security settings for online accounts can have a huge impact on someone's safety.

Second, using empathetic language in consumer communication makes security less intimidating and more accessible. This means using terms and concepts that are easily understood within local cultural and languages, even if they differ from the terms technical experts would use. Research shows that over time, fearful communications designed to scare people actually have a diminishing rate of return in helping consumers avoid online threats. On the other hand, building resiliency can help people better understand potential threats, recover from mistakes, and identify the most important preventative actions.

If you want to increase empathy on your team, one of the best ways to do it is to invite a diverse set of disciplines to be part of the product development process, both through hiring and through collaborating with other teams. Professionals with experience in psychology, behavioral sciences, or communications can bring invaluable perspectives for building an empathetic team. Then invest in research to understand the experience and security concerns of the people using your products; don't guess or assume you know what they are.

Empathy is not easy. It requires a commitment to deeply understanding the people you're protecting—but it also leads to significantly better security. And that's the whole point.

MELISSA LUU-VAN is a product manager at Facebook, where she leads a cross-functional team focused on helping people maintain access to their accounts and keep them secure.

Adapted from content posted on hbr.org
on April 28, 2016 (product #H02U0U).

9

The Limits of Empathy

By Adam Waytz

A few years ago, Ford Motor Company started asking its (mostly male) engineers to wear the Empathy Belly, a simulator that allows them to experience symptoms of pregnancy first-hand—the back pain, the bladder pressure, the 30 or so pounds of extra weight. They can even feel "movements" that mimic fetal kicking. The idea is to get them to understand the ergonomic challenges that pregnant women face when driving, such as limited reach, shifts in posture and center of gravity, and general bodily awkwardness.

It's unclear whether this has improved Ford's cars or increased customer satisfaction, but the engineers claim benefits from the experience. They're still using the belly; they're also simulating the foggy vision and stiff joints of elderly drivers with an "age suit." If nothing more, these exercises are certainly an attempt to "get the other person's point of view," which Henry Ford once famously said was the key to success.

Empathy is all the rage pretty much everywhere—not just at Ford and not just on engineering and product development teams. It's at the heart of design thinking and innovation more broadly defined. It's also touted as a critical leadership skill—one that helps you influence others in your organization, anticipate stakeholders' concerns, respond to social media followers, and even run better meetings.

But recent research (by me and many others) suggests that all this heat and light may be a bit too intense. Though empathy is essential to leading and managing others—without it, you'll make disastrous decisions and forfeit the benefits just described—

failing to recognize its limits can impair individual and organizational performance.

Here are some of the biggest problems you can run into and recommendations for getting around them.

Problem #1: It's exhausting

Like heavy-duty cognitive tasks, such as keeping multiple pieces of information in mind at once or avoiding distractions in a busy environment, empathy depletes our mental resources. So jobs that require constant empathy can lead to "compassion fatigue," an acute inability to empathize that's driven by stress, and burnout, a more gradual and chronic version of this phenomenon.

Health and human services professionals (doctors, nurses, social workers, corrections officers) are especially at risk, because empathy is central to their day-to-day jobs. In a study of hospice nurses, for example, the key predictors for compassion fatigue were psychological: anxiety, feelings of trauma, life demands, and what the researchers call excessive empathy, meaning the tendency to sacrifice one's own needs for others' (rather than simply "feeling" for people).[1] Variables such as long hours and heavy caseloads also had an impact, but less than expected. And in a survey of Korean nurses, self-reported compassion fatigue strongly predicted their intentions to leave their jobs in the near future.[2] Other studies of nurses show additional consequences of compassion fatigue, such as absenteeism and increased errors in administering medication.

People who work for charities and other nonprofits (think animal shelters) are similarly at risk. Voluntary turnover is exceedingly high, in part because of the empathically demanding nature of the work; low pay exacerbates the element of self-sacrifice. What's more, society's strict views of how nonprofits should operate mean they face a backlash when they act like businesses (for instance, investing in "overhead" to keep the organization running smoothly). They're expected to thrive through selfless outpourings of compassion from workers.

The demand for empathy is relentless in other sectors as well. Day after day, managers must motivate knowledge workers by understanding their experiences and perspectives and helping them find personal meaning in their work. Customer service professionals must continually quell the concerns of distressed callers. Empathy is exhausting in any setting or role in which it's a primary aspect of the job.

Problem #2: It's zero-sum

Empathy doesn't just drain energy and cognitive resources—it also depletes itself. The more empathy I devote to my spouse, the less I have left for my mother; the more I give to my mother, the less I can give my son. Both our desire to be empathic and the effort it requires are in limited supply, whether we're dealing with family and friends or customers and colleagues.

Consider this study: Researchers examined the trade-offs associated with empathic behaviors at work and at home by surveying 844 workers from various sectors, including hairstylists, firefighters, and telecom professionals.[3] People who reported workplace behaviors such as taking "time to listen to coworkers' problems and worries" and helping "others who have heavy workloads" felt less capable of connecting with their families. They felt emotionally drained and burdened by work-related demands.

Sometimes the zero-sum problem leads to another type of trade-off: Empathy toward insiders—say, people on our teams or in our organizations—can limit our capacity to empathize with people outside our immediate circles. We naturally put more time and effort into understanding the needs of our close friends and colleagues. We simply find it easier to do, because we care more about them to begin with. This uneven investment creates a gap that's widened by our limited supply of empathy: As we use up most of what's available on insiders, our bonds with them get stronger, while our desire to connect with outsiders wanes.

Preferential empathy can antagonize those who see us as protecting our own (think about how people reacted when the Pope praised the Catholic Church's handling of sexual abuse). It can also, a bit more surprisingly, lead to insiders' aggression toward outsiders. For example, in a study I conducted with University of Chicago professor Nicholas Epley, we looked at how two sets of participants—those sitting with a friend (to prime empathic connection) and those sitting with a stranger—would treat a group of terrorists, an outgroup with particularly negative associations. After describing the terrorists, we asked how much participants endorsed statements portraying them as subhuman, how acceptable waterboarding them would be, and how much voltage of electric shock they would be willing to administer to them. Merely sitting in a room with a friend significantly increased people's willingness to torture and dehumanize.

Although this study represents an extreme case, the same principle holds for organizations. Compassion for one's own employees and colleagues sometimes produces aggressive responses toward others. More often, insiders are simply uninterested in empathizing with outsiders—but even that can cause people to neglect opportunities for constructive collaboration across functions or organizations.

Problem #3: It can erode ethics

Finally, empathy can cause lapses in ethical judgment. We saw some of that in the study about terrorists. In many cases, though, the problem stems not from aggression toward outsiders but, rather, from extreme loyalty toward insiders. In making a focused effort to see and feel things the way people who are close to us do, we may take on their interests as our own. This can make us more willing to overlook transgressions or even behave badly ourselves.

Multiple studies in behavioral science and decision making show that people are more inclined to cheat when it serves another person.[4] In various settings, with the benefits ranging from financial to reputational, people use this ostensible altruism to rationalize their dishonesty. It only gets worse when they empathize with another's plight or feel the pain of someone who is treated unfairly: In those cases, they're even more likely to lie, cheat, or steal to benefit that person.

In the workplace, empathy toward fellow employees can inhibit whistle-blowing—and when that happens, it seems scandals often follow. Just ask the police, the military, Penn State University, Citigroup, JPMorgan, and WorldCom. The kinds of problems that have plagued those organizations—brutality, sexual abuse, fraud—tend to be exposed by outsiders who don't identify closely with the perpetrators.

In my research with Liane Young and James Dungan of Boston College, we studied the effects of loyalty on people using Amazon's Mechanical Turk, an online marketplace where users earn money for completing tasks. At the beginning of the study, we asked some participants to write an essay about loyalty and others to write about fairness. Later in the study, they were each exposed to poor work by someone else. Those who had received the loyalty nudge were less willing to blow the whistle on a fellow user for inferior performance. This finding complements research showing that bribery is more common in countries that prize collectivism.[5] The sense of group belonging and interdependence among members often leads people to tolerate the offense. It makes them feel less accountable for it, diffusing responsibility to the collective whole instead of assigning it to the individual.

In short, empathy for those within one's immediate circle can conflict with justice for all.

How to rein in excessive empathy

These three problems may seem intractable, but as a manager you can do a number of things to mitigate them in your organization.

Split up the work

You might start by asking each employee to zero in on a certain set of stakeholders, rather than empathize with anyone and everyone. Some people can focus primarily on customers, for instance, and others on coworkers—think of it as creating task forces to meet different stakeholders' needs. This makes the work of developing relationships and gathering perspectives less consuming for individuals. You'll also accomplish more in the aggregate, by distributing "caring" responsibilities across your team or company. Although empathy is finite for any one person, it's less bounded when managed across employees.

Make it less of a sacrifice

Our mindsets can either intensify or lessen our susceptibility to empathy overload. For example, we exacerbate the zero-sum problem when we assume that our own interests and others' are fundamentally opposed. (This often happens in deal making, when parties with different positions on an issue get stuck because they're obsessed with the gap between them.) An adversarial mindset not only prevents us from understanding and responding to the other party but also makes us feel as though we've "lost" when we don't get our way. We can avoid burnout by seeking integrative solutions that serve both sides' interests.

Take this example: A salary negotiation between a hiring manager and a promising candidate will become a tug-of-war contest if they have different numbers in mind and fixate on the money alone. But let's suppose that the candidate actually cares more about job security, and the manager is keenly interested in avoiding turnover. Building security into the contract would be a win-win: an empathic act by the manager that wouldn't drain his empathy reserves the way making a concession on salary would, because keeping new hires around is in line with his own desires.

There's only so much empathy to go around, but it's possible to achieve economies of sorts. By asking questions instead of letting assumptions go unchecked, you can bring such solutions to the surface.

Give people breaks

As a management and organizations professor, I cringe when students refer to my department's coursework—on leadership, teams, and negotiation—as "soft skills." Understanding and responding to the needs, interests, and desires of other human beings involves some of the *hardest* work of all. Despite claims that empathy comes naturally, it takes arduous mental effort to get into another person's mind—and then to respond with compassion rather than indifference.

We all know that people need periodic relief from technical and analytical work and from rote jobs like data entry. The same is true of empathy. Look for ways to give employees breaks. It's not sufficient to encourage self-directed projects that also benefit the company (and often result in more work), as Google did with its 20% time policy. Encourage individuals to take time to focus on their interests alone. Recent research finds that people who take lots of self-focused breaks subsequently report feeling more empathy for others.[6] That might seem counterintuitive, but when people feel restored, they're better able to perform the demanding tasks of figuring out and responding to what others need.

How do you give people respite from thinking and caring about others? Some companies are purchasing isolation chambers like Orrb Technologies' wellness and learning pods so that people can literally put themselves in a bubble to relax, meditate, or do whatever else helps them recharge. McLaren, for example, uses the pods to train F1 supercar drivers to focus. Other companies, such as electrical parts distributor Van Meter, are relying on much simpler interventions like shutting off employee email accounts when workers go on vacation to allow them to concentrate on themselves without interruption.

Despite its limitations, empathy is essential at work. So managers should make sure employees are investing it wisely.

When trying to empathize, it's generally better to talk with people about their experiences than to imagine how they might be feeling, as Nicholas Epley suggests in his book *Mindwise*. A recent study bears this out.[7] Participants were asked how capable they thought blind people were of working and living independently. But before answering the question, some were asked to complete difficult physical tasks while wearing a blindfold. Those who had done the blindness simulation judged blind people to be much less capable. That's because the exercise led them to ask "What would it be like if *I* were blind?" (the answer: very difficult!) rather than "What is it like for *a blind person* to be blind?" This finding speaks to why Ford's use of the Empathy Belly, while well-intentioned, may be misguided: After wearing it, engineers may overestimate or misidentify the difficulties faced by drivers who actually are pregnant.

Talking to people—asking them how they feel, what they want, and what they think—may seem simplistic, but it's more accurate. It's also less taxing to employees and their organizations, because it involves collecting real information instead of endlessly speculating. It's a smarter way to empathize.

ADAM WAYTZ is an associate professor of management and organizations at Northwestern University's Kellogg School of Management.

Notes

1. M. Abendroth and J. Flannery, "Predicting the Risk of Compassion Fatigue: A Study of Hospice Nurses," *Journal of Hospice and Palliative Nursing* 8, no. 6 (November–December 2006): 346–356.

2. K. Sung et al., "Relationships Between Compassion Fatigue, Burnout, and Turnover Intention in Korean Hospital Nurses," *Journal of Korean Academy of Nursing* 42, no. 7 (December 2012): 1087–1094.

3. J. Halbesleben et al., "Too Engaged? A Conservation of Resources View of the Relationships Between Work Engagement and Work Interference with Family," *Journal of Applied Psychology* 94, no. 6 (November 2009): 1452–1465.

4. F. Gino et al., "Self-Serving Altruism? The Lure of Unethical Actions That Benefit Others," *Journal of Economic Behavior & Organization* 93 (September 2013); and F. Gino and L. Pierce, "Dishonesty in the Name of Equity," *Psychological Science* 20, no. 9 (December 2009): 1153–1160.

5. N. Mazar and P. Aggarwal, "Greasing the Palm: Can Collectivism Promote Bribery?" *Psychological Science* 22, no. 7 (June 2011): 843–848.

6. G. Boyraz and J. B. Waits, "Reciprocal Associations Among Self-Focused Attention, Self-Acceptance, and Empathy: A Two-Wave Panel Study," *Personality and Individual Differences* 74 (2015): 84–89.

7. A. M. Silverman et al., "Stumbling in Their Shoes: Disability Simulations Reduce Judge Capabilities of Disabled People," *Social Psychological & Personality Science* 6, no. 4 (May 2015): 464–471.

Reprinted from *Harvard Business Review*,
January–February 2016 (product #R1601D).

10

What the Dalai Lama Taught Daniel Goleman About Emotional Intelligence

An interview with Daniel Goleman by Andrea Ovans

wo decades before Daniel Goleman first wrote about emotional intelligence in the pages of HBR, he met the Dalai Lama at Amherst College. The Dalai Lama mentioned to the young science journalist for the *New York Times* that he was interested in meeting with scientists. Thus began a long, rich friendship as Goleman became involved over the years in arranging a series of what he calls "extended dialogues" between the Buddhist spiritual leader and researchers in fields ranging from ecology to neuroscience. Over the next 30 years, as Goleman has pursued his own work as a psychologist and business thinker, he has come to see the Dalai Lama as a highly uncommon leader. And so he was understandably delighted when, on the occasion of his friend's 80th birthday, he was asked to write a book describing the Dalai Lama's compassionate approach to addressing the world's most intractable problems. Published in June 2015, *Force for Good: The Dalai Lama's Vision for Our World*, which draws both on Goleman's background in cognitive science and his long relationship with the Dalai Lama, is both an exploration of the science and the power of compassion and a call to action. Curious about the book and about how the Dalai Lama's views on compassion informed Goleman's thinking on emotional intelligence, I caught up with Goleman over the phone. What follows are edited excerpts from our conversation.

HBR: *Let's start with some definitions here. What is compassion, as you are describing it? It sounds a lot like empathy, one of the major components of emotional intelligence. Is there a difference?*

Goleman: Yes, an important difference. As I've written about recently in HBR, three kinds of empathy are important to emotional intelligence: *cognitive empathy*—the ability to understand another person's point of view, *emotional empathy*—the ability to feel what someone else feels, and *empathic concern*—the ability to sense what another person needs from you [see chapter 1, "What Is Empathy?"]. Cultivating all three kinds of empathy, which originate in different parts of the brain, is important for building social relationships.

But compassion takes empathy a step further. When you feel compassion, you feel distress when you witness someone else in distress—and because of that you want to help that person.

Why draw this distinction?

Simply put, compassion makes the difference between understanding and caring. It's the kind of love that a parent has for a child. Cultivating it more broadly means extending that to the other people in our lives and to people we encounter. I think that in the workplace, that attitude has a hugely positive effect, whether it's in how we relate to our peers, how we are as a leader, or how we relate to clients and customers. A positive disposition toward another person creates the kind of resonance that builds trust and loyalty and makes interactions harmonious. And the opposite of that—when you do nothing to show that you care—creates distrust and disharmony and causes huge dysfunction at home and in business.

When you put it that way, it's hard to disagree that if you treat people well things would go better than if you don't or that if you cared about them they would care a lot more about you. So why do you think that doesn't just happen naturally? Is it a cultural thing? Or a misplaced confusion about when competition is appropriate?

I think too often there's a muddle in people's thinking that if I'm nice to another person or if I have their interests at heart it means that I don't have my own interests at heart. The pathology of that is, "Well, I'll just care about me and not the other person." And that, of course, is the kind of attitude that leads to lots of problems in the business realm and in the personal realm. But compassion also includes yourself. If we protect ourselves and make sure we're okay—and also make sure the other person is okay—that creates a different framework for working with and cooperating with other people.

Could you give me an example of how that might work in the business world?

There's research that was done on star salespeople and on client managers that found that the lowest level of performance was a kind of "I'm going to get the best deal I can now, and I don't care how this affects the other person" attitude, which means that you might make the sale but that you lose the relationship. But at the top end, the stars were typified by the attitude, "I am working for the client as well as myself. I'm going to be completely straight with them, and I'm going to act as their advisor. If the deal I have is not the best deal they can get I'm going to let them know because that's going to strengthen the relationship, even though I might lose this specific sale." And I think that captures the difference between the "me first" and the "let's all do well" attitude that I'm getting at.

How would we cultivate compassion if we just weren't feeling it?

Neuroscientists have been studying compassion recently, and places like Stanford, Yale, UC Berkeley, and the University of Wisconsin, Madison, among others, have been testing methodologies for increasing compassion. Right now there's a kind of a trend toward incorporating mindfulness into the workplace, and it turns out there's data from the Max Planck Institute showing that enhancing mindfulness does have an effect in brain function but that the circuitry that's affected is not the circuitry for concern or compassion. In other words, there's no automatic boost in compassion from mindfulness alone.

Still, in the traditional methods of meditation that mindfulness in the workplace is based on, the two were always linked, so that you would practice mindfulness in a context in which you'd also cultivate compassion.

Stanford, for example, has developed a program that incorporates secularized versions of methods that have originally come from religious practices. It involves a meditation in which you cultivate an attitude of loving-kindness or of concern, or of compassion, toward people. First you do this for yourself, then for people you love, then for people you just know. And finally you do it for everyone. And this has the effect of priming the circuitry responsible for compassion within the brain so that you are more inclined to act that way when the opportunity arises.

You've remarked that the Dalai Lama is a very distinctive kind of leader. Is there something we could learn as leaders ourselves from his unique form of leadership?

Observing him over the years, and then doing this book for which I interviewed him extensively, and of course being immersed in leadership literature myself, three things struck me.

The first is that he's not beholden to any organization at all. He's not in any business. He's not a party leader. He's a citizen of the world at large. And this has freed him to tackle the largest problems we face. I think that to the extent that a leader is beholden to a particular organization or outcome, that creates a kind of myopia of what's possible and what matters. Focus narrows to the next quarter's results or the next election. He's way beyond that. He thinks in terms of generations and of what's best for humanity as a whole. Because his vision is so expansive, he can take on the largest challenges, rather than small, narrowly defined ones.

So I think there's a lesson here for all of us, which is to ask ourselves if there is something that limits our vision—that limits our capacity to care. And is there a way to enlarge it?

The second thing that struck me is that he gathers information from everywhere. He meets with heads of state, and he meets with beggars. He's getting information from people at every level of society worldwide. This casting a large net lets him understand situations in a very deep way, and he can analyze them in many different ways and come up with solutions that aren't confined by anyone. And I think that's another lesson everyday leaders can take from him.

The third thing would be the scope of his compassion, which I think is an ideal that we could strive for. It's pretty unlimited. He seems to care about everybody and the world at large.

You've said that the book is a call to action. What do you hope people will do after reading it?

The book is a call to action, but it is a very reasoned call to action. The Dalai Lama is a great believer in a deep analysis of problems and letting solutions come from that analysis. And then he is also passionate about people acting now. Not feeling passive, not feeling helpless, not feeling, "What's the point? I won't live to see the benefit," but rather having them start changes now even if the change won't come to fruition until future generations.

So my hope, and his, is to help people understand what they can do in the face of problems that are so vast: creating a more inclusive economy; making work meaningful; doing good and not just well; cleaning up injustice and unfairness, corruption and collusion in society, whether in business, politics, or religion; helping the environment heal; the hope that one day conflict will be settled by dialogue rather than war.

These are very big issues. But everyone can do something to move things in the right direction, even if it's just reaching across the divide and becoming friendly with someone who belongs to some other group. That actually has a very powerful end result: If you have two groups somewhere in the world that have deep enmity toward each other, and yet a few people in each group like each other because they've had personal contact—they have a friend in that other group. So something as simple as reaching out across a divide is actually a profound thing. In each of these areas, with whatever leverage we have, the point is to use it, not just to stand back.

DANIEL GOLEMAN is a codirector of the Consortium for Research on Emotional Intelligence in Organizations at Rutgers University, coauthor of *Primal Leadership: Leading with Emotional Intelligence* (Harvard Business Review Press, 2013), and author of *The Brain and Emotional Intelligence: New Insights* and *Leadership: Selected Writings* (More Than Sound, 2011). His latest book is *A Force For Good: The Dalai Lama's Vision for Our World* (Bantam, 2015). ANDREA OVANS is a former senior editor at *Harvard Business Review*.

Adapted from content published on hbr.org
on May 4, 2015 (product #H021KQ).

Index

How to be human at work.

HBR's Emotional Intelligence Series features smart, essential reading on the human side of professional life from the pages of *Harvard Business Review*. Each book in the series offers uplifting stories, practical advice, and research from leading experts on how to tend to our emotional well-being at work.

Harvard Business Review Emotional Intelligence Series

Available in paperback or ebook format. The specially priced six-volume set includes:

- Mindfulness
- Resilience
- Influence and Persuasion

- Authentic Leadership
- Happiness
- Empathy

The most important management ideas all in one place.

We hope you enjoyed this book from *Harvard Business Review*. For the best ideas HBR has to offer turn to HBR's 10 Must Reads Boxed Set. From books on leadership and strategy to managing yourself and others, this 6-book collection delivers articles on the most essential business topics to help you succeed.

HBR's 10 Must Reads Series

The definitive collection of ideas and best practices on our most sought-after topics from the best minds in business.

- Change Management
- Collaboration
- Communication
- Emotional Intelligence
- Innovation
- Leadership
- Making Smart Decisions

- Managing Across Cultures
- Managing People
- Managing Yourself
- Strategic Marketing
- Strategy
- Teams
- The Essentials

hbr.org/mustreads

Happiness

HBR EMOTIONAL INTELLIGENCE SERIES

HBR Emotional Intelligence Series

How to be human at work

The HBR Emotional Intelligence Series features smart, essential reading on the human side of professional life from the pages of *Harvard Business Review*.

Empathy

Happiness

Mindfulness

Resilience

Other books on emotional intelligence from *Harvard Business Review*:

HBR's 10 Must Reads on Emotional Intelligence

HBR Guide to Emotional Intelligence

Happiness

HBR EMOTIONAL INTELLIGENCE SERIES

Harvard Business Review Press

Boston, Massachusetts

Copyright 2017 Harvard Business School Publishing Corporation
All rights reserved
Printed in the United States of America

10 9 8 7 6

No part of this publication may be reproduced, stored in or introduced into a retrieval system, or transmitted, in any form, or by any means (electronic, mechanical, photocopying, recording, or otherwise), without the prior permission of the publisher. Requests for permission should be directed to permissions@hbsp.harvard.edu, or mailed to Permissions, Harvard Business School Publishing, 60 Harvard Way, Boston, Massachusetts 02163.

The web addresses referenced in this book were live and correct at the time of the book's publication but may be subject to change.

Library of Congress Cataloging-in-Publication Data

Title: Happiness.
Other titles: HBR emotional intelligence series.
Description: Boston, Massachusetts : Harvard Business Review Press, [2017]
    Series: HBR emotional intelligence series
Identifiers: LCCN 2016056298 | ISBN 9781633693210 (pbk. : alk. paper)
Subjects: LCSH: Happiness. | Work—Psychological aspects.
Classification: LCC BF575.H27 H362 2017 | DDC 152.4/2—dc23 LC record available at https://lccn.loc.gov/2016056298

ISBN: 978-1-63369-321-0
eISBN: 978-1-63369-322-7

The paper used in this publication meets the requirements of the American National Standard for Permanence of Paper for Publications and Documents in Libraries and Archives Z39.48-1992.

Contents

Contents

Happiness

HBR EMOTIONAL INTELLIGENCE SERIES

1

Happiness Isn't the Absence of Negative Feelings

By Jennifer Moss

Happiness feels intolerably elusive for many of us. Like fog, you can see it from afar, dense and full of shape. But upon approach, its particles loosen, and suddenly it becomes out of reach, even though it's all around you.

We put so much emphasis on the pursuit of happiness, but if you stop and think about it, to pursue is to chase something without a guarantee of ever catching it.

Up until about six years ago, I was fervently and ineffectively chasing happiness. My husband, Jim, and I were living in San Jose, California, with our two-year-old son and a second baby on the way. On paper, our life appeared rosy. Still, I couldn't seem to find the joy. I always felt so guilty about my sadness. My problems were embarrassingly "first world."

Then in September 2009, my world tilted. Jim fell severely ill. He was diagnosed with Swine Flu (H1N1) and West Nile virus, then Guillain-Barré Syndrome, due to his compromised immune system.

Jim never worried about death. I did.

When we were told Jim's illness was letting up, that he'd won this round, we were relieved. When we were told Jim might not walk for some time—likely a year, maybe longer—we were alarmed. We knew this prognosis meant the end of Jim's career as a pro lacrosse player. What we didn't know was how we'd pay the medical bills or how much energy Jim would have for parenting.

With 10 weeks to go until the baby arrived, I had very little time to think and reflect. Jim, on the other hand, *only* had time. He was used to moving at high speeds, both in life and on the field, so minutes passed like hours in the hospital. He was kept busy with physical and occupational therapy, but he was also in need of psychological support.

He put out a note to people in his social networks, asking them for reading suggestions that would help him to mentally heal. Suggestions flowed in. Books and audio tapes were delivered bedside with notes about how they'd "helped so much" after whatever difficulty this person had also experienced but overcame.

Jim would spend his days reading motivational books from Tony Robbins and Oprah or watching TED talks, like Jill Bolte Taylor's "My Stroke of Insight," about the impacts of brain trauma. He would analyze spiritual books by Deepak Chopra and the Dalai Lama. Or review scientific research papers about happiness and gratitude written by researchers Martin Seligman, Shawn Achor, Sonja Lyubomirsky, and many others.

There was a repeated theme throughout all the literature—gratitude. It would weave in and out of the science, the true stories, and the drivers for success. Jim responded by starting a gratitude journal of his own. He got very thankful—thankful for the people who changed his sheets, thankful for the family that would bring him hot meals at dinner. Thankful for the nurse who would encourage him and thankful for the extra attention his rehab team would give him on their own time. (The team once told Jim that they were only putting in extra time because they knew how grateful he was for their efforts.)

He asked that I participate in his approach, and because I wanted to help him to heal so badly and I was seeing how hard it was for him, I tried hard to be in a positive place when I came into his world inside that hospital room. I wasn't always at my best. I sometimes resented that I couldn't break down—but after a while I started to see how rapidly he was getting better. And although our paths weren't congruent, we were making it work. I was "coming around."

It was shaky and scary, but when Jim walked out of the hospital on crutches (he stubbornly refused the wheelchair) only six weeks after he was rushed by ambulance to the ER, we decided there was something more to his healing than just dumb luck.

One of those early books that influenced Jim was Seligman's *Flourish*. A psychologist and former president of the American Psychology Association, Seligman was responsible for defining the term "PERMA," the root of many positive psychology research projects around the world. The acronym stands for the five elements essential to lasting contentment:

- *Positive emotion*: Peace, gratitude, satisfaction, pleasure, inspiration, hope, curiosity, and love fall into this category.

- *Engagement*: Losing ourselves in a task or project provides us with a sense of "disappeared time" because we are so highly engaged.

- *Relationships*: People who have meaningful, positive relationships with others are happier than those who do not.

- *Meaning*: Meaning comes from serving a cause bigger than ourselves. Whether it's a religion or a cause that helps humanity in some way, we all need meaning in our lives.

- *Accomplishment/achievement*: To feel significant life satisfaction, we must strive to better ourselves.

We slowly brought these five tenets back into our lives. Jim returned to Wilfrid Laurier University in Ontario to research neuroscience, and we promptly started up Plasticity Labs to help teach others what we'd learned about the pursuit of happiness. As our lives came to include more empathy, gratitude, and meaning, I stopped feeling sad.

So when I see skepticism directed at the positive psychology movement, I take it personally. Do these critics have a problem with gratitude? Relationships? Meaning? Hope?

Perhaps part of the problem is that we oversimplify happiness in our pop culture and media, which makes it easy to discard as unproven. As Vanessa Buote, a postdoctoral fellow in social psychology, put it to me in an email:

One of the misconceptions about happiness is that happiness is being cheerful, joyous, and content all the time; always having a smile on your face. It's not—being happy and leading rich lives is about taking the good with the bad, and learning how to reframe the bad. In fact, in the recent [article in the Journal of Experimental Psychology*], "Emodiversity and the Emotional Ecosystem," by Harvard [researcher Jordi] Quoidbach, found that experiencing a wide range of* *emotions—both positive and negative—was linked to positive mental and physical well-being.*

Not only do we tend to misunderstand what happiness is, we also tend to chase it the wrong way. Shawn Achor, the researcher and corporate trainer who wrote the HBR article "Positive Intelligence," told me that most people think about happiness the wrong way: "The biggest misconception of the happiness industry is that happiness is an end, not a means. We think that if we get what we want, then we'll be happy. But it turns out that our brains actually work in the opposite direction."

Buote agrees: "We sometimes tend to see 'being happy' as the end goal, but we forget that what's really important is the journey; finding out what makes us the happiest and regularly engaging in those activities to help us lead a more fulfilling life."

In other words, we're not happy when we're chasing happiness. We're happiest when we're not thinking about it, when we're enjoying the present moment because we're lost in a meaningful project, working toward a higher goal, or helping someone who needs us.

Healthy positivity doesn't mean cloaking your authentic feelings. Happiness is not the absence of suffering; it's the ability to rebound from it. And happiness is not the same as joy or ecstasy; happiness includes contentment, well-being, and the emotional flexibility to experience a full range of emotions. At our company, some of us have dealt with anxiety and depression. Some have experienced PTSD. Some of us have witnessed severe mental illness in our families, and some of us have not. We openly share. Or we don't—either way is fine. We support tears in the office, if the situation calls for it (in both sorrow and in laughter).

Some people—perhaps looking for a fresh angle—have even argued that happiness is harmful (see, for example, the last two articles in this book). But the point of practicing exercises that help increase mental and emotional fitness is not to learn to paste a smile on your face or wish away your problems. It's to learn how to handle stressors with more resilience through training, just as you would train to run a marathon.

During my time with Jim in the hospital, I watched him change. It happened in subtle ways at first, but then all at once I realized that practicing gratitude and the happiness that comes with it had given me a gift: It gave me back Jim. If happiness is harmful—then I say, bring it on.

JENNIFER MOSS is a cofounder and chief communications officer of Plasticity Labs.

Adapted from content posted on hbr.org on
August 20, 2015 (product #H02AEB).

2

Being Happy at Work Matters

By Annie McKee

People used to believe that you didn't have to be happy at work to succeed. And you didn't need to like the people you worked with, or even share their values. "Work is *not* personal," the thinking went. This is bunk.

My research with dozens of companies and hundreds of people—along with the research conducted by neuroscientists like Richard Davidson and V.S. Ramachandran and scholars such as Shawn Achor— increasingly points to a simple fact: Happy people are better workers. Those who are engaged with their jobs and colleagues work harder—and smarter.

And yet, an alarmingly high number of people aren't engaged. According to a sobering 2013 Gallup report, only 30% of the U.S. workforce *is* engaged. This echoes what I've seen in my work. Not very many people are truly "emotionally and intellectually committed" to their organizations.[1] Far too many couldn't care less about what's happening around them. For them, Wednesday is "hump day" and they're just working to get to Friday. And then there's the other end of the bell curve—the nearly one out of five employees who is actively *disengaged*, according to the same Gallup report. These people are sabotaging projects, backstabbing colleagues, and generally wreaking havoc in their workplaces.

The Gallup report also notes that employee engagement has remained largely constant over the years despite economic ups and downs. Scary: We're not engaged with work, and we haven't been for a long time.

Disengaged, unhappy people aren't any fun to work with and don't add much value; they impact our organizations (and our economy) in profoundly negative ways. It's even worse when leaders are disengaged because they infect others with their attitude. Their emotions and mindsets impact others' moods and performance tremendously. After all, how we feel is linked to what and how we think. In other words, thought influences emotion, and emotion influences thinking.[2]

It's time to finally blow up the myth that feelings don't matter at work. Science is on our side: There are clear neurological links between feelings, thoughts, and actions.[3] When we are in the grip of strong negative emotions, it's like having blinders on. We focus mostly—sometimes only—on the source of the pain. We don't process information as well, think creatively, or make good decisions. Frustration, anger, and stress cause an important part of us to shut down—the part that's thinking and engaged.[4] Disengagement is a natural neurological and psychological response to pervasive negative emotions.

But it's not just negative emotions we need to watch out for. Extremely strong positive emotions can have the same effect.[5] Some studies show that too much happiness can make you less creative and prone to engaging in riskier behaviors (think about how we act like fools when we fall in love). On the work front: I've seen groups of people worked up into a frenzy at sales conferences and corporate pep rallies. Little learning or innovation comes out of these meetings. Throw in a lot of alcohol, and you've got a whole host of problems.

If we can agree that our emotional states at work matter, what can we do to increase engagement and improve performance?

Over the past few years, my team at the Teleos Leadership Institute and I have studied dozens of organizations and interviewed thousands of people. The early findings about the links between people's feelings and engagement are fascinating. There are clear similarities in what people say they want and

need, no matter where they are from, whom they
work for, or what field they're in. We often assume
that there are huge differences across industries and
around the world, but the research challenges that
assumption.

To be fully engaged and happy, virtually everyone
tells, we need three things:

1. *A meaningful vision of the future.* When people talked with our research team about what
   was working and what wasn't in their organizations and what helped or hindered them the
   most, they talked about *vision.* People want to
   be able to see the future and know how they
   fit in. And, as we know from our work with
   organizational behavior expert Richard Boyatzis on intentional change, people learn and
   change when they have a personal vision that
   is linked to an organizational vision.[6] Sadly, far
   too many leaders don't paint a very compelling

vision of the future, they don't try to link it to people's personal visions, and they don't communicate well. And they lose people as a result.

2. *A sense of purpose.* People want to feel as if their work matters, that their contributions help achieve something really important. And except for those at the tippy top, shareholder value isn't a meaningful goal that excites and engages them. They want to know that they— and their organizations—are doing something big that matters to other people.

3. *Great relationships.* We know that people join an organization and leave a boss.[7] A dissonant relationship with one's boss is downright painful. So too are bad relationships with colleagues. Leaders, managers, and employees have all told us that close, trusting, and supportive relationships are hugely important to their state of mind—and their willingness contribute to a team.

Added up, brain science and organizational research are in fact debunking the old myths: Emotions matter a lot at work. Happiness is important. To be fully engaged, people need vision, meaning, purpose, and resonant relationships.

It's on us as individuals to find ways to live our values at work and build great relationships. And it's on leaders to create an environment where people can thrive. It's simple and it's practical: If you want an engaged workforce, pay attention to how you create a vision, link people's work to your company's larger purpose, and reward individuals who resonate with others.

ANNIE MCKEE is a senior fellow at the University of Pennsylvania, director of the PennCLO executive doctoral program, and the founder of the Teleos Leadership Institute. She is a co-author with Daniel Goleman and Richard Boyatzis of *Primal Leadership, Resonant Leadership*, and *Becoming a Resonant Leader.* The ideas in this article are expanded in McKee's latest book, *How to Be Happy at Work*, forthcoming from Harvard Business Review Press.

Notes

1. A. K. Goel et al., "Measuring the Level of Employee Engagement: A Study from the Indian Automobile Sector." *International Journal of Indian Culture and Business Management* 6, no. 1 (2013): 5–21.
2. J. Lite, "*MIND* Reviews: *The Emotional Life of Your Brain,*" *Scientific American MIND*, July 1, 2012, http://www.scientificamerican.com/article/mind-reviews-the-emotional-life-of/.
3. D. Goleman, *Destructive Emotions: A Scientific Dialogue with the Dalai Lama.* (New York: Bantam, 2004).
4. D. Goleman et al., *Primal Leadership: Unleashing the Power of Emotional Intelligence.* (Boston: Harvard Business Review Press, 2013).
5. J. Gruber, "Four Ways Happiness Can Hurt You," *Greater Good*, May 3, 2012, http://greatergood.berkeley.edu/article/item/four_ways_happiness_can_hurt_you.
6. R. E. Boyatzis and C. Soler, "Vision, Leadership, and Emotional Intelligence Transforming Family Business," *Journal of Family Business Management* 2, no. 1 (2012) 23–30; and A. McKee et al., *Becoming a Resonant Leader: Develop Your Emotional Intelligence, Renew Your Relationships, Sustain Your Effectiveness.* (Boston: Harvard Business Review Press, 2008). http://www.amazon.com/Becoming-Resonant-Leader-Relationships-Effectiveness/dp/1422117340.

7. "How Managers Trump Companies," *Gallup Business Journal*, August 12, 1999, http://businessjournal.gallup .com/content/523/how-managers-trump-companies.aspx.

Adapted from content posted on hbr.org on
November 14, 2014 (product #H012CE).

3

The Science
Behind the Smile

An interview with Daniel Gilbert by Gardiner Morse

Harvard psychology professor Daniel Gilbert is widely known for his 2006 best seller, *Stumbling on Happiness*. His work reveals, among other things, the systematic mistakes we all make in imagining how happy (or miserable) we'll be. In this edited interview with HBR's Gardiner Morse, Gilbert surveys the field of happiness research and explores its frontiers.

HBR: *Happiness research has become a hot topic in the past 20 years. Why?*

Gilbert: It's only recently that we realized we could marry one of our oldest questions—"What is the nature of human happiness?"—to our newest way of getting answers: science. Until just a few decades ago, the problem of happiness was mainly in the hands of philosophers and poets.

Psychologists have always been interested in emotion, but in the past two decades the study of emotion has exploded, and one of the emotions that psychologists have studied most intensively is happiness. Recently economists and neuroscientists joined the party. All these disciplines have distinct but intersecting interests: Psychologists want to understand what people feel, economists want to know what people value, and neuroscientists want to know how people's brains respond to rewards. Having three separate disciplines all interested in a single topic has put that topic on the scientific map. Papers on happiness are published in *Science*, people who study happiness win Nobel prizes, and governments all over the world are rushing to figure out how to measure and increase the happiness of their citizens.

How is it possible to measure something as subjective as happiness?

Measuring subjective experiences is a lot easier than you think. It's what your eye doctor does when she fits you for glasses. She puts a lens in front of your eye and asks you to report your experience, and then she puts another lens up, and then another. She uses your reports as data, submits the data to scientific analysis, and designs a lens that will give you perfect vision—all on the basis of your reports of your subjective experience. People's real-time reports are very good approximations of their experiences, and they make it possible for us to see the world through their eyes. People may not be able to tell us how happy they were yesterday or how happy they will be tomorrow, but they *can* tell us how they're feeling at the moment we ask them. "How are you?" may be the world's most frequently asked question, and nobody's stumped by it.

There are many ways to measure happiness. We can ask people "How happy are you right now?" and have them rate it on a scale. We can use magnetic resonance imaging to measure cerebral blood flow, or electromyography to measure the activity of the "smile muscles" in the face. But in most circumstances those measures are highly correlated, and you'd have to be the federal government to prefer the complicated, expensive measures over the simple, inexpensive one.

But isn't the scale itself subjective? Your five might be my six.

Imagine that a drugstore sold a bunch of cheap thermometers that weren't very well calibrated. People with normal temperatures might get readings other than 98.6, and two people with the same temperature might get different readings. These inaccuracies could cause people to seek medical treatment they didn't need or to miss getting treatment they did need. So buggy thermometers are sometimes a problem—but not always. For example, if I brought 100 people to my lab, exposed half of them to a flu virus, and then used those buggy thermometers to take their temperatures a week later, the average temperature of the people who'd been exposed would almost surely be higher than the average temperature of the others. Some thermometers would underestimate, some would overestimate, but as long as I measured enough people, the inaccuracies would cancel themselves out. Even with poorly calibrated instruments, we can compare large groups of people.

A rating scale is like a buggy thermometer. Its inaccuracies make it inappropriate for some kinds of measurement (for example, saying exactly how happy John was at 10:42 am on July 3, 2010), but it's perfectly appropriate for the kinds of measurements most psychological scientists make.

What did all these happiness researchers discover?

Much of the research confirms things we've always suspected. For example, in general people who are in good romantic relationships are happier than those who aren't. Healthy people are happier than sick people. People who participate in their churches are happier than those who don't. Rich people are happier than poor people. And so on.

That said, there have been some surprises. For example, while all these things do make people happier, it's astonishing how little any one of them matters. Yes, a new house or a new spouse will make you happier, but not much and not for long. As it turns out, people are not very good at predicting what will make them happy or how long that happiness will last. They expect positive events to make them much happier than those events actually do, and they expect negative events to make them unhappier than they actually do. In both field and lab studies, we've found that winning or losing an election, gaining or losing a romantic partner, getting or not getting a promotion, passing or failing an exam all have less impact on happiness than people think they will. A recent study showed that very few experiences affect us for more than three months. When good things happen, we celebrate for a while and then sober up. When bad things happen, we weep and whine for a while and then pick ourselves up and get on with it.

Why do events have such a fleeting effect on happiness?

One reason is that people are good at synthesizing happiness—at finding silver linings. As a result, they usually end up happier than they expect after almost any kind of trauma or tragedy. Pick up any newspaper, and you'll find plenty of examples. Remember Jim Wright, who resigned in disgrace as

Speaker of the House of Representatives because of a shady book deal? A few years later he told the *New York Times* that he was "so much better off, physically, financially, emotionally, mentally and in almost every other way." Then there's Moreese Bickham, who spent 37 years in the Louisiana State Penitentiary; after his release he said, "I don't have one minute's regret. It was a glorious experience." These guys appear to be living in the best of all possible worlds. Speaking of which, Pete Best, the original drummer for the Beatles, was replaced by Ringo Starr in 1962, just before the Beatles got big. Now he's a session drummer. What did he have to say about missing out on the chance to belong to the most famous band of the 20th century? "I'm happier than I would have been with the Beatles."

One of the most reliable findings of the happiness studies is that we do not have to go running to a therapist every time our shoelaces break. We have a remarkable ability to make the best of things. Most people are more resilient than they realize.

Aren't they deluding themselves? Isn't real happiness better than synthetic happiness?

Let's be careful with terms. Nylon is real; it's just not natural. Synthetic happiness is perfectly real; it's just man-made. Synthetic happiness is what we produce when we don't get what we want, and natural happiness is what we experience when we do. They have different origins, but they are not necessarily different in terms of how they feel. One is not obviously better than the other.

Of course, most folks don't see it that way. Most folks think that synthetic happiness isn't as "good" as the other kind—that people who produce it are just fooling themselves and aren't really happy. I know of no evidence demonstrating that that's the case. If you go blind or lose a fortune, you'll find that there's a whole new life on the other side of those events. And you'll find many things about that new life that are quite good. In fact, you'll undoubtedly find a few things that are even better than what you had before. You're not lying to yourself; you're not delusional. You're discovering things you didn't know—*couldn't* know—until you were in that new life. You are looking for things that make your new life better, you are finding them, and they are making you happy. What is most striking to me as a scientist is that most of us don't realize how good we're going to be at finding these things. We'd never say, "Oh, of course, if I lost my money or my wife left me, I'd find a way to be just as happy as I am now." We'd never say it—but it's true.

Is being happy always desirable? Look at all the unhappy creative geniuses—Beethoven, van Gogh, Hemingway. Doesn't a certain amount of unhappiness spur good performance?

Nonsense! Everyone can think of a historical example of someone who was both miserable and creative, but that doesn't mean misery generally promotes creativity. There's certainly someone out there who smoked two packs of cigarettes a day and lived to be 90, but that doesn't mean cigarettes are good for you. The difference between using anecdotes to prove a point and using science to prove a point is that in science you can't just cherry-pick the story that suits you best. You have to examine *all* the stories, or at least take a fair sample of them, and see if there are more miserable creatives or happy creatives, more miserable noncreatives or happy noncreatives. If misery promoted creativity, you'd see a higher percentage of creatives among the miserable than among the delighted. And you don't. By and large, happy people are more creative and more productive. Has there ever been a human being whose misery was the source of his creativity? Of course. But that person is the exception, not the rule.

Many managers would say that contented people aren't the most productive employees, so you want to keep people a little uncomfortable, maybe a little anxious, about their jobs.

Managers who collect data instead of relying on intuition don't say that. I know of no data showing that anxious, fearful employees are more creative or productive. Remember, contentment doesn't mean sitting and staring at the wall. That's what people do when they're bored, and people *hate* being bored. We know that people are happiest when they're appropriately challenged—when they're trying to achieve goals that are difficult but not out of reach. Challenge and threat are not the same thing. People blossom when challenged and wither when threatened. Sure, you can get results from threats: Tell someone, "If you don't get this to me by Friday, you're fired," and you'll probably have it by Friday. But you'll also have an employee who will thereafter do his best to undermine you, who will feel no loyalty to the organization, and who will never do more than he must. It would be much more effective to tell your employee, "I don't think most people could get this done by Friday. But I have full faith and confidence that you can. And it's hugely important to the entire team." Psychologists have studied reward and punishment for a century, and the bottom line is perfectly clear: Reward works better.

So challenge makes people happy. What else do we know now about the sources of happiness?

If I had to summarize all the scientific literature on the causes of human happiness in one word, that word would be "social." We are by far the most social species on Earth. Even ants have nothing on us. If I wanted to predict your happiness, and I could know only one thing about you, I wouldn't want to know your gender, religion, health, or income. I'd want to know about your social network—about your friends and family and the strength of your bonds with them.

Beyond having rich networks, what makes us happy day to day?

The psychologist Ed Diener has a finding I really like. He essentially shows that the *frequency* of your positive experiences is a much better predictor of your happiness than is the *intensity* of your positive experiences. When we think about what would make us happy, we tend to think of intense events—going on a date with a movie star, winning a Pulitzer, buying a yacht. But Diener and his colleagues have shown that how good your experiences are doesn't matter nearly as much as how many good experiences you have. Somebody who has a dozen mildly nice things happen each day is likely to be happier than somebody who has a single truly amazing thing happen. So wear comfortable shoes, give your wife a big kiss, sneak a french fry. It sounds like small stuff, and it is. But the small stuff matters.

I think this helps explain why it's so hard for us to forecast our affective states. We imagine that one or two big things will have a profound effect. But it looks like happiness is the sum of hundreds of small things. Achieving happiness requires the same approach as losing weight. People trying to lose weight want a magic pill that will give them instant results. Ain't no such thing. We know exactly how people lose weight: They eat less and exercise more. They don't have to eat *much* less or exercise *much* more— they just have to do those things consistently. Over time it adds up. Happiness is like that. The things you can do to increase your happiness are obvious and small and take just a little time. But you have to do them every day and wait for the results.

What are those little things we can do to increase our happiness?

They won't surprise you any more than "eat less and exercise more" does. The main things are to commit to some simple behaviors—meditating, exercising, getting enough sleep—and to practice altruism. One of the most selfish things you can do is help others. Volunteer at a homeless shelter. You may or may not help the homeless, but you will almost surely help yourself. And nurture your social connections. Twice a week, write down three things you're grateful for, and tell someone why. I know these sound like homilies from your grandmother. Well, your grandmother was smart. The secret of happiness is like the secret of weight loss: It's not a secret!

If there's no secret, what's left to study?

There's no shortage of questions. For decades psychologists and economists have been asking,

"Who's happy? The rich? The poor? The young? The old?" The best we could do was divide people into groups, survey them once or maybe twice, and try to determine if the people in one group were, on average, happier than those in the others. The tools we used were pretty blunt instruments. But now millions of people are carrying little computers in their pockets—smartphones—and this allows us to collect data in real time from huge numbers of people about what they are doing and feeling from moment to moment. That's never been possible before.

One of my collaborators, Matt Killingsworth, has built an experience-sampling application called Track Your Happiness. He follows more than 15,000 people by iPhone, querying them several times a day about their activities and emotional states. Are they at home? On a bus? Watching television? Praying? How are they feeling? What are they thinking about? With this technology, Matt's beginning to answer a much better question than the one we've been asking for decades. Instead of asking *who* is happy, he can ask *when* they are happy. He doesn't get the answer by asking, "When are you happy?"—because frankly, people don't know. He gets it by tracking people over days, months, and years and measuring what they are doing and how happy they are while they are doing it. I think this kind of technology is about to revolutionize our understanding of daily emotions and human well-being. (See the sidebar "The Future of Happiness Research.")

What are the new frontiers of happiness research?

We need to get more specific about what we are measuring. Many scientists say they are studying happiness, but when you look at what they're measuring, you find they are actually studying depression or life satisfaction. These things are related to happiness, of course, but they are not the same as happiness. Research shows that people with children are typically less happy on a moment-to-moment basis than people without children. But people who have kids may feel fulfilled in a way that people without kids do not. It doesn't make sense to say that people with kids are happier, or that people without kids are happier; each group is happier in some ways and less happy in others. We need to stop painting our portrait of happiness with such a fat brush.

Will all this research ultimately make us happier?

We are learning and will continue to learn how to maximize our happiness. So yes, there is no doubt that the research has helped and will continue to help us increase our happiness. But that still leaves the big question: What kind of happiness *should* we want? For example, do we want the average happiness of our moments to be as large as possible, or do we want the sum of our happy moments to be as large as possible? Those are different things.

Do we want lives free of pain and heartache, or is there value in those experiences? Science will soon be able to tell us how to live the lives we want, but it will never tell us what kinds of lives we should want to live. That will be for us to decide.

THE FUTURE OF HAPPINESS RESEARCH

by Matthew Killingsworth

You'd think it would be easy to figure out what makes us happy. Until recently, though, researchers have had to rely mainly on people's reports about their average emotional states over long periods of time and on easily surveyed predictors of happiness, such as demographic variables. As a result, we know that married or wealthy people are, on average, happier than unmarried or less-well-off people. But what is it about being married or having money that makes people happy?

Focusing on average emotional states also smoothes out short-term fluctuations in happiness and consequently diminishes our ability to understand the causes of those fluctuations. For example, how do the moment-by-moment details of a person's day affect that person's happiness?

We can now begin to answer questions like these, thanks to the smartphone. For an ongoing research project called Track Your Happiness, I have recruited more than 15,000 people in 83 countries to report their emotional states in real time, using devices they carry with them every day. I created an iPhone web app that queries users at random intervals, asking them about their mood (respondents slide a button along a scale that ranges from "very bad" to "very good"), what they are doing (they can select from 22 options, including commuting, working, exercising,

(Continued)

and eating), and factors such as their level of productivity, the nature of their environment, the amount and quality of their sleep, and their social interactions. Since 2009 we have collected more than half a million data points—making this, to my knowledge, the first-ever large-scale study of happiness in daily life.

One major finding is that people's minds wander nearly half the time, and this appears to lower their mood. Wandering to unpleasant or even neutral topics is associated with sharply lower happiness; straying to positive topics has no effect either way. The amount of mind-wandering varies greatly depending on the activity, from roughly 60% of the time while commuting to 30% when talking to someone or playing a game to 10% during sex. But no matter what people are doing, they are much less happy when their minds are wandering than when their minds are focused.

All of this strongly suggests that to optimize our emotional well-being, we should pay at least as much attention to where our minds are as to what our bodies are doing. Yet for most of us, the focus of our thoughts isn't part of our daily planning. When you wake up on a Saturday morning and ask, "What am I going to do today?" the answer is usually about where you'll take your body—to the beach, to the kids' soccer practice, for a run. You ought to also ask, "What am I going to do with my mind today?"

A related stream of research examines the relationship between mind-wandering and productivity. Many managers, particularly those whose employees do creative knowledge work, may sense that a certain amount of daydreaming is a good thing, providing a mental break and perhaps leading people to reflect on related work matters. Unfortunately, the data so far suggest that, in addition to reducing happiness, mind-wandering on the job reduces productivity. And employees' minds stray much more than managers

(Continued)

probably imagine—about 50% of the workday—and almost always veer toward personal concerns. Managers may want to look for ways to help employees stay focused, for the employees' *and* the company's sakes.

The data are also beginning to paint a picture of variations in happiness within an individual and from one individual to the next. The most striking finding here is that happiness differs more from moment to moment than it does from person to person. This suggests that it's not the stable conditions of our lives, such as where we live or whether we're married, that are the principal drivers of happiness; it could be the small, everyday things that count the most.

It also suggests that happiness on the job may depend more on our moment-to-moment experiences— our routine interactions with coworkers, the projects we're involved in, our daily contributions—than on the

A focused mind is a happy mind

Participants were queried about mood and mind-wandering during 22 activities. The balls represent their activities and thoughts. The farther to the right a ball is, the happier people were, on average. The larger the ball, the more frequently they engaged in the activity or thought.

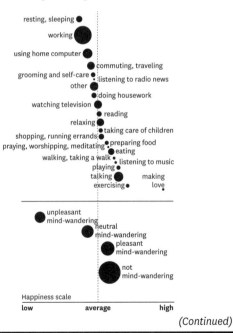

(Continued)

stable conditions thought to promote happiness, such as a high salary or a prestigious title. A priority of my current and future research is to deploy this tracking technology in the workplace and, I hope, at last reveal what actually makes employees happy.

Matthew Killingsworth is a doctoral student in psychology at Harvard University. He is the creator of www.trackyour happiness.com.

DANIEL GILBERT is the Edgar Pierce Professor of Psychology at Harvard University. He has won numerous awards for his research and teaching, including the American Psychological Association's Distinguished Scientific Award for an Early Career Contribution to Psychology. He is the author of *Stumbling on Happiness* and host and co-writer of the PBS television series *This Emotional Life*. GARDINER MORSE is a senior editor at *Harvard Business Review*.

Reprinted from *Harvard Business Review*, January–February 2012 (product #R1201E).

4

The Power of Small Wins

By Teresa M. Amabile and Steven J. Kramer

What is the best way to drive innovative work inside organizations? Important clues hide in the stories of world-renowned creators. It turns out that ordinary scientists, marketers, programmers, and other unsung knowledge workers, whose jobs require creative productivity every day, have more in common with famous innovators than most managers realize. The workday events that ignite their emotions, fuel their motivation, and trigger their perceptions are fundamentally the same.

The Double Helix, James Watson's 1968 memoir about discovering the structure of DNA, describes the roller coaster of emotions he and Francis Crick experienced through the progress and setbacks of the work that eventually earned them the Nobel Prize. After the excitement of their first attempt to build a DNA model, Watson and Crick noticed some serious flaws. According to Watson, "Our first minutes with the models . . . were not joyous." Later that evening, "a shape began to emerge which brought back our spirits." But when they showed their "breakthrough" to colleagues, they found that their model would not work. Dark days of doubt and ebbing motivation followed. When the duo finally had their bona fide breakthrough, and their colleagues found no fault with it, Watson wrote, "My morale skyrocketed, for I suspected that we now had the answer to the riddle." Watson and Crick were so driven by this success that they practically lived in the lab, trying to complete the work.

Throughout these episodes, Watson and Crick's progress—or lack thereof—ruled their reactions. In our recent research on creative work inside businesses, we stumbled upon a remarkably similar phenomenon. Through exhaustive analysis of diaries kept by knowledge workers, we discovered the "progress principle": Of all the things that can boost emotions, motivation, and perceptions during a workday, the single most important is making progress in meaningful work. And the more frequently people experience that sense of progress, the more likely they are to be creatively productive in the long run. Whether they are trying to solve a major scientific mystery or simply produce a high-quality product or service, everyday progress—even a small win—can make all the difference in how they feel and perform.

The power of progress is fundamental to human nature, but few managers understand it or know how to leverage progress to boost motivation. In fact, work motivation has been a subject of long-standing debate. In a survey asking about the keys to motivating workers, we found that some managers ranked recognition for good work as most important, while others put more stock in tangible incentives. Some focused on the value of interpersonal support, while still others thought clear goals were the answer. Interestingly, very few of our surveyed managers ranked progress first. (See the sidebar "A Surprise for Managers.")

If you are a manager, the progress principle holds clear implications for where to focus your efforts. It suggests that you have more influence than you may realize over employees' well-being, motivation, and creative output. Knowing what serves to catalyze and nourish progress—and what does the opposite— turns out to be the key to effectively managing people and their work.

In this article, we share what we have learned about the power of progress and how managers can leverage it. We spell out how a focus on progress translates into concrete managerial actions and provide a checklist to help make such behaviors habitual. But to clarify why those actions are so potent, we first

A SURPRISE FOR MANAGERS

In a 1968 issue of HBR, Frederick Herzberg published a now-classic article titled "One More Time: How Do you Motivate Employees?" Our findings are consistent with his message: People are most satisfied with their jobs (and therefore most motivated) when those jobs give them the opportunity to experience achievement. The diary research we describe in this article—in which we microscopically examined the events of thousands of workdays, in real time—uncovered the mechanism underlying the sense of achievement: making consistent, meaningful progress.

But managers seem not to have taken Herzberg's lesson to heart. To assess contemporary awareness of the importance of daily work progress, we recently administered a survey to 669 managers of varying levels from dozens of companies around the world. We asked about the managerial tools that can affect employees'

(Continued)

motivation and emotions. The respondents ranked five tools—support for making progress in the work, recognition for good work, incentives, interpersonal support, and clear goals—in order of importance.

Of the managers who took our survey, 95% would probably be surprised to learn that supporting progress is the primary way to elevate motivation—because that's the percentage who failed to rank progress number one. In fact, only 35 managers ranked progress as the number one motivator—a mere 5%. The vast majority of respondents ranked support for making progress dead last as a motivator and third as an influence on emotion. They ranked "recognition for good work (either public or private)" as the most important factor in motivating workers and making them happy. In our diary study, recognition certainly did boost inner work life. But it wasn't nearly as prominent as progress. Besides, without work achievements, there is little to recognize.

describe our research and what the knowledge workers' diaries revealed about their "inner work lives."

Inner work life and performance

For nearly 15 years, we have been studying the psychological experiences and the performance of people doing complex work inside organizations. Early on, we realized that a central driver of creative, productive performance was the quality of a person's inner work life: the mix of emotions, motivations, and perceptions over the course of a workday. How happy workers feel; how motivated they are by an intrinsic interest in the work; how positively they view their organization, their management, their team, their work, and themselves—all these combine either to push them to higher levels of achievement or to drag them down.

To understand such interior dynamics better, we asked members of project teams to respond individually to an end-of-day email survey during the course of the project—just over four months, on average. (For more on this research, see our article "Inner Work Life: Understanding the Subtext of Business Performance," HBR May 2007.) The projects—inventing kitchen gadgets, managing product lines of cleaning tools, and solving complex IT problems for a hotel empire, for example—all involved creativity. The daily survey inquired about participants' emotions and moods, motivation levels, and perceptions of the work environment that day, as well as what work they did and what events stood out in their minds.

Twenty-six project teams from seven companies participated, comprising 238 individuals. This yielded nearly 12,000 diary entries. Naturally, every individual in our population experienced ups and downs. Our goal was to discover the states of inner work life and the workday events that correlated with the highest levels of creative output.

In a dramatic rebuttal to the commonplace claim that high pressure and fear spur achievement, we found that, at least in the realm of knowledge work, people are more creative and productive when their inner work lives are positive—when they feel happy, are intrinsically motivated by the work itself, and have positive perceptions of their colleagues and the organization. Moreover, in those positive states, people are more committed to the work and more collegial toward those around them. Inner work life, we saw, can fluctuate from one day to the next— sometimes wildly—and performance along with it. A person's inner work life on a given day fuels his or her performance for the day and can even affect performance the *next* day.

Once this "inner work-life effect" became clear, our inquiry turned to whether and how managerial action could set it in motion. What events could evoke positive or negative emotions, motivations, and perceptions? The answers were tucked within our research participants' diary entries. There are predictable triggers that inflate or deflate inner work life, and, even accounting for variation among individuals, they are pretty much the same for everyone.

The power of progress

Our hunt for inner work-life triggers led us to the progress principle. When we compared our research participants' best and worst days (based on their overall mood, specific emotions, and motivation levels), we found that the most common event triggering a "best day" was any progress in the work by the individual or the team. The most common event triggering a "worst day" was a setback.

Consider, for example, how progress relates to one component of inner work life: overall mood ratings. Steps forward occurred on 76% of people's best-mood days. By contrast, setbacks occurred on only 13% of those days. (See the figure "What happens on good days and bad days?")

Two other types of inner work-life triggers also occur frequently on best days: *catalysts*, actions that directly support work, including help from a person or group, and *nourishers*, events such as shows of respect and words of encouragement. Each has an opposite: *inhibitors*, actions that fail to support or actively hinder work, and *toxins*, discouraging or undermining events. Whereas catalysts and inhibitors are directed at the project, nourishers and toxins are directed at the person. Like setbacks, inhibitors and toxins are rare on days of great inner work life.

Events on worst-mood days are nearly the mirror image of those on best-mood days. Here, setbacks predominated, occurring on 67% of those days; progress occurred on only 25% of them. Inhibitors and toxins also marked many worst-mood days, and catalysts and nourishers were rare.

This is the progress principle made visible: If a person is motivated and happy at the end of a workday, it's a good bet that he or she made some progress.

If the person drags out of the office disengaged and joyless, a setback is most likely to blame.

When we analyzed all 12,000 daily surveys filled out by our participants, we discovered that progress and setbacks influence all three aspects of inner work life. On days when they made progress, our participants reported more positive *emotions*. They not only were in a more upbeat mood in general but also expressed more joy, warmth, and pride. When they suffered setbacks, they experienced more frustration, fear, and sadness.

Motivations were also affected: On progress days, people were more intrinsically motivated—by interest in and enjoyment of the work itself. On setback days, they were not only less intrinsically motivated but also less extrinsically motivated by recognition. Apparently, setbacks can lead a person to feel generally apathetic and disinclined to do the work at all.

Perceptions differed in many ways, too. On progress days, people perceived significantly more positive

What happens on good days and bad days?

Progress—even a small step forward—occurs on many of the days people report being in a good mood. Events on bad days—setbacks and other hindrances—are nearly the mirror image of those on good days.

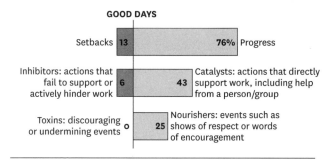

GOOD DAYS

Setbacks 13   **76%** Progress

Inhibitors: actions that fail to support or actively hinder work 6   43 Catalysts: actions that directly support work, including help from a person/group

Toxins: discouraging or undermining events 0   25 Nourishers: events such as shows of respect or words of encouragement

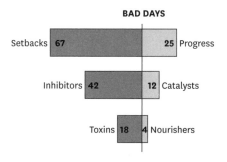

BAD DAYS

Setbacks 67   25 Progress

Inhibitors 42   12 Catalysts

Toxins 18   4 Nourishers

challenge in their work. They saw their teams as more mutually supportive and reported more positive interactions between the teams and their supervisors. On a number of dimensions, perceptions suffered when people encountered setbacks. They found less positive challenge in the work, felt that they had less freedom in carrying it out, and reported that they had insufficient resources. On setback days, participants perceived both their teams and their supervisors as less supportive.

To be sure, our analyses establish correlations but do not prove causality. Were these changes in inner work life the result of progress and setbacks, or was the effect the other way around? The numbers alone cannot answer that. However, we do know, from reading thousands of diary entries, that more-positive perceptions, a sense of accomplishment, satisfaction, happiness, and even elation often followed progress. Here's a typical post-progress entry, from a programmer: "I smashed that bug that's been frustrating me for almost a calendar week. That may not be an event to you, but I live a very drab life, so I'm all hyped."

Likewise, we saw that deteriorating perceptions, frustration, sadness, and even disgust often followed setbacks. As another participant, a product marketer, wrote, "We spent a lot of time updating the cost reduction project list, and after tallying all the numbers, we are still coming up short of our goal. It is discouraging to not be able to hit it after all the time spent and hard work."

Almost certainly, the causality goes both ways, and managers can use this feedback loop between progress and inner work life to support both.

Minor milestones

When we think about progress, we often imagine how good it feels to achieve a long-term goal or experience a major breakthrough. These big wins are great—but they are relatively rare. The good news is that even small wins can boost inner work life tremendously. Many of the progress events our research participants reported represented only minor steps forward. Yet they often evoked outsize positive reactions. Consider this diary entry from a programmer in a high-tech company, which was accompanied by very positive self-ratings of her emotions, motivations, and perceptions that day: "I figured out why something was not working correctly. I felt relieved and happy because this was a minor milestone for me."

Even ordinary, incremental progress can increase people's engagement in the work and their happiness during the workday. Across all the types of events our participants reported, a notable proportion (28%) that had a minor impact on the project had a major impact on people's feelings about it. Because inner work life has such a potent effect on creativity and productivity, and because small but consistent steps forward shared by many people can accumulate into excellent execution, progress events that often go unnoticed are critical to the overall performance of organizations.

Unfortunately, there is a flip side. Small losses or setbacks can have an extremely negative effect on inner work life. In fact, our study and research by others show that negative events can have a more powerful impact than positive ones. Consequently, it is especially important for managers to minimize daily hassles. (See again the figure "What happens on good days and bad days?")

Progress in meaningful work

We've shown how gratifying it is for workers when they are able to chip away at a goal, but recall what we said earlier: The key to motivating performance is supporting progress in *meaningful* work. Making headway boosts your inner work life, but only if the work matters to you.

Think of the most boring job you've ever had. Many people nominate their first job as a teenager—washing pots and pans in a restaurant kitchen, for example, or checking coats at a museum. In jobs like those, the power of progress seems elusive. No matter how hard you work, there are always more pots to wash and coats to check; only punching the time clock at the end of the day or getting the paycheck at the end of the week yields a sense of accomplishment.

In jobs with much more challenge and room for creativity, like the ones our research participants had, simply "making progress"—getting tasks done—doesn't guarantee a good inner work life, either. You may have experienced this rude fact in your own job, on days (or in projects) when you felt demotivated, devalued, and frustrated, even though you worked hard and got things done. The likely cause is your perception of the completed tasks as peripheral or irrelevant. For the progress principle to operate, the work must be meaningful to the person doing it.

In 1983, Steve Jobs was trying to entice John Sculley to leave a wildly successful career at PepsiCo to become Apple's new CEO. Jobs reportedly asked him, "Do you want to spend the rest of your life selling sugared water or do you want a chance to change the world?" In making his pitch, Jobs leveraged a potent psychological force: the deep-seated human desire to do meaningful work.

Fortunately, to feel meaningful, work doesn't have to involve putting the first personal computers in the hands of ordinary people, or alleviating poverty, or helping to cure cancer. Work with less profound importance to society can matter if it contributes value to something or someone important to the worker. Meaning can be as simple as making a useful and high-quality product for a customer or providing a genuine service for a community. It can be supporting a colleague or boosting an organization's profits by reducing inefficiencies in a production process. Whether the goals are lofty or modest, as long as they are meaningful to the worker and it is clear how his or her efforts contribute to them, progress toward them can galvanize inner work life.

In principle, managers shouldn't have to go to extraordinary lengths to infuse jobs with meaning. Most jobs in modern organizations are potentially meaningful for the people doing them. However, managers can make sure that employees know just how their work is contributing. And, most important, they can avoid actions that negate its value. (See the sidebar "How Work Gets Stripped of Its Meaning.") All the participants in our research were doing work that should have been meaningful; no one was washing pots or checking coats. Shockingly often, however, we saw potentially important, challenging work losing its power to inspire.

HOW WORK GETS STRIPPED OF ITS MEANING

Diary entries from 238 knowledge workers who were members of creative project teams revealed four primary ways in which managers unwittingly drain work of its meaning.

Managers may dismiss the importance of employees' work or ideas. Consider the case of Richard, a senior lab technician at a chemical company, who found meaning in helping his new-product development team solve complex technical problems. However, in team meetings over the course of a three-week period, Richard perceived that his team leader was ignoring his suggestions and those of his teammates. As a result, he felt that his contributions were not meaningful, and his spirits flagged. When at last he believed that he was again making a substantive contribution to the success of the project, his mood

(Continued)

improved dramatically: "I felt much better at today's team meeting. I felt that my opinions and information were important to the project and that we have made some progress."

They may destroy employees' sense of ownership of their work. Frequent and abrupt reassignments often have this effect. This happened repeatedly to the members of a product development team in a giant consumer products company, as described by team member Bruce: "As I've been handing over some projects, I do realize that I don't like to give them up. Especially when you have been with them from the start and are nearly to the end. You lose ownership. This happens to us way too often."

Managers may send the message that the work employees are doing will never see the light of day. They can signal this—unintentionally—by shifting their priorities or changing their minds about how something should be done. We saw the latter in an internet technology company after user-interface developer Burt had spent weeks designing seamless transitions for non-English-speaking users. Not surprisingly, Burt's mood was seriously marred on the day he reported this incident: "Other options for the international [interfaces] were [given] to the team during a team meeting, which could render the work I am doing useless."

They may neglect to inform employees about unexpected changes in a customer's priorities. Often, this arises from poor customer management or inadequate communication within the company. For example, Stuart, a data transformation expert at an IT company, reported deep frustration and low

(Continued)

motivation on the day he learned that weeks of the team's hard work might have been for naught: "Found out that there is a strong possibility that the project may not be going forward, due to a shift in the client's agenda. Therefore, there is a strong possibility that all the time and effort put into the project was a waste of our time."

Supporting progress: catalysts and nourishers

What can managers do to ensure that people are motivated, committed, and happy? How can they support workers' daily progress? They can use catalysts and nourishers, the other kinds of frequent "best day" events we discovered.

Catalysts are actions that support work. They include setting clear goals, allowing autonomy, providing sufficient resources and time, helping with the work, openly learning from problems and successes, and allowing a free exchange of ideas. Their opposites, inhibitors, include failing to provide support and actively interfering with the work. Because of their impact on progress, catalysts and inhibitors ultimately affect inner work life. But they also have a more immediate impact: When people realize that they have clear and meaningful goals, sufficient resources, helpful colleagues, and so on, they get an instant boost to their emotions, their motivation to do a great job, and their perceptions of the work and the organization.

Nourishers are acts of interpersonal support, such as respect and recognition, encouragement, emotional comfort, and opportunities for affiliation. Toxins, their opposites, include disrespect, discouragement, disregard for emotions, and interpersonal conflict. For good and for ill, nourishers and toxins affect inner work life directly and immediately.

Catalysts and nourishers—and their opposites—can alter the meaningfulness of work by shifting people's perceptions of their jobs and even themselves. For instance, when a manager makes sure that people have the resources they need, it signals to them that what they are doing is important and valuable. When managers recognize people for the work they do, it signals that they are important to the organization. In this way, catalysts and nourishers can lend greater meaning to the work—and amplify the operation of the progress principle.

The managerial actions that constitute catalysts and nourishers are not particularly mysterious; they may sound like Management 101, if not just common sense and common decency. But our diary study reminded us how often they are ignored or forgotten. Even some of the more attentive managers in the companies we studied did not consistently provide catalysts and nourishers. For example, a supply chain specialist named Michael was, in many ways and on most days, an excellent subteam manager. But he was occasionally so overwhelmed that he became toxic toward his people. When a supplier failed to complete a "hot" order on time and Michael's team had to resort to air shipping to meet the customer's deadline, he realized that the profit margin on the sale would be blown. In irritation, he lashed out at his subordinates, demeaning the solid work they had done and disregarding their own frustration with the supplier. In his diary, he admitted as much: "As of Friday, we have spent $28,000 in air freight to send 1,500 $30 spray jet mops to our number two customer. Another 2,800 remain on this order, and there is a good probability that they too will gain wings. I have turned from the kindly supply chain manager into the black-masked executioner. All similarity to civility is gone, our backs are against the wall, flight is not possible, therefore fight is probable."

Even when managers don't have their backs against the wall, developing long-term strategy and launching new initiatives can often seem more important—and perhaps sexier—than making sure subordinates have what they need to make steady progress and feel supported as human beings. But as we saw repeatedly in our research, even the best strategy will fail if managers ignore the people working in the trenches to execute it.

A model manager—and a tool for emulating him

We could explain the many (and largely unsurprising) moves that can catalyze progress and nourish spirits, but it may be more useful to give an example of a manager who consistently used those moves—and then to provide a simple tool that can help any manager do so.

Our model manager is Graham, whom we observed leading a small team of chemical engineers within a multinational European firm we'll call Kruger-Bern. The mission of the team's NewPoly project was clear and meaningful enough: Develop a safe, biodegradable polymer to replace petrochemicals in cosmetics and, eventually, in a wide range of consumer products. As in many large firms however, the project was nested in a confusing and sometimes threatening corporate setting of shifting top-management priorities, conflicting signals, and wavering commitments. Resources were uncomfortably tight, and uncertainty loomed over the project's future—and every team member's career. Even worse, an incident early in the project, in which an important customer reacted angrily to a sample, left the team reeling. Yet Graham was able to sustain team members' inner work lives by repeatedly and visibly removing obstacles, materially supporting progress, and emotionally supporting the team.

Graham's management approach excelled in four ways. First, he established a positive climate, one event at a time, which set behavioral norms for the entire team. When the customer complaint stopped the project in its tracks, for example, he engaged immediately with the team to analyze the problem, without recriminations, and develop a plan for repairing the relationship. In doing so, he modeled how to respond to crises in the work: not by panicking or pointing fingers but by identifying problems and their causes and developing a coordinated action plan. This is both a practical approach and a great way to give subordinates a sense of forward movement even in the face of the missteps and failures inherent in any complex project.

Second, Graham stayed attuned to his team's everyday activities and progress. In fact, the nonjudgmental climate he had established made this happen naturally. Team members updated him frequently—

without being asked—on their setbacks, progress, and plans. At one point, one of his hardest-working colleagues, Brady, had to abort a trial of a new material because he couldn't get the parameters right on the equipment. It was bad news, because the New-Poly team had access to the equipment only one day a week, but Brady immediately informed Graham. In his diary entry that evening, Brady noted, "He didn't like the lost week but seemed to understand." That understanding assured Graham's place in the stream of information that would allow him to give his people just what they needed to make progress.

Third, Graham targeted his support according to recent events in the team and the project. Each day, he could anticipate what type of intervention—a catalyst or the removal of an inhibitor; a nourisher or some antidote to a toxin—would have the most impact on team members' inner work lives and progress. And if he could not make that judgment, he asked. Most days it was not hard to figure out, as on the day he received some uplifting news about his bosses' commitment to the project. He knew the team was jittery about a rumored corporate reorganization and could use the encouragement. Even though the clarification came during a well-earned vacation day, he immediately got on the phone to relay the good news to the team.

Finally, Graham established himself as a resource for team members rather than a micromanager; he was sure to check in while never seeming to check *up* on them. Superficially, checking in and checking up seem quite similar, but micromanagers make four kinds of mistakes. First, they fail to allow autonomy in carrying out the work. Unlike Graham, who gave the NewPoly team a clear strategic goal but respected members' ideas about how to meet it, micromanagers dictate every move. Second, they frequently ask subordinates about their work without providing any real help. By contrast, when one of Graham's team members reported problems, Graham helped analyze them—remaining open to alternative interpretations—and often ended up helping to get things back on track. Third, micromanagers are quick to affix personal blame when problems arise, leading subordinates to hide problems rather than honestly discuss how to surmount them, as Graham did with Brady. And fourth, micromanagers tend to hoard information to use as a secret weapon. Few realize how damaging this is to inner work life. When subordinates perceive that a manager is withholding potentially useful information, they feel infantilized, their motivation wanes, and their work is handicapped. Graham was quick to communicate upper management's views of the project, customers' opinions and needs, and possible sources of assistance or resistance within and outside the organization.

In all those ways, Graham sustained his team's positive emotions, intrinsic motivation, and favorable perceptions. His actions serve as a powerful example of how managers at any level can approach each day determined to foster progress.

We know that many managers, however well-intentioned, will find it hard to establish the habits that seemed to come so naturally to Graham. Awareness, of course, is the first step. However, turning an awareness of the importance of inner work life into routine action takes discipline. With that in mind, we developed a checklist for managers to consult on a daily basis (see the sidebar "The Daily Progress Checklist"). The aim of the checklist is managing for meaningful progress, one day at a time.

The progress loop

Inner work life drives performance; in turn, good performance, which depends on consistent progress, enhances inner work life. We call this the "progress loop"—it reveals the potential for self-reinforcing benefits.

So, the most important implication of the progress principle is this: By supporting people and their daily progress in meaningful work, managers improve not only the inner work lives of their employees but also the organization's long-term performance, which enhances inner work life even more. Of course, there is a dark side—the possibility of negative feedback loops. If managers fail to support progress and the people trying to make it, inner work life suffers and so does performance; and degraded performance further undermines inner work life.

A second implication of the progress principle is that managers needn't fret about trying to read the psyches of their workers or manipulate complicated incentive schemes to ensure that employees are motivated and happy. As long as managers show basic respect and consideration, they can focus on supporting the work itself.

To become an effective manager, you must learn to set this positive feedback loop in motion. That may require a significant shift. Business schools, business books, and managers themselves usually focus on managing organizations or people. But if you focus on managing progress, the management of people—and even of entire organizations—becomes much more feasible. You won't have to figure out how to x-ray the inner work lives of subordinates; if you facilitate their steady progress in meaningful work, make that progress salient to them, and treat them well, they will experience the emotions, motivations, and perceptions necessary for great performance. Their superior work will contribute to organizational success. And here's the beauty of it: They will love their jobs.

TERESA M. AMABILE is the Edsel Bryant Ford Professor of Business Administration at Harvard Business School and the author of *Creativity in Context* (Westview Press, 1996). STEVEN J. KRAMER is an independent researcher, writer, and consultant. He is a coauthor of "Creativity Under the Gun" (HBR August 2002) and "Inner Work Life" (HBR May 2007). Amabile and Kramer are the coauthors of *The Progress*

Principle: Using Small Wins to Ignite Joy, Engagement, and Creativity at Work (Harvard Business Review Press, 2011).

Reprinted from *Harvard Business Review*,
May 2011 (product # R1105C).

THE DAILY PROGRESS CHECKLIST

Near the end of each workday, use this checklist to review the day and plan your managerial actions for the next day. After a few days, you will be able to identify issues by scanning the boldface words.

First, focus on **progress** and **setbacks** and think about specific events (**catalysts**, **nourishers**, **inhibitors**, and **toxins**) that contributed to them. Next, consider any clear inner-work-life clues and what further information they provide about progress and other events. Finally, prioritize for action.

The action plan for the next day is the most important part of your daily review: What is the one thing you can do to best facilitate progress?

(Continued)

_____

Progress

Which 1 or 2 events today indicated either a small win or a possible breakthrough? (Describe briefly.)

_____

_____

Catalysts

- ☐ Did the team have clear short- and long-term **goals** for meaningful work?

- ☐ Did team members have sufficient **autonomy** to solve problems and take ownership of the project?

- ☐ Did they have all the **resources** they needed to move forward efficiently?

- ☐ Did they have sufficient **time** to focus on meaningful work?

- ☐ Did I discuss **lessons** from today's successes and problems with my team?

- ☐ Did I give or get them **help** when they needed or requested it? Did I encourage team members to help one another?

- ☐ Did I help **ideas** flow freely within the group?

Nourishers

- ☐ Did I show **respect** to team members by recognizing their contributions to progress, attending to their ideas, and treating them as trusted professionals?

- ☐ Did I **encourage** team members who faced difficult challenges?

- ☐ Did I **support** team members who had a personal or professional problem?

- ☐ Is there a sense of personal and professional **affiliation** and camaraderie within the team?

(Continued)

Setbacks

Which 1 or 2 events today indicated either a small setback or a possible crisis? (Describe briefly.)

_____

_____

Inhibitors

- ☐ Was there any confusion regarding long- or short-term **goals** for meaningful work?

- ☐ Were team members overly **constrained** in their ability to solve problems and feel ownership of the project?

- ☐ Did they lack any of the **resources** they needed to move forward effectively?

- ☐ Did they lack sufficient **time** to focus on meaningful work?

- ☐ Did I or others fail to provide needed or requested **help**?

☐ Did I "punish" failure or neglect to find **lessons** and/or opportunities in problems and successes?

☐ Did I or others cut off the presentation or debate of **ideas** prematurely?

Toxins

☐ Did I **disrespect** any team members by failing to recognize their contributions to progress, not attending to their ideas, or not treating them as trusted professionals?

☐ Did I **discourage** a member of the team in any way?

☐ Did I **neglect** a team member who had a personal or professional problem?

☐ Is there tension or **antagonism** among members of the team or between team members and me?

(Continued)

Inner work life

- Did I see any indications of the quality of my subordinates' inner work lives today? _____

  _____

  _____

- Perceptions of the work, team, management, firm _____

  _____

- Emotions_____

  _____

  _____

- Motivation _____

  _____

- What specific events might have affected inner work life today? _____

  _____

Action plan

- What can I do tomorrow to strengthen the catalysts and nourishers identified and provide the ones that are lacking? _____

  _____

  _____

  _____

  _____

- What can I do tomorrow to start eliminating the inhibitors and toxins identified? _____

  _____

  _____

  _____

  _____

5

Creating Sustainable Performance

By Gretchen Spreitzer and Christine Porath

When the economy's in terrible shape, when any of us is lucky to have a job—let alone one that's financially and intellectually rewarding—worrying about whether or not your employees are happy might seem a little over the top. But in our research into what makes for a consistently high-performing workforce, we've found good reason to care: Happy employees produce more than unhappy ones over the long term. They routinely show up at work, they're less likely to quit, they go above and beyond the call of duty, and they attract people who are just as committed to the job. Moreover, they're not sprinters; they're more like marathon runners, in it for the long haul.

So what does it mean to be happy in your job? It's not about *contentment,* which connotes a degree of complacency. When we and our research partners at the Ross School of Business's Center for Positive Organizational Scholarship started looking into the factors involved in sustainable individual and organizational performance, we found a better word: *thriving.* We think of a thriving workforce as one in which employees are not just satisfied and productive but also engaged in creating the future—the company's and their own. Thriving employees have a bit of an edge: They are highly energized—but they know how to avoid burnout.

Across industries and job types, we found that people who fit our description of thriving demonstrated 16% better overall performance (as reported by their managers) and 125% less burnout (self-reported) than their peers. They were 32% more committed to the organization and 46% more satisfied with their jobs. They also missed much less work and reported significantly fewer doctor visits, which meant health care savings and less lost time for the company.

We've identified two components of thriving. The first is *vitality*: the sense of being alive, passionate, and excited. Employees who experience vitality spark energy in themselves and others. Companies generate vitality by giving people the sense that what they do on a daily basis makes a difference.

The second component is *learning*: the growth that comes from gaining new knowledge and skills. Learning can bestow a technical advantage and status as an expert. Learning can also set in motion a virtuous cycle: People who are developing their abilities are likely to believe in their potential for further growth.

The two qualities work in concert; one without the other is unlikely to be sustainable and may even damage performance. Learning, for instance, creates momentum for a time, but without passion it can lead to burnout. What will I do with what I've learned? Why should I stick with this job? Vitality alone—even when you love the kudos you get for delivering results—can be deadening: When the work doesn't give you opportunities to learn, it's just the same thing over and over again.

The combination of vitality and learning leads to employees who deliver results and find ways to grow. Their work is rewarding not just because they successfully perform what's expected of them today but also because they have a sense of where they and the company are headed. In short, they are thriving, and the energy they create is contagious. (See the sidebar "About the Research.")

How organizations can help employees thrive

Some employees thrive no matter the context. They naturally build vitality and learning into their jobs, and they inspire the people around them. A smart

ABOUT THE RESEARCH

Over the past seven years, we have been researching the nature of thriving in the workplace and the factors that enhance or inhibit it.

Across several studies with our colleagues Cristina Gibson and Flannery Garnett, we surveyed or interviewed more than 1,200 white- and blue-collar employees in an array of industries, including higher education, health care, financial services, maritime, energy, and manufacturing. We also studied metrics reflecting energy, learning, and growth, based on information supplied by employees and bosses, along with retention rates, health, overall job performance, and organizational citizenship behaviors.

We developed a definition of thriving that breaks the concept into two factors: *vitality*—the sense that

(Continued)

you're energized and alive; and *learning*—the gaining of knowledge and skills.

When you put the two together, the statistics are striking. For example, people who were high energy and high learning were 21% more effective as leaders than those who were only high energy. The outcomes on one measure in particular—health—were even more extreme. Those who were high energy and low learning were 54% worse when it came to health than those who were high in both.

hiring manager will look for those people. But most employees are influenced by their environment. Even those predisposed to flourish can fold under pressure.

The good news is that—without heroic measures or major financial investments—leaders and managers can jump-start a culture that encourages employees to thrive. That is, managers can overcome organizational inertia to promote thriving and the productivity that follows it—in many cases with a relatively modest shift in attention.

Ideally, you'd be blessed with a workforce full of people who naturally thrive. But there's a lot you can do to release and sustain enthusiasm. Our research has uncovered four mechanisms that create the conditions for thriving employees: providing decision-making discretion, sharing information, minimizing incivility, and offering performance feedback. The mechanisms overlap somewhat. For instance, if you let people make decisions but give them incomplete information, or leave them exposed to hostile reactions, they'll suffer rather than thrive. One mechanism by itself will get you part of the way, but all four are necessary to create a culture of thriving. Let's look at each in turn.

Providing decision-making discretion

Employees at every level are energized by the ability to make decisions that affect their work. Empowering them in this way gives them a greater sense of control, more say in how things get done, and more opportunities for learning.

The airline industry might seem like an unlikely place to find decision-making discretion (let alone a thriving workforce), but consider one company we studied, Alaska Airlines, which created a culture of empowerment that has contributed to a major turnaround over the past decade. In the early 2000s the airline's numbers were flagging, so senior management launched the 2010 Plan, which explicitly invited employee input into decisions that would improve service while maintaining a reputation for timely departures. Employees were asked to set aside their current perceptions of "good" service and consider new ways to contribute, coming up with ideas that could take service from good to truly great. Agents embraced the program, which gave them, for instance, the discretion to find solutions for customers who had missed flights or were left behind for any other reason. Ron Calvin, the director of the eastern region, told us of a call he had recently received on his cell phone from a customer he hadn't seen or spoken to since working at the Seattle airport, five years earlier. The customer had a three-month-old grandchild who had just gone into cardiac arrest. The grandparents were trying to get back to Seattle from Honolulu. Everything was booked. Ron made a few calls and got them on a flight right away. That day the grandfather sent Ron a text saying, simply, "We made it."

Efforts like this to meet individual needs without holding up flights have led to a number one rating for on-time performance and a full trophy case. The airline has also expanded considerably into new markets, including Hawaii, the Midwest, and the East Coast.

Southwest is a better-known story, largely because of the company's reputation for having a fun and caring culture. Flight attendants are often eager to sing, joke around, and in general entertain customers. They also radiate energy and a passion for learning. One decided to offer the preflight safety instructions in rap format. He was motivated to put his special talents to work, and the passengers loved it, reporting that it was the first time they had actually paid attention to the instructions.

At Facebook, decision-making discretion is fundamental to the culture. One employee posted a note on the site expressing his surprise, and pleasure, at the company's motto, "Move fast and break things," which encourages employees to make decisions and act. On just his second day of work, he found a fix to a complicated bug. He expected some sort of hierarchical review, but his boss, the vice president of product, just smiled and said, "Ship it." He marveled that so early on he had delivered a solution that would instantly reach millions of people.

The challenge for managers is to avoid cutting back on empowerment when people make mistakes. Those situations create the best conditions for learning—not only for the parties concerned but also for others, who can learn vicariously.

Sharing information

Doing your job in an information vacuum is tedious and uninspiring; there's no reason to look for innovative solutions if you can't see the larger impact. People can contribute more effectively when they understand how their work fits with the organization's mission and strategy.

Alaska Airlines has chosen to invest management time in helping employees gain a broad view of the company's strategy. The 2010 Plan was launched with traditional communications but also with a months-long road show and training classes designed to help employees share ideas. The CEO, the president, and the COO still go on the road quarterly to gather information about the idiosyncrasies of various markets; they then disseminate what they've learned. The benefits show up in yearly measures of employee pride in the company—now knocking it out of the park at 90%.

At Zingerman's (an Ann Arbor, Michigan, community of food-related businesses that has worked closely with Wayne Baker, a colleague of ours at the Center for Positive Organizational Scholarship), information is as transparent as possible. The organization had never consciously withheld its numbers—financial information was tacked up for employees to see—but when cofounders Ari Weinzweig and Paul Saginaw studied open book management in the mid-

1990s, they came to believe that employees would show more interest if they got involved in the "game."

Implementation of a more formal and meaningful open book policy was not easy. People could look at the numbers, but they had little reason to pay attention and didn't get much insight into how the data related to their daily work. For the first five or six years, the company struggled to build the concept into its systems and routines and to wrap people's minds around what Baker calls "the rigor of the huddle": weekly gatherings around a whiteboard at which teams track results, "keep score," and forecast the next week's numbers. Although people understood the rules of open book management, at first they didn't see the point of adding yet another meeting to their busy schedules. It wasn't until senior leaders made huddling non-negotiable that employees grasped the true purpose of the whiteboards, which displayed not just financial figures but also service and food quality measures, check averages, internal satisfaction figures, and "fun," which could mean anything from weekly contests to customer satisfaction ratings to employees' ideas for innovation.

Some Zingerman's businesses began instituting "mini games": short-term incentives to find a problem or capitalize on an opportunity. For instance, the staff at Zingerman's Roadhouse restaurant used the greeter game to track how long it took for customers to be greeted. "Ungreeted" customers expressed less satisfaction, and employees found themselves frequently comping purchases to make up for service lapses. The greeter game challenged the host team to greet every customer within five minutes of being seated, with a modest financial reward for 50 straight days of success. It inspired hosts to quickly uncover and fill holes in the service process. Service scores improved considerably over the course of a month. Other Zingerman's businesses started similar games, with incentives for faster delivery, fewer knife injuries in the bakery (which would lower insurance costs), and neater kitchens.

The games have naturally created some internal tensions by delivering the bad news along with the good, which can be demoralizing. But overall they have greatly increased frontline employees' sense of ownership, contributing to better performance. From 2000 to 2010 Zingerman's revenue grew by almost 300%, to more than $35 million. The company's leaders credit open book management as a key factor in that success.

Simple anecdotes lend credence to their claim. For instance, a couple of years ago we saw Ari Weinzweig give a talk at the Roadhouse. A guest asked him whether it was realistic to expect the average waiter or busboy to understand company strategy and finance. In response, Ari turned to a busboy, who had been oblivious to the conversation: Would the teenager mind sharing Zingerman's vision and indicating how well the restaurant was meeting its weekly goals?

Without batting an eye, the busboy stated the vision in his own words and then described how well the restaurant was doing that week on "meals sent back to the kitchen."

While Zingerman's is a fairly small business, much larger ones—such as Whole Foods and the transportation company YRC Worldwide—have also adopted open book management. Systems that make information widely available build trust and give employees the knowledge they need to make good decisions and take initiative with confidence.

Minimizing incivility

The costs of incivility are great. In our research with Christine Pearson, a professor at Arizona State University's Thunderbird School of Global Management, we discovered that half of employees who had experienced uncivil behavior at work intentionally decreased their efforts. More than a third deliberately decreased the quality of their work. Two-thirds spent a lot of time avoiding the offender, and about the same number said their performance had declined.

Most people have experienced rude behavior at work. Here are a few quotes from our research:

> "My boss asked me to prepare an analysis. This was my first project, and I was not given any instructions or examples. He told me the assignment was crap."

> "My boss said, 'If I wanted to know what you thought, I'd ask you.'"

> "My boss saw me remove a paper clip from some documents and drop it in my wastebasket. In front of my 12 subordinates he rebuked me for being wasteful and required me to retrieve it."

"On speakerphone, in front of peers, my boss told me that I'd done 'kindergarten work.'"

We have heard hundreds of stories, and they're sadly familiar to most working people. But we don't hear so much about the costs.

Incivility prevents people from thriving. Those who have been the targets of bad behavior are often, in turn, uncivil themselves: They sabotage their peers. They "forget" to copy colleagues on memos. They spread gossip to deflect attention. Faced with incivility, employees are likely to narrow their focus to avoid risks—and lose opportunities to learn in the process.

A management consultancy we studied, Caiman Consulting, was founded as an alternative to the larger firms. Headquartered in Redmond, Washington, in offices that are not particularly sleek, the firm is recognized for its civil culture. Background checks in its hiring process include a candidate's record of civility.

"People leave a trail," says Caiman's director, Greg Long. "You can save yourself from a corrosive culture by being careful and conscientious up front." The managing director, Raazi Imam, told us, "I have no tolerance for anyone to berate or disrespect someone." When it does happen, he pulls the offender aside to make his policy clear. Long attributes the firm's 95% retention rate to its culture.

Caiman passes up highly qualified candidates who don't match that culture. It also keeps a list of consultants who might be good hires when an appropriate spot opens up. The HR director, Meg Clara, puts strong interpersonal skills and emotional intelligence among her prime criteria for candidates.

At Caiman, as at all companies, managers establish the tone when it comes to civility. A single bad player can set the culture awry. One young manager told us about her boss, an executive who had a habit of yelling from his office "You made a mistake!" for a sin as minor as a typo. His voice would resonate across the floor, making everyone cringe and the recipient feel acutely embarrassed. Afterward, colleagues would gather in a common area for coffee and commiseration. An insider told us that those conversations focused not on how to get ahead at the company or learn to cope by developing a thick skin but on how to get even and get out.

In our research, we were surprised by how few companies consider civility—or incivility—when evaluating candidates. Corporate culture is inherently contagious; employees assimilate to their environment. In other words, if you hire for civility, you're more likely to breed it into your culture. (See the sidebar "Individual Strategies for Thriving.")

Offering performance feedback

Feedback creates opportunities for learning and the energy that's so critical for a culture of thriving. By resolving feelings of uncertainty, feedback keeps

INDIVIDUAL STRATEGIES FOR THRIVING

Although organizations benefit from enabling employees to thrive, leaders have so much on their plates that attention to this important task can slip. However, anyone can adopt strategies to enhance learning and vitality without significant organizational support. And because thriving can be contagious, you may find your ideas quickly spreading.

Take a break

Research by Jim Loehr and Tony Schwartz has shown that breaks and other renewal tactics, no matter how small, can create positive energy.

In our teaching, we let students design regular breaks and activities into the class to ensure that they stay energized. In one term, students decided to halt every class for two minutes at the midpoint to get up and do something active. Each week a different

(Continued)

foursome designed the quick activity—watching a funny YouTube video, doing the cha-cha slide, or playing a game. The point is that the students figure out what is energizing for them and share it with the class.

Even if your organization doesn't offer formal mechanisms for renewal, it's nearly always possible to schedule a short walk, a bike ride, or a quick lunch in the park. Some people write it into their schedules so that meetings can't impinge.

Craft your own work to be more meaningful

You can't ignore the requirements of your job, but you can watch for opportunities to make it more meaningful. Consider Tina, the staff administrator of a policy think tank within a large organization. When her boss took a six-month sabbatical, Tina needed to find a short-term replacement project. After some scouting, she uncovered a budding initiative to develop staff members' ability to speak up with their ideas about the organization. The effort needed an innovative spirit to kick it off. The pay was lower, but the nature of the work energized Tina. When her boss returned, she renegotiated the terms of her think tank job to consume only 80% of her time, leaving the rest for the staff development project.

Look for opportunities to innovate and learn

Breaking out of the status quo can trigger the learning that is so essential to thriving. When Roger became the head of a prestigious high school in the Midwest, he was brimming with innovative ideas. He quickly ascertained, however, that quite a few staff members were not open to new ways of doing things.

(Continued)

He made sure to listen to their concerns and tried to bring them along, but he invested more of his effort in the growth and learning of those who shared his passion for breakthrough ideas. Mentoring and encouraging them, Roger began to achieve small wins, and his initiatives gained some momentum. A few of the resisters ended up leaving the school, and others came around when they saw signs of positive change. By focusing on those bright spots rather than the points of resistance, Roger was able to launch an effort that is propelling the school toward a radically different future.

Invest in relationships that energize you

All of us have colleagues who may be brilliant but are difficult and corrosive to work with. Individuals who thrive look for opportunities to work closely with colleagues who generate energy and to minimize interaction with those who deplete it. In fact, when we built the research team to study thriving, we chose colleagues we enjoyed, who energized us, with whom we looked forward to spending time, and from whom we knew we could learn. We seek to build good relationships by starting every meeting with good news or expressions of gratitude.

Recognize that thriving can spill over outside the office

There's evidence that high levels of engagement at work will not lessen your ability to thrive in your personal life but instead can enhance it. When one of us (Gretchen) was dealing with her husband's difficult medical diagnosis, she found that her work,

(Continued)

even though it was demanding, gave her the energy to thrive professionally and in her family life. Thriving is not a zero-sum game. People who feel energized at work often bring that energy to their lives beyond work. And people inspired by outside activities—volunteering, training for a race, taking a class—can bring their drive back to the office.

people's work-related activities focused on personal and organizational goals. The quicker and more direct the feedback, the more useful it is.

The Zingerman's huddle, described earlier, is a tool for sharing near-real-time information about individual as well as business performance. Leaders outline daily ups and downs on the whiteboard, and employees are expected to "own" the numbers and come up with ideas for getting back on track when necessary. The huddles also include "code reds" and "code greens," which document customer complaints and compliments so that all employees can learn and grow on the basis of immediate and tangible feedback.

Quicken Loans, a mortgage finance company that measures and rewards employee performance like no other organization, offers continually updated performance feedback using two types of dashboards: a ticker and kanban reports. (*Kanban*, a Japanese word meaning "signal," is used frequently in operations.)

The ticker has several panels that display group and individual metrics along with data feeds that show how likely an employee is to meet his or her daily goals. People are hardwired to respond to scores and goals, so the metrics help keep them energized through the day; essentially, they're competing against their own numbers.

The kanban dashboard allows managers to track people's performance so that they know when an employee or a team needs some coaching or other type of assistance. A version of the kanban chart is also displayed on monitors, with a rotating list of the top 15 salespeople for each metric. Employees are constantly in competition to make the boards, which are almost like a video game's ranking of high scorers.

Employees could feel overwhelmed or even oppressed by the constant nature of the feedback. Instead, the company's strong norms for civility and respect and for giving employees a say in how they accomplish their work create a context in which the feedback is energizing and promotes growth.

The global law firm O'Melveny & Myers lauds the use of 360-degree evaluations in helping workers thrive. The feedback is open-ended and summarized rather than shared verbatim, which has encouraged a 97% response rate. Carla Christofferson, the managing partner of the Los Angeles offices, learned from her evaluation that people saw her behavior as not matching the firm's stated commitment to work-life balance—which was causing stress among employees. She started to spend more time away from the office and to limit weekend work to things she could do at home. She became a role model for balance, which went a long way toward eliminating the worry of employees who wanted a life outside of work.

The four mechanisms that help employees thrive don't require enormous efforts or investments. What they do require is leaders who are open to empowering employees and who set the tone. As we've noted, each mechanism provides a different angle that's necessary for thriving. You can't choose one or two from the menu; the mechanisms reinforce one another. For example, can people be comfortable making decisions if they don't have honest information about current numbers? Can they make effective decisions if they're worried about being ridiculed?

Creating the conditions for thriving requires your concerted attention. Helping people grow and remain energized at work is valiant on its own merits—but it can also boost your company's performance in a sustainable way.

GRETCHEN SPREITZER is the Keith E. and Valerie J. Alessi Professor of Business Administration at the University of Michigan's Ross School of Business where she is a core faculty member in the Center for Positive Organizations. CHRISTINE PORATH is an associate professor of management at Georgetown University, the author of *Mastering Civility: A Manifesto for the Workplace* (Grand Central Publishing, 2016), and a coauthor of *The Cost of Bad Behavior* (Portfolio, 2009).

Reprinted from *Harvard Business Review*,
January–February 2012 (product #R1201F).

6

The Research We've Ignored About Happiness at Work

By André Spicer and Carl Cederström

Recently, we found ourselves in motivational seminars at our respective places of employment. Both events preached the gospel of happiness. In one, a speaker explained that happiness could make you healthier, kinder, more productive, and even more likely to get promoted.

The other seminar involved mandatory dancing of the wilder kind. It was supposed to fill our bodies with joy. It also prompted one of us to sneak out and take refuge in the nearest bathroom.

Ever since a group of scientists switched the lights on and off at the Hawthorne factory in the mid-1920s, scholars and executives alike have been obsessed with increasing their employees' productivity. In particular, happiness as a way to boost productivity seems to have gained traction in corporate circles as of late.[1] Firms spend money on happiness coaches, team-building exercises, gameplays, funsultants, and chief happiness officers (yes, you'll find one of those at Google). These activities and titles may appear jovial or even bizarre, but companies are taking them extremely seriously. Should they?

When you look closely at the research—which we did after the dancing incident—it's not clear that encouraging happiness at work is always a good idea. Sure, there is evidence to suggest that happy employees are less likely to leave, more likely to satisfy customers, are safer, and more likely to engage in citizenship behavior.[2] However, we also discovered alternate findings, which indicates that some of the taken-for-granted wisdoms about what happiness can achieve in the workplace are mere myths.

To start, we don't really know what happiness is or how to measure it. Measuring happiness is about as easy as taking the temperature of the soul or determining the exact color of love. As historian Darrin M. McMahon shows in his illuminating book *Happiness: A History*, ever since the sixth century BC, when Croesus is said to have quipped "No one who lives is happy," this slippery concept has served as a proxy for all sorts of other concepts, from pleasure and joy to plenitude and contentment. Being happy in the moment, Samuel Johnson said, could be achieved only when drunk.[3] For Jean-Jacques Rousseau, happiness was to lie in a boat, drifting aimlessly, feeling like a God (not exactly the picture of productivity). There are other definitions of happiness, too, but they are neither less nor more plausible than those of Johnson or Rousseau.

And just because we have more-advanced technology today doesn't mean we're any closer to pinning down a definition, as Will Davies reminds us in his book *The Happiness Industry*. He concludes that even as we have developed more-advanced techniques for measuring emotions and predicting behaviors, we have also adopted increasingly simplified notions of what it means to be human, let alone what it means to pursue happiness. A brain scan that lights up may *seem* like it's telling us something concrete about an elusive emotion, for example, when it actually isn't.

Happiness doesn't necessarily lead to increased productivity. A stream of research shows some contradictory results about the relationship between happiness—which is often defined as "job satisfaction"—and productivity.[4] One study on British supermarkets even suggests there might be a negative correlation between job satisfaction and corporate productivity: The more miserable the employees were, the better the profits.[5] Sure, other studies have pointed in the opposite direction, saying that there is a link between feeling content with work and being productive. But even these studies, when considered as a whole, demonstrate a relatively weak correlation.

Happiness can also be exhausting. The pursuit of happiness may not be wholly effective, but it doesn't really hurt, right? Wrong. Ever since the eighteenth century, people have been pointing out that the demand to be happy brings with it a heavy burden, a responsibility that can never be perfectly fulfilled. Focusing on happiness can actually make us feel less happy.

A psychological experiment recently demonstrated this.[6] The researchers asked their subjects to watch a film that would usually make them happy: a figure skater winning a medal. But before watching the film, half of the group was asked to read a statement aloud about the importance of happiness in life. The other half did not read the statement. The researchers were surprised to find that those who had read the statement were actually *less* happy after watching the film. Essentially, when happiness becomes a duty, it can make people feel worse if they fail to accomplish it.

This is particularly problematic at the present era, in which happiness is preached as a moral obligation.[7] As the French philosopher Pascal Bruckner put it, "Unhappiness is not only unhappiness; it is, worse yet, a failure to be happy."[8]

Happiness won't necessarily get you through the workday. If you've worked in a frontline customer service job, like a call center or a fast food restaurant, you know that being upbeat is not optional—it's compulsory. And as tiring as that may be, it makes some sense when you're in front of customers.

But today, many non-customer-facing employees are also asked to be upbeat. This could have some unforeseen consequences. One study found that people who were in a good mood were worse at picking out acts of deception than those who were in a bad mood.[9] Another piece of research found that people who were angry during a negotiation achieved better outcomes than people who were happy.[10] This suggests that being happy may not be good for all aspects of our work or for jobs that rely heavily on certain abilities. In fact, in some cases, happiness can actually make our performance worse.

Happiness could damage your relationship with your boss. If we believe that work is where we will find happiness, we might, in some cases, start to mistake our boss for a surrogate spouse or parent. In her study of a media company, researcher Susanne Ekmann found that those who expected work to make them happy would often become emotionally needy.[11] They wanted their managers to provide them with a steady stream of recognition and emotional reassurance. And when they *didn't* receive the expected emotional response (which was often), these employees felt neglected and started overreacting. Even minor setbacks were interpreted as being rejected by their bosses. So in many ways, expecting a boss to bring happiness makes us emotionally vulnerable.

Happiness could also hurt your relationships with friends and family. In her book *Cold Intimacies*, sociology professor Eva Illouz points out a strange side effect of people trying to live more emotionally at work: They started to treat their private lives like work tasks. The people she spoke with saw their personal lives as something that needed to be carefully administered using a range of tools and techniques they had learned from corporate life. As a result, their home lives became increasingly cold and calculating. It's no wonder then that many of the people she spoke with preferred to spend time at work rather than at home.

Happiness could make losing your job that much more devastating. When we expect the workplace to provide happiness and meaning in our lives, we become dangerously dependent on it. When studying professionals, sociology professor Richard Sennett noticed that people who saw their employer as an important source of personal meaning were those who became most devastated if they were fired.[12] When these people lost their jobs, they weren't just losing an income—they were losing the promise of happiness. This suggests that, when we see our work as a great source of happiness, we make ourselves emotionally vulnerable during periods of change. In an era of constant corporate restructuring, this can be dangerous.

Happiness could also make you selfish. Being happy makes you a better person, right? Not so, according to an interesting piece of research.[13] Participants were given lottery tickets and then given a choice about how many tickets they wanted to give to others and how many they wished to keep for themselves. Those who were in a good mood ended up keeping more tickets for themselves. This implies that, at least in some settings, being happy doesn't necessarily mean we will be generous. In fact, the opposite could be true.

Finally, happiness could also make you lonely. In one experiment, psychologists asked a number of people to keep a detailed diary for two weeks. What they found at the end of the study was that those who greatly valued happiness felt lonelier than those who valued happiness less.[14] It seems that focusing too much on the pursuit of happiness can make us feel disconnected from other people.

So why, contrary to all of this evidence, do we continue to hold on to the belief that happiness can improve a workplace? The answer, according to one study, comes down to aesthetics and ideology. Happiness is a convenient idea that looks good on paper (the aesthetic part). But it's also an idea that helps us shy away from more serious issues at work, such as conflicts and workplace politics (the ideological part).[15]

When we assume that happy workers are better workers, we may sweep more uncomfortable questions under the rug, especially since happiness is often seen as a choice. It becomes a convenient way of dealing with negative attitudes, party poopers, miserable bastards, and other unwanted characters in corporate life. Invoking happiness, in all its ambiguity, is an excellent way of getting away with controversial decisions, such as choosing to let people go. As Barbara Ehrenreich points out in her book *Bright-Sided*, positive messages about happiness have proved particularly popular in times of crisis and mass layoffs.

Given all these potential problems, we think there is a strong case for rethinking our expectation that work should always make us happy. It can be exhausting, make us overreact, drain our personal life of meaning, increase our vulnerability, and make us more gullible, selfish, and lonely. Most striking is that consciously pursuing happiness can actually drain the sense of joy we usually get from the really good things we experience.

In reality, work—like all other aspects of life—is likely to make us feel a wide range of emotions. If your job feels depressing and meaningless, it might be because it *is* depressing and meaningless. Pretending otherwise can just make it worse. Happiness, of course, is a great thing to experience, but it can't be willed into existence. Maybe the less we seek to actively pursue happiness through our jobs, the more likely we will be to actually experience a sense of joy in our work—a joy that is spontaneous and pleasurable rather than constructed and oppressive. But most important, we will be better equipped to cope with work in a sober manner. To see it for what it is and not what we—whether as executives, employees, or dancing motivational seminar leaders—pretend that it is.

ANDRÉ SPICER is a professor of organizational behavior at Cass Business School in London. CARL CEDERSTRÖM is an associate professor of organization theory at Stockholm University. They are the coauthors of *The Wellness Syndrome* (Polity 2015).

Notes

1. C. D. Fisher, "Happiness at Work." *International Journal of Management Reviews* 12, no. 4 (December 2010): 384–412.
2. Ibid.
3. D. M. McMahon, *Happiness: A History.* (New York: Atlantic Monthly Press, 2006.)
4. Fisher, "Happiness at Work."
5. McMahon, *Happiness: A History.*
6. I. B. Mauss et al., "Can Seeking Happiness Make People Happy? Paradoxical Effects of Valuing Happiness." *Emotion* 11, no. 4 (August 2011): 807–815.
7. P. Bruckner, *Perpetual Euphoria: On the Duty to Be Happy*, tr. Steven Rendall. (Princeton, New Jersey: Princeton University Press, 2011.)
8. Ibid, 5.
9. J. P. Forgas and R. East, "On Being Happy and Gullible: Mood Effects on Skepticism and the Detection of Deception." *Journal of Experimental Social Psychology* 44 (2008): 1362–1367.

10. G. A. van Kleef et al., "The Interpersonal Effects of Anger and Happiness in Negotiations." *Journal of Personality and Social Psychology* 86, no. 1 (2004): 57–76.

11. S. Ekman, "Fantasies About Work as Limitless Potential—How Managers and Employees Seduce Each Other through Dynamics of Mutual Recognition." *Human Relations* 66, no. 9 (December 2012): 1159–1181.

12. R. Sennett, *The Corrosion of Character: The Personal Consequences of Work in New Capitalism.* (New York: W.W. Norton, 2000.)

13. H. B. Tan and J. Forgas, "When Happiness Makes Us Selfish, But Sadness Makes Us Fair: Affective Influences on Interpersonal Strategies in the Dictator Game." *Journal of Experimental Social Psychology* 46, no. 3 (May 2010): 571–576.

14. I. B. Mauss, "The Pursuit of Happiness Can Be Lonely." *Emotion* 12, no. 5 (2012): 908–912.

15. G. E. Ledford, "Happiness and Productivity Revisited." *Journal of Organizational Behavior* 20, no. 1 (January 1999): 25–30.

Adapted from content posted on hbr.org on
July 21, 2015 (product #H027TW).

7

The Happiness Backlash

By Alison Beard

Nothing depresses me more than reading about happiness. Why? Because there's entirely too much advice out there about how to achieve it. As Frédéric Lenoir points out in *Happiness: A Philosopher's Guide* (recently translated from its original French), great thinkers have been discussing this topic for more than 2,000 years. But opinions on it still differ. Just scan the 14,700 titles listed in the "happiness" subgenre of self-help books on Amazon, or watch the 55 TED talks tagged in the same category. What makes us happy? Health, money, social connection, purpose, "flow," generosity, gratitude, inner peace, positive thinking . . . research shows that any (or all?) of the above answers are correct. Social scientists tell us that even the simplest of tricks—counting our blessings, meditating for 10 minutes a day, forcing smiles—can push us into a happier state of mind.

And yet for me and many others, happiness remains elusive. Of course, I sometimes feel joyful and content—reading a bedtime story to my kids, interviewing someone I greatly admire, finishing a tough piece of writing. But despite having good health, supportive family and friends, and a stimulating and flexible job, I'm often awash in negative emotions: worry, frustration, anger, disappointment, guilt, envy, regret. My default state is dissatisfied.

The huge and growing body of happiness literature promises to lift me out of these feelings. But the effect is more like kicking me when I'm down. I know I should be happy. I know I have every reason to be and that I'm better off than most. I know that happier people are more successful. I know that just a few mental exercises might help me. Still, when I'm in a bad mood, it's hard to break out of it. And—I'll admit—a small part of me regards my nonbliss not as unproductive negativity but as highly productive realism. I can't imagine being happy all the time; indeed, I'm highly suspicious of anyone who claims to be.

I agreed to write this essay because over the past several years I've sensed a swell of support for this point of view. Barbara Ehrenreich's 2009 book *Bright-Sided*, about the "relentless promotion" and undermining effects of positive thinking, was followed last year by *Rethinking Positive Thinking*, by the NYU psychology professor Gabriele Oettingen, and *The Upside of Your Dark Side*, by two experts in positive psychology, Todd Kashdan and Robert Biswas-Diener. This year brought a terrific *Psychology Today* article by Matthew Hutson titled "Beyond Happiness: The Upside of Feeling Down"; *The Upside of Stress*, by Stanford's Kelly McGonigal; *Beyond Happiness*, by the British historian and commentator Anthony Seldon; and *The Happiness Industry:*

How the Government and Big Business Sold Us Well-Being, by another Brit, the Goldsmiths lecturer in politics William Davies.

Are we finally seeing a backlash against happiness? Sort of. Most of these recent releases rail against our modern obsession with *feeling* happy and *thinking* positively. Oettingen explains the importance of damping sunny fantasies with sober analysis of the obstacles in one's way. Kashdan and Biswas-Diener's book and Hutson's article detail the benefits we derive from all the negative emotions I cited earlier; taken together, those feelings spur us to better our circumstances and ourselves. (The Harvard psychologist Susan David, a coauthor of the HBR article "Emotional Agility," also writes thoughtfully on this topic.)

McGonigal shows how viewing one unhappy condition—stress—in a kinder light can turn it into something that improves rather than hurts our health. Those who accept feeling stressed as the body's natural response to a challenge are more resilient and live longer than those who try to fight it.

Seldon describes his own progression from pleasure seeking to more-meaningful endeavors that bring him (and should bring us) joy. Sadly, he trivializes his advice by alphabetizing it: Accepting oneself; Belonging to a group; having good Character, Discipline, Empathy, Focus, Generosity, and Health; using Inquiry; embarking on an inner Journey; accepting Karma; and embracing both Liturgy and Meditation. (One wonders what he'll use for X and Z in the next book.)

Davies comes at the issue from a different angle. He's fed up with organizational attempts to tap into what is essentially a "grey mushy process inside our brains." In his view, there's something sinister about the way advertisers, HR managers, governments, and pharmaceutical companies are measuring, manipulating, and ultimately making money from our insatiable desire to be happier.

But none of these authors is arguing against individuals' aspiring to have a generally happy life. We call that the pursuit of "happiness," but what we really mean is "long-term fulfillment." Martin Seligman, the father of positive psychology, calls it "flourishing" and said years ago that positive emotion (that is, feeling happy) is only one element of it, along with engagement, relationships, meaning, and achievement. In the parlance Arianna Huffington uses in her recent book, it's "thriving," and Lenoir, whose history of happiness philosophy is probably the most enlightening and entertaining of the bunch, describes it as simply "love of life." Who can argue against any of those things?

Where most of the happiness gurus go wrong is insisting that daily if not constant happiness is a means to long-term fulfillment. For some glass-half-full optimists, that may be true. They can "stumble on happiness" the way the field's most prominent researcher, Dan Gilbert, suggests; or gain "the happiness advantage" that the professor-turned-consultant Shawn Achor talks about; or "broadcast happiness," as Michelle Gielan, Achor's wife and partner at the firm GoodThink, recommends in her new book. As I said, it apparently takes just a few simple tricks.

But for the rest of us, that much cheer feels forced, so it's unlikely to help us mold meaningful relationships or craft the perfect career. It certainly can't be drawn out of us by employers or other external forces. We pursue fulfillment in different ways, without reading self-help books. And I suspect that in the long run we'll be OK—perhaps even happy.

ALISON BEARD is a senior editor at *Harvard Business Review*.

Reprinted from *Harvard Business Review*,
July–August 2015.

Index

How to be human at work.

HBR's Emotional Intelligence Series features smart, essential reading on the human side of professional life from the pages of *Harvard Business Review*. Each book in the series offers uplifting stories, practical advice, and research from leading experts on how to tend to our emotional well-being at work.

Harvard Business Review Emotional Intelligence Series

Available in paperback or ebook format. The specially priced six-volume set includes:

- Mindfulness
- Resilience
- Influence and Persuasion
- Authentic Leadership
- Happiness
- Empathy

The most important management ideas all in one place.

We hope you enjoyed this book from *Harvard Business Review*. For the best ideas HBR has to offer turn to HBR's 10 Must Reads Boxed Set. From books on leadership and strategy to managing yourself and others, this 6-book collection delivers articles on the most essential business topics to help you succeed.

HBR's 10 Must Reads Series

The definitive collection of ideas and best practices on our most sought-after topics from the best minds in business.

- Change Management
- Collaboration
- Communication
- Emotional Intelligence
- Innovation
- Leadership
- Making Smart Decisions

- Managing Across Cultures
- Managing People
- Managing Yourself
- Strategic Marketing
- Strategy
- Teams
- The Essentials

hbr.org/mustreads

Influence and Persuasion

HBR EMOTIONAL INTELLIGENCE SERIES

HBR Emotional Intelligence Series

How to be human at work

The HBR Emotional Intelligence Series features smart, essential reading on the human side of professional life from the pages of *Harvard Business Review*.

Authentic Leadership

Empathy

Happiness

Influence and Persuasion

Mindfulness

Resilience

Other books on emotional intelligence from *Harvard Business Review*:

HBR's 10 Must Reads on Emotional Intelligence

HBR Guide to Emotional Intelligence

Influence and Persuasion

HBR EMOTIONAL INTELLIGENCE SERIES

Harvard Business Review Press

Boston, Massachusetts

Copyright 2018 Harvard Business School Publishing Corporation
All rights reserved
Printed in the United States of America

10 9 8 7 6

The web addresses referenced in this book were live and correct at the time of the book's publication but may be subject to change.

Library of Congress cataloging information is forthcoming

ISBN 978-1-63369-393-7
eISBN 978-1-63369-394-4

The paper used in this publication meets the requirements of the American National Standard for Permanence of Paper for Publications and Documents in Libraries and Archives Z39.48-1992.

Contents

Contents

Influence and
Persuasion

1

Understand the Four Components of Influence

By Nick Morgan

We've all encountered people who say less but what they say matters more; people who know how to use silence to dominate an exchange. So having influence means more than just doing all the talking; it's about taking charge and understanding the roles that positional power, emotion, expertise, and nonverbal signals play. These four aspects of influence are essential to master if you want to succeed as a leader.

Take *positional power*. If you have it, influence becomes a relatively simple proposition. People with power over others tend to talk more, to interrupt more, and to guide the conversation more, by picking the topics, for example.

If you don't have the positional power in a particular situation, then, expect to talk less, interrupt less, and choose the topics of conversation less. After all, exercising their right to talk more about the subjects they care for is one of the ways that people with positional power demonstrate it.

What do you do if you want to challenge the positional authority? Perhaps you have a product, or an idea, or a company you want to sell, and you have the ear of someone who can buy it. How do you get control in that kind of situation?

The second aspect of influence is *emotion*, and using it is one way to counteract positional power and generally to dominate a conversation. When the other side has the power and you have the emotion, something closer to parity is possible. Indeed, passion can sweep away authority, when it's well supported and the speaker is well prepared. We've all witnessed that happen when a young unknown performer disarms and woos the judges, devastating the competition, in one of those talent competitions. The purity and power of the emotion in the performance is enough to silence—and enlist—the judges despite their positional authority. Indeed, the impassioned speech, the plea for clemency, the summation to the jury that brings them to tears and wins the case for the defendant—this is the stuff of Hollywood climaxes.

Passion often links with *expertise*, the third aspect of influence. And indeed, you can dominate the conversation, beating out positional power, if you have both passion and expertise. The diffident expert's voice is sometimes lost in the clamor of people wanting to be heard. So expertise without passion is not always effective, but if it's patient, it can be the last person standing in a debate and thereby get its turn.

The final aspect of influence is the subtlest of the four and as such rarely can trump either positional authority or passion. But in rare instances, artfully manipulated, I have seen it prevail. What is it? It is the mastery of the dance of human interaction.

We have very little conscious awareness of this aspect of influence, but we are all participants in it with more or less expertise. We learn at a very early age that conversation is a pas de deux, a game that two (or more) people play that involves breathing, winking, nodding, eye contact, head tilts, hand gestures, and a whole series of subtle nonverbal signals that help both parties communicate with each other.

Indeed, conversation is much less functional without these *nonverbal signals*. That's why phone conversations are nowhere near as satisfying as in-person encounters and why conference calls inevitably involve lots more interruptions, miscues, and cross talking. We're not getting the signals we're used to getting to help us know when the other person is ready to hand the conversational baton on to us, and vice versa.

Can you manage influence only using this fourth aspect? I have seen it done in certain situations, but the other three aspects will usually trump this one. Nonetheless, I once watched a senior executive effortlessly dominate a roomful of people who were ostensibly equal—a group of researchers gathered from around the world to discuss the future of IT. Within a few minutes, everyone in the room was unconsciously deferring to this executive, even though he had no positional power and was not particularly passionate about the subject. His mastery of the subtle signals of conversational cuing was profound, and soon he had everyone dancing to his verbal beat. It was beautiful to watch; he showed complete conversational mastery in action.

Influence, then, is a measure of how much skin the participants have in the game, and most of us are unconscious experts at measuring it. To wield it, you need to have the edge in at least one of its four aspects—and preferably more than one.

NICK MORGAN is an author, speaker, coach, and the president and founder of Public Words, a communications consulting firm.

Excerpted from the author's book *Power Cues: The Subtle Science of Leading Groups, Persuading Others, and Maximizing Your Personal Impact* (product #11710), Harvard Business Review Press, 2014.

2

Harnessing the Science of Persuasion

By Robert Cialdini

A lucky few have it; most of us do not. A handful of gifted "naturals" simply know how to capture an audience, sway the undecided, and convert the opposition. Watching these masters of persuasion work their magic is at once impressive and frustrating. What's impressive is not just the easy way they use charisma and eloquence to convince others to do as they ask. It's also how eager those others are to do what's requested of them, as if the persuasion itself were a favor they couldn't wait to repay.

The frustrating part of the experience is that these born persuaders are often unable to account for their remarkable skill or pass it on to others. Their way with people is an art, and artists as a rule are far better at doing than at explaining. Most of them can't offer much help to those of us who possess no more than the ordinary quotient of charisma and eloquence but who still have to wrestle with leadership's fundamental challenge: getting things done through others. That challenge is painfully familiar to corporate executives, who every day have to figure out how to motivate and direct a highly individualistic work force. Playing the "Because I'm the boss" card is out. Even if it weren't demeaning and demoralizing for all concerned, it would be out of place in a world where cross-functional teams, joint ventures, and intercompany partnerships have blurred the lines of authority. In such an environment, persuasion skills exert far greater influence over others' behavior than formal power structures do.

Which brings us back to where we started. Persuasion skills may be more necessary than ever, but how can executives acquire them if the most talented practitioners can't pass them along? By looking to science. For the past five decades, behavioral scientists have conducted experiments that shed considerable light on the way certain interactions lead people to concede, comply, or change. This research shows that persuasion works by appealing to a limited set of deeply rooted human drives and needs, and it does so in predictable ways. Persuasion, in other words, is governed by basic principles that can be taught, learned, and applied. By mastering these principles, executives can bring scientific rigor to the business of securing consensus, cutting deals, and winning concessions. In the pages that follow, I describe six fundamental principles of persuasion and suggest a few ways that executives can apply them in their own organizations.

The principle of liking:
People like those who like them.

*The application: Uncover real similarities
and offer genuine praise.*

The retailing phenomenon known as the Tupperware party is a vivid illustration of this principle in action. The demonstration party for Tupperware products is hosted by an individual, almost always a woman, who invites to her home an array of friends, neighbors, and relatives. The guests' affection for their hostess predisposes them to buy from her, a dynamic that was confirmed by a 1990 study of purchase decisions made at demonstration parties. The researchers, Jonathan Frenzen and Harry Davis, writing in the *Journal of Consumer Research*, found that the guests' fondness for their hostess weighed twice as heavily in their purchase decisions as their regard for the products they bought. So when guests at a Tupperware party buy something, they aren't just buying to please themselves. They're buying to please their hostess as well.

What's true at Tupperware parties is true for business in general: If you want to influence people, win friends. How? Controlled research has identified several factors that reliably increase liking, but two stand out as especially compelling—similarity and praise. Similarity literally draws people together. In one experiment, reported in a 1968 article in the *Journal of Personality*, participants stood physically closer to one another after learning that they shared political beliefs and social values. And in a 1963 article in *American Behavioral Scientists*, researcher F. B. Evans used demographic data from insurance company records to demonstrate that prospects were more willing to purchase a policy from a salesperson who was akin to them in age, religion, politics, or even cigarette-smoking habits.

Managers can use similarities to create bonds with a recent hire, the head of another department, or even a new boss. Informal conversations during the workday create an ideal opportunity to discover at least one common area of enjoyment, be it a hobby, a college basketball team, or reruns of *Seinfeld*. The important thing is to establish the bond early because it creates a presumption of goodwill and trustworthiness in every subsequent encounter. It's much easier to build support for a new project when the people you're trying to persuade are already inclined in your favor.

Praise, the other reliable generator of affection, both charms and disarms. Sometimes the praise doesn't even have to be merited. Researchers at the University of North Carolina writing in the *Journal of Experimental Social Psychology* found that men felt the greatest regard for an individual who flattered them unstintingly even if the comments were untrue. And in their book *Interpersonal Attraction* (Addison-Wesley, 1978), Ellen Berscheid and Elaine

Hatfield Walster presented experimental data showing that positive remarks about another person's traits, attitude, or performance reliably generates liking in return, as well as willing compliance with the wishes of the person offering the praise.

Along with cultivating a fruitful relationship, adroit managers can also use praise to repair one that's damaged or unproductive. Imagine you're the manager of a good-sized unit within your organization. Your work frequently brings you into contact with another manager—call him Dan—whom you have come to dislike. No matter how much you do for him, it's not enough. Worse, he never seems to believe that you're doing the best you can for him. Resenting his attitude and his obvious lack of trust in your abilities and in your good faith, you don't spend as much time with him as you know you should; in consequence, the performance of both his unit and yours is deteriorating.

The research on praise points toward a strategy for fixing the relationship. It may be hard to find, but there has to be something about Dan you can sincerely admire, whether it's his concern for the people in his department, his devotion to his family, or simply his work ethic. In your next encounter with him, make an appreciative comment about that trait. Make it clear that in this case at least, you value what he values. I predict that Dan will relax his relentless negativity and give you an opening to convince him of your competence and good intentions.

The principle of reciprocity: People repay in kind.

The application: Give what you want to receive.

Praise is likely to have a warming and softening effect on Dan because, ornery as he is, he is still human and subject to the universal human tendency to treat people the way they treat him. If you have ever caught yourself smiling at a coworker just because he or she smiled first, you know how this principle works.

Charities rely on reciprocity to help them raise funds. For years, for instance, the Disabled American Veterans organization, using only a well-crafted fund-raising letter, garnered a very respectable 18% rate of response to its appeals. But when the group started enclosing a small gift in the envelope, the response rate nearly doubled to 35%. The gift—personalized address labels—was extremely modest, but it wasn't what prospective donors received that made the difference. It was that they had gotten anything at all.

What works in that letter works at the office, too. It's more than an effusion of seasonal spirit, of course, that impels suppliers to shower gifts on purchasing departments at holiday time. In 1996, purchasing managers admitted to an interviewer from *Inc.* magazine that after having accepted a gift from a supplier, they were willing to purchase products and services they would have otherwise declined. Gifts also have a startling effect on retention. I have encouraged readers of my book to send me examples of the principles of influence at work in their own lives. One reader, an employee of the State of Oregon, sent a letter in which she offered these reasons for her commitment to her supervisor:

He gives me and my son gifts for Christmas and gives me presents on my birthday. There is no promotion for the type of job I have, and my only choice for one is to move to another department. But I find myself resisting trying to move. My boss is reaching retirement age, and I am thinking I will be able to move out after he retires . . . [F]or now, I feel obligated to stay since he has been so nice to me.

Ultimately, though, gift giving is one of the cruder applications of the rule of reciprocity. In its more sophisticated uses, it confers a genuine first-mover advantage on any manager who is trying to foster positive attitudes and productive personal relationships in the office: Managers can elicit the desired behavior from coworkers and employees by displaying it first. Whether it's a sense of trust, a spirit of cooperation, or a pleasant demeanor, leaders should model the behavior they want to see from others.

The same holds true for managers faced with issues of information delivery and resource allocation. If you lend a member of your staff to a colleague who is shorthanded and staring at a fast-approaching deadline, you will significantly increase your chances of getting help when you need it. Your odds will improve even more if you say, when your colleague thanks you for the assistance, something like, "Sure, glad to help. I know how important it is for me to count on your help when I need it."

The principle of social proof: People follow the lead of similar others.

The application: Use peer power whenever it's available.

Social creatures that they are, human beings rely heavily on the people around them for cues on how to think, feel, and act. We know this intuitively, but intuition has also been confirmed by experiments, such as the one first described in 1982 in the *Journal of Applied Psychology*. A group of researchers went door-to-door in Columbia, South Carolina, soliciting donations for a charity campaign and displaying a list of neighborhood residents who had already donated to the cause. The researchers found that the longer the donor list was, the more likely those solicited would be to donate as well.

To the people being solicited, the friends' and neighbors' names on the list were a form of social evidence about how they should respond. But the evidence would not have been nearly as compelling had the names been those of random strangers. In an experiment from the 1960s, first described in the *Journal of Personality and Social Psychology*, residents of New York City were asked to return a lost wallet to its owner. They were highly likely to attempt to return the wallet when they learned that another New Yorker had previously attempted to do so. But learning that someone from a foreign country had tried to return the wallet didn't sway their decision one way or the other.

The lesson for executives from these two experiments is that persuasion can be extremely effective when it comes from peers. The science supports what most sales professionals already know: Testimonials from satisfied customers work best when the satisfied customer and the prospective customer share similar circumstances. That lesson can help a manager faced with the task of selling a new corporate initiative.

Imagine that you're trying to streamline your department's work processes. A group of veteran employees is resisting. Rather than try to convince the employees of the move's merits yourself, ask an old-timer who supports the initiative to speak up for it at a team meeting. The compatriot's testimony stands a much better chance of convincing the group than yet another speech from the boss. Stated simply, influence is often best exerted horizontally rather than vertically.

The principle of consistency: People align with their clear commitments.

The application: Make their commitments active, public, and voluntary.

Liking is a powerful force, but the work of persuasion involves more than simply making people feel warmly toward you, your idea, or your product. People need not only to like you but to feel committed to what you want them to do. Good turns are one reliable way to make people feel obligated to you. Another is to win a public commitment from them.

My own research has demonstrated that most people, once they take a stand or go on record in favor of a position, prefer to stick to it. Other studies reinforce that finding and go on to show how even a small, seemingly trivial commitment can have a powerful effect on future actions. Israeli researchers writing in 1983 in the *Personality and Social Psychology Bulletin* recounted how they asked half the residents of a large apartment complex to sign a petition favoring the establishment of a recreation center for the handicapped. The cause was good and the request was small, so almost everyone who was asked agreed to sign. Two weeks later, on National Collection Day for the Handicapped, all residents of the complex were approached at home and asked to give to the cause.

A little more than half of those who were not asked to sign the petition made a contribution. But an astounding 92% of those who did sign donated money. The residents of the apartment complex felt obligated to live up to their commitments because those commitments were active, public, and voluntary. These three features are worth considering separately.

There's strong empirical evidence to show that a choice made actively—one that's spoken out loud or written down or otherwise made explicit—is considerably more likely to direct someone's future conduct than the same choice left unspoken. Writing in 1996 in the *Personality and Social Psychology Bulletin*, Delia Cioffi and Randy Garner described an experiment in which college students in one group were asked to fill out a printed form saying they wished to volunteer for an AIDS education project in the public schools. Students in another group volunteered for the same project by leaving blank a form stating that they didn't want to participate. A few days later, when the volunteers reported for duty, 74% of those who showed up were students from the group that signaled their commitment by filling out the form.

The implications are clear for a manager who wants to persuade a subordinate to follow some particular course of action: Get it in writing. Let's suppose you want your employee to submit reports in a more timely fashion. Once you believe you've won agreement, ask him to summarize the decision in a memo and send it to you. By doing so, you'll have greatly increased the odds that he'll fulfill the commitment because, as a rule, people live up to what they have written down.

Research into the social dimensions of commitment suggests that written statements become even more powerful when they're made public. In a classic experiment, described in 1955 in the *Journal of Abnormal and Social Psychology*, college students were asked to estimate the length of lines projected on a screen. Some students were asked to write down their choices on a piece of paper, sign it, and hand the paper to the experimenter. Others wrote their choices on an erasable slate, then erased the slate immediately. Still others were instructed to keep their decisions to themselves.

The experimenters then presented all three groups with evidence that their initial choices may have been wrong. Those who had merely kept their decisions in their heads were the most likely to reconsider their original estimates. More loyal to their first guesses were the students in the group that had written them down and immediately erased them. But by a wide margin, the ones most reluctant to shift from their original choices were those who had signed and handed them to the researcher.

This experiment highlights how much most people wish to appear consistent to others. Consider again the matter of the employee who has been submitting late reports. Recognizing the power of this desire, you should, once you've successfully convinced him of the need to be more timely, reinforce the commitment by making sure it gets a public airing. One way to do that would be to send the employee an email that reads, "I think your plan is just what we need. I showed it to Diane in manufacturing and Phil in shipping, and they thought it was right on target, too." Whatever way such commitments are formalized, they should never be like the New Year's resolutions people privately make and then abandon with no one the wiser. They should be publicly made and visibly posted.

More than 300 years ago, Samuel Butler wrote a couplet that explains succinctly why commitments must be voluntary to be lasting and effective: "He that complies against his will/Is of his own opinion still." If an undertaking is forced, coerced, or imposed from the outside, it's not a commitment; it's an unwelcome burden. Think how you would react if your boss pressured you to donate to the campaign of a political candidate. Would that make you more apt to opt for that candidate in the privacy of a voting booth? Not likely. In fact, in their 1981 book *Psychological Reactance* (Academic Press), Sharon S. Brehm and Jack W. Brehm present data that suggest you'd vote the opposite way just to express your resentment of the boss's coercion.

This kind of backlash can occur in the office, too. Let's return again to that tardy employee. If you want to produce an enduring change in his behavior, you should avoid using threats or pressure tactics to gain his compliance. He'd likely view any change in his behavior as the result of intimidation rather than a personal commitment to change. A better approach would be to identify something that the employee genuinely values in the workplace—high-quality workmanship, perhaps, or team spirit—and then describe how timely reports are consistent with those values. That gives the employee reasons for improvement that he can own. And because he owns them, they'll continue to guide his behavior even when you're not watching.

The principle of authority:
People defer to experts.

The application: Expose your expertise;
don't assume it's self-evident.

Two thousand years ago, the Roman poet Virgil offered this simple counsel to those seeking to choose correctly: "Believe an expert." That may or may not be good advice, but as a description of what people actually do, it can't be beaten. For instance, when the news media present an acknowledged expert's views on a topic, the effect on public opinion is dramatic. A single expert-opinion news story in the *New York Times* is associated with a 2% shift in public opinion nationwide, according to a 1993 study described in the *Public Opinion Quarterly*. And researchers writing in the *American Political Science Review* in 1987 found that when the expert's view was aired on national television, public opinion shifted as much as 4%. A cynic might argue that these findings only illustrate the docile submissiveness of the public. But a fairer explanation is that, amid the teeming complexity of contemporary life, a well-selected expert offers a valuable and efficient shortcut to good decisions. Indeed, some questions, be they legal, financial, medical, or technological, require so much specialized knowledge to answer, we have no choice but to rely on experts.

Since there's good reason to defer to experts, executives should take pains to ensure that they establish their own expertise before they attempt to exert influence. Surprisingly often, people mistakenly assume that others recognize and appreciate their experience. That's what happened at a hospital where some colleagues and I were consulting. The physical therapy staffers were frustrated because so many of their stroke patients abandoned their exercise routines as soon as they left the hospital. No matter how often the staff emphasized the importance of regular home exercise—it is, in fact, crucial to the process of regaining independent function—the message just didn't sink in.

Interviews with some of the patients helped us pinpoint the problem. They were familiar with the background and training of their physicians, but the patients knew little about the credentials of the physical therapists who were urging them to exercise. It was a simple matter to remedy that lack of information: We merely asked the therapy director to display all the awards, diplomas, and certifications of her staff on the walls of the therapy rooms. The result was startling: Exercise compliance jumped 34% and has never dropped since.

What we found immensely gratifying was not just how much we increased compliance, but how. We didn't fool or browbeat any of the patients. We *informed* them into compliance. Nothing had to be invented; no time or resources had to be spent in the process. The staff's expertise was real—all we had to do was make it more visible.

The task for managers who want to establish their claims to expertise is somewhat more difficult. They can't simply nail their diplomas to the wall and wait for everyone to notice. A little subtlety is called for. Outside the United States, it is customary for people to spend time interacting socially before getting down to business for the first time. Frequently they gather for dinner the night before their meeting or negotiation. These get-togethers can make discussions easier and help blunt disagreements—remember the findings about liking and similarity—and they can also provide an opportunity to establish expertise. Perhaps it's a matter of telling an anecdote about successfully solving a problem similar to the one that's on the agenda at the next day's meeting. Or perhaps dinner is the time to describe years spent mastering a complex discipline—not in a boastful way but as part of the ordinary give-and-take of conversation.

Granted, there's not always time for lengthy introductory sessions. But even in the course of the

PERSUASION EXPERTS, SAFE AT LAST

Thanks to several decades of rigorous empirical research by behavioral scientists, our understanding of the how and why of persuasion has never been broader, deeper, or more detailed. But these scientists aren't the first students of the subject. The history of persuasion studies is an ancient and honorable one, and it has generated a long roster of heroes and martyrs.

A renowned student of social influence, William McGuire, contends in a chapter of the *Handbook of Social Psychology*, 3rd edition (Oxford University Press, 1985), that scattered among the more than four millennia of recorded Western history are four centuries in which the study of persuasion flourished as a craft. The first was the Periclean Age of ancient Athens, the second occurred during the years of the

(Continued)

PERSUASION EXPERTS, SAFE AT LAST

Roman Republic, the next appeared in the time of the European Renaissance, and the last extended over the hundred years that have just ended, which witnessed the advent of large-scale advertising, information, and mass media campaigns. Each of the three previous centuries of systematic persuasion study was marked by a flowering of human achievement that was suddenly cut short when political authorities had the masters of persuasion killed. The philosopher Socrates is probably the best known of the persuasion experts to run afoul of the powers that be.

Information about the persuasion process is a threat because it creates a base of power entirely separate from the one controlled by political authorities. Faced with a rival source of influence, rulers in previous centuries had few qualms about eliminating those rare individuals who truly understood how to marshal forces that heads of state have never been able to monopolize, such as cleverly crafted language, strategically placed information, and, most important, psychological insight.

It would perhaps be expressing too much faith in human nature to claim that persuasion experts no longer face a threat from those who wield political power. But because the truth about persuasion is no longer the sole possession of a few brilliant, inspired individuals, experts in the field can presumably breathe a little easier. Indeed, since most people in power are interested in remaining in power, they're likely to be more interested in acquiring persuasion skills than abolishing them.

preliminary conversation that precedes most meetings, there is almost always an opportunity to touch
lightly on your relevant background and experience
as a natural part of a sociable exchange. This initial
disclosure of personal information gives you a chance
to establish expertise early in the game, so that when
the discussion turns to the business at hand, what you
have to say will be accorded the respect it deserves.

The principle of scarcity:
People want more of what
they can have less of.

*The application: Highlight unique benefits
and exclusive information.*

Study after study shows that items and opportunities are seen to be more valuable as they become less
available. That's a tremendously useful piece of in-

formation for managers. They can harness the scarcity principle with the organizational equivalents of limited-time, limited-supply, and one-of-a-kind offers. Honestly informing a coworker of a closing window of opportunity—the chance to get the boss's ear before she leaves for an extended vacation, perhaps—can mobilize action dramatically.

Managers can learn from retailers how to frame their offers not in terms of what people stand to gain but in terms of what they stand to lose if they don't act on the information. The power of "loss language" was demonstrated in a 1988 study of California homeowners written up in the *Journal of Applied Psychology*. Half were told that if they fully insulated their homes, they would save a certain amount of money each day. The other half were told that if they failed to insulate, they would lose that amount each day. Significantly more people insulated their homes when exposed to the loss language. The same phenomenon occurs in business. According to a 1994 study in the journal *Organizational Behavior and Human Decision Processes*, potential losses figure far more heavily in managers' decision making than potential gains.

In framing their offers, executives should also remember that exclusive information is more persuasive than widely available data. A doctoral student of mine, Amram Knishinsky, wrote his 1982 dissertation on the purchase decisions of wholesale beef buyers. He observed that they more than doubled their orders when they were told that, because of certain weather conditions overseas, there was likely to be a scarcity of foreign beef in the near future. But their orders increased 600% when they were informed that no one else had that information yet.

The persuasive power of exclusivity can be harnessed by any manager who comes into possession of information that's not broadly available and that supports an idea or initiative he or she would like the organization to adopt. The next time that kind of information crosses your desk, round up your organization's key players. The information itself may seem dull, but exclusivity will give it a special sheen. Push it across your desk and say, "I just got this report today. It won't be distributed until next week, but I want to give you an early look at what it shows." Then watch your listeners lean forward.

Allow me to stress here a point that should be obvious. No offer of exclusive information, no exhortation to act now or miss this opportunity forever should be made unless it is genuine. Deceiving colleagues into compliance is not only ethically objectionable, it's foolhardy. If the deception is detected—and it certainly will be—it will snuff out any enthusiasm the offer originally kindled. It will also invite dishonesty toward the deceiver. Remember the rule of reciprocity.

Putting it all together

There's nothing abstruse or obscure about these six principles of persuasion. Indeed, they neatly codify our intuitive understanding of the ways people evaluate information and form decisions. As a result, the principles are easy for most people to grasp, even those with no formal education in psychology. But in the seminars and workshops I conduct, I have learned that two points bear repeated emphasis.

First, although the six principles and their applications can be discussed separately for the sake of clarity, they should be applied in combination to compound their impact. For instance, in discussing the importance of expertise, I suggested that managers use informal, social conversations to establish their credentials. But that conversation affords an opportunity to gain information as well as convey it. While you're showing your dinner companion that you have the skills and experience your business problem demands, you can also learn about your companion's background, likes, and dislikes—information that will help you locate genuine similarities and give sincere compliments. By letting your expertise surface and also establishing rapport, you double your persuasive power. And if you succeed in bringing your dinner partner on board, you may encourage other people to sign on as well, thanks to the persuasive power of social evidence.

The other point I wish to emphasize is that the rules of ethics apply to the science of social influence just as they do to any other technology. Not only is it ethically wrong to trick or trap others into assent, it's ill-advised in practical terms. Dishonest or high-pressure tactics work only in the short run, if at all. Their long-term effects are malignant, especially within an organization that can't function properly without a bedrock level of trust and cooperation.

That point is made vividly in the following account, which a department head for a large textile manufacturer related at a training workshop I conducted. She described a vice president in her company who wrung public commitments from department heads in a highly manipulative manner. Instead of giving his subordinates time to talk or think through his proposals carefully, he would approach them individually at the busiest moment of their workday and describe the benefits of his plan in exhaustive, patience-straining detail. Then he would move in for the kill. "It's very important for me to see you as being on my team on this," he would say. "Can I count on your support?" Intimidated, frazzled, eager to chase the man from their offices so they could get back to work, the department heads would invariably go along with his request. But because the commitments never felt voluntary, the department heads never followed through, and as a result the vice president's initiatives all blew up or petered out.

This story had a deep impact on the other participants in the workshop. Some gulped in shock as they recognized their own manipulative behavior. But what stopped everyone cold was the expression on the department head's face as she recounted the damaging collapse of her superior's proposals. She was smiling.

Nothing I could say would more effectively make the point that the deceptive or coercive use of the principles of social influence is ethically wrong and pragmatically wrongheaded. Yet the same principles, if applied appropriately, can steer decisions correctly. Legitimate expertise, genuine obligations, authentic similarities, real social proof, exclusive news, and freely made commitments can produce choices that are likely to benefit both parties. And any approach that works to everyone's mutual benefit is good business, don't you think? Of course, I don't want to press you into it, but, if you agree, I would love it if you could just jot me a memo to that effect.

ROBERT CIALDINI is the author of *Influence and Pre-Suasion: A Revolutionary Way to Influence and Persuade* (Simon & Schuster, 2016). He is Regents' Professor Emeritus of Psychology and Marketing at Arizona State University and president and CEO of INFLUENCE AT WORK, a global training and keynote company.

Reprinted from *Harvard Business Review*, October 2001 (product #R0109D).

3

Three Things Managers Should Be Doing Every Day

By Linda A. Hill and Kent Lineback

When are we supposed to do all *that*?" That's the question we constantly get from new managers, only weeks or months into their positions, when we describe the three key activities they should be focusing on to be successful as leaders: building trust, building a team, and building a broader network. To their dismay, most of them have found they rarely end a day in their new positions having done what they planned to do. They spend most of their time solving unexpected problems and making sure their groups do their work on time, on budget, and up to standard. They feel desperately out of control because what's *urgent*—the daily work—always seems to highjack what's *important*—their ongoing work as managers and leaders.

So they push back because they think we've just made their to-do list even longer. And these key elements (we call them the "Three Imperatives of Leading and Managing") are not quick and easy wins—they are substantial and fundamental to one's ability to function effectively as a leader. Here's why:

- *Building trust.* Successful leadership is, at root, about influencing others, and trust is the foundation of all ability to influence others. You cannot influence anyone who does not trust you. Thus the manager must work to cultivate the trust of everyone they work with. They do this by demonstrating the two basic components of trust: competence and character. Competence doesn't mean being the resident expert in everything the group does; it does mean understanding the work well enough to make solid decisions about it and having the courage to ask questions where they may be less knowledgeable. Character means basing decisions and actions on values that go beyond self-interest and truly caring about the work, about the customers (internal or external) for whom they do the work, and about the people doing the work. If people believe in your competence and character, they will trust you to do the right thing.

- *Building a real team and managing through it.* An effective team is bound together by a common, compelling purpose, based on shared values. In a genuine team, the bonds among members are so strong that they truly believe they will all succeed or fail together and that no individual can win if the team loses. Besides purpose and values, strong teams also have rules of engagement: explicit and implicit understandings of how members work together. For example, what kinds of conflict are allowed, and what kinds are not? Smart leaders make sure all the elements that create a real team are in place—purpose, values, rules— and then manage *through* the team. So instead of saying, "Do it because I'm the boss," they say, "Do it for the team," which is a much more powerful approach. In a real team, members value their membership and strive mightily not to let their comrades down. The smart leader builds and uses these powerful ties to shape behavior.

- *Building a network.* Every team depends on the support and collaboration of outside people and groups. Effective group leaders proactively build and maintain a network of these outsiders, which includes not just those needed for today's work but also those the group will need to achieve future goals. This is without a doubt the imperative that most troubles new managers. They think "networking" is manipulative organizational politicking that requires them to pretend they like people just because they want something from them. They strive to be above that sort of thing. Alas, in the process, they unnecessarily limit their own and their group's ability to influence others for good ends. Building a network can be politicking, but it need not be if they do it honestly, openly, and with the genuine intent of creating relationships that benefit both sides.

It is here, after covering these imperatives, that we hear the question, "When are we supposed to build trust, build a team, and create a network? How do we do that on top of everything else we have to do?"

Our answer is that the "Three Imperatives" and all that each embodies are not discrete tasks to put on a to-do. Instead, strong, effective leaders manage and lead *through* the daily work. They do this in the way they define, assign, structure, talk about, review, and generally guide that work. They are masters at using the daily work and its inevitable crises to perform their work as managers and leaders.

How do they do this?

They build *trust* by taking the opportunity to demonstrate their ability as they do their daily work, by asking knowledgeable questions and offering insightful suggestions. They use daily decisions and choices to illustrate their own values, expressing their concern for those who work for them or those for whom the group does its work. They reveal themselves, but not in an egotistical way, showing what they know, what they believe, and what they value—and in doing this, they show themselves to be trustworthy.

They build a *team* by using problems and crises in the daily work to remind members of the team's purpose and what it values most. They explain their decisions in these terms. They immediately call out team members who violate a rule of engagement—treating each other disrespectfully, for example—or who place their interests above those of the team. And since the rules apply to all members, including the leader, they ask team members to hold the leader accountable if she ever forgets one of those rules.

They build a *network* by taking opportunities afforded by routine activities—a regular meeting of department heads, for example, or even a chance meeting in the elevator—to build and maintain relationships with colleagues outside their group. They consciously approach problems that involve another group leader in a way that both solves the problem and fosters a long-term relationship. They proactively share information with outsiders who would benefit from it. They encourage their group members to take the same approach when they deal with outsiders.

These are obviously only a few of the ways good managers use their daily work to fulfill the deeper imperatives of leadership, but you get the idea. In fact, if there's anything that might be called a "secret" for not getting overwhelmed by the challenges of becoming an effective manager, this is surely it. We've seen new managers light up when they finally grasp this principle: that the daily work isn't an impediment to doing what good leaders do. Instead, it's *the way*, the vehicle, to do most of what good managers do.

Once they learn this lesson, they look at their daily work differently. For every new task, for every unexpected problem, they take a moment to step back and ask, How can I use this to foster trust? To build and strengthen us as a team? To expand our network and make it stronger?

LINDA A. HILL is the Wallace Brett Donham Professor of Business Administration at Harvard Business School. She is the author of *Becoming a Manager* and a coauthor of *Being the Boss* and *Collective Genius: The Art and Practice of Leading Innovation* (Harvard Business Review Press, 2014). KENT LINEBACK spent many years as a manager and an executive in business and government. He is a coauthor of *Collective Genius: The Art and Practice of Leading Innovation* (Harvard Business Review Press, 2014).

Reprinted from hbr.org, originally published September 24, 2015 (product #H02DCU).

4

Learning
Charisma

By John Antonakis, Marika Fenley, and Sue Liechti

J ana stands at the podium, palms sweaty, looking out at hundreds of colleagues who are waiting to hear about her new initiative. Bill walks into a meeting after a failed product launch to greet an exhausted and demotivated team that desperately needs his direction. Robin gets ready to confront a brilliant but underperforming subordinate who needs to be put back on track.

We've all been in situations like these. What they require is charisma—the ability to communicate a clear, visionary, and inspirational message that captivates and motivates an audience. So how do you learn charisma? Many people believe that it's impossible.

They say that charismatic people are born that way—as naturally expressive and persuasive extroverts. After all, you can't teach someone to be Winston Churchill.

While we agree with the latter contention, we disagree with the former. Charisma is not all innate; it's a learnable skill or, rather, a set of skills that have been practiced since antiquity. Our research with managers in the laboratory and in the field indicates that anyone trained in what we call "charismatic leadership tactics" (CLTs) can become more influential, trustworthy, and "leader like" in the eyes of others. In this article we'll explain these tactics and how we help managers master them. Just as athletes rely on hard training and the right game plan to win a competition, leaders who want to become charismatic must study the CLTs, practice them religiously, and have a good deployment strategy.

What is charisma?

Charisma is rooted in values and feelings. It's influence born of the alchemy that Aristotle called the *logos*, the *ethos*, and the *pathos*; that is, to persuade others, you must use powerful and reasoned rhetoric, establish personal and moral credibility, and then rouse followers' emotions and passions. If a leader can do those three things well, he or she can then tap into the hopes and ideals of followers, give them a sense of purpose, and inspire them to achieve great things.

Several large-scale studies have shown that charisma can be an invaluable asset in any work context—small or large, public or private, Western or Asian. Politicians know that it's important. Yet many business managers don't use charisma, perhaps because they don't know how to or because they believe it's not as easy to master as transactional (carrot-and-stick) or instrumental (task-based) leadership. Let's be clear: Leaders need technical expertise to win the trust of followers, manage operations, and set strategy; they also benefit from the ability to punish and reward. But the most effective leaders layer charismatic leadership on top of transactional and instrumental leadership to achieve their goals.

In our research, we have identified a dozen key CLTs. Some of them you may recognize as long-standing techniques of oratory. Nine of them are verbal: metaphors, similes, and analogies; stories and anecdotes; contrasts; rhetorical questions; three-part lists; expressions of moral conviction; reflections of the group's sentiments; the setting of high goals; and conveying confidence that they can be achieved. Three tactics are nonverbal: animated voice, facial expressions, and gestures.

There are other CLTs that leaders can use—such as creating a sense of urgency, invoking history, using repetition, talking about sacrifice, and using humor— but the 12 described in this article are the ones that have the greatest effect and can work in almost any context. In studies and experiments, we have found that people who use them appropriately can unite followers around a vision in a way that others can't. In 8 of the past 10 U.S. presidential races, for instance, the candidate who deployed verbal CLTs more often won. And when we measured "good" presentation skills— such as speech structure, clear pronunciation, use of easy-to-understand language, tempo of speech, and speaker comfort—and compared their impact against that of the CLTs, we found that the CLTs played a much bigger role in determining who was perceived to be more leader like, competent, and trustworthy.

Still, these tactics don't seem to be widely known or taught in the business world. The managers who practice them typically learned them by trial and error, without thinking consciously about them. As one manager who attended our training remarked, "I use a lot of these tactics, some without even knowing it." Such learning should not be left to chance.

We teach managers the CLTs by outlining the concepts and then showing news and film clips that highlight examples from business, sports, and politics. Managers must then experiment with and practice the tactics—on video, in front of peers, and on their own. A group of midlevel European executives (with an average age of 35) that did so as part of our training almost doubled their use of CLTs in presentations. As a result, they saw observers' numerical ratings of their competence as leaders jump by about 60% on average. They were then able to take the tactics back to their jobs. We saw the same thing happen with another group of executives (with an average age of 42) in a large Swiss firm. Overall, we've found that about 65% of people who have been trained in the CLTs receive above-average ratings as leaders, in contrast with only 35% of those who have not been trained.

The aim is to use the CLTs not only in public speaking but also in everyday conversations—to be more charismatic all the time. The tactics work because they help you create an emotional connection with followers, even as they make you appear more powerful, competent, and worthy of respect. In Greek, the word "charisma" means special gift. Start to use the CLTs correctly, and that's what people will begin to think you have.

Let's now look at the tactics in detail.

Connect, compare, and contrast

Charismatic speakers help listeners understand, relate to, and remember a message. A powerful way to do this is by using *metaphors*, *similes*, and *analogies*. Martin Luther King Jr. was a master of the metaphor. In his "I Have a Dream" speech, for example, he likened the U.S. Constitution to "a promissory note" guaranteeing the unalienable rights of life, liberty, and the pursuit of happiness to all people but noted that America had instead given its black citizens "a bad check," one that had come back marked "insufficient funds." Everyone knows what it means to receive a bad check. The message is crystal clear and easy to retain.

Metaphors can be effective in any professional context, too. Joe, a manager we worked with, used one to predispose his team to get behind an urgent relocation. He introduced it by saying, "When I heard about this from the board, it was like hearing about a long-awaited pregnancy. The difference is that we have four months instead of nine months to prepare." The team instantly understood it was about to experience an uncomfortable but ultimately rewarding transition.

Stories and anecdotes also make messages more engaging and help listeners connect with the speaker. Even people who aren't born raconteurs can employ them in a compelling way. Take this example from a speech Bill Gates gave at Harvard, urging graduates to consider their broader responsibilities: "My mother . . . never stopped pressing me to do more for others. A few days before my wedding, she hosted a bridal event, at which she read aloud a letter about marriage that she had written to Melinda. My mother was very ill with cancer at the time, but she saw one more opportunity to deliver her message, and at the close of the letter she [quoted]: 'From those to whom much is given, much is expected.'"

Lynn, another manager we studied, used the following story to motivate her reports during a crisis: "This reminds me of the challenge my team and I faced when climbing the Eiger peak a few years ago. We got caught in bad weather, and we could have died up there. But working together, we managed to survive. And we made what at first seemed impossible, possible. Today we are in an economic storm, but by pulling together, we can turn this situation around and succeed." The story made her team feel reassured and inspired.

Contrasts are a key CLT because they combine reason and passion; they clarify your position by pitting it against the opposite, often to dramatic effect. Think of John F. Kennedy's "Ask not what your country can do for you—ask what you can do for your country." In our experience, contrasts are one of the easiest tactics to learn and use, and yet they aren't used enough. Here are some examples from managers newly trained in the CLTs. Gilles, a senior VP, speaking to a direct report managing a stagnant team: "It seems to me that you're playing too much defense when you need to be playing more offense." (That's also a metaphor.) And Sally, introducing herself to her new team: "I asked to lead the medical division not because it has the best location but because I believe we can accomplish something great for our company and at the same time help save lives."

Engage and distill

Rhetorical questions might seem hackneyed, but charismatic leaders use them all the time to encourage engagement. Questions can have an obvious answer or pose a puzzle to be answered later. Think again of Martin Luther King Jr., who said, "There are those who are asking the devotees of civil rights, 'When will you be satisfied?'" and then went on to show that oppressed people can never be satisfied. Anita Roddick—founder of the Body Shop—once used three rhetorical questions to explain what led her to help start the social responsibility movement. The thinking, she said, "was really simple: How do you make business kinder? How do you embed it in the community? How do you make community a social purpose for business?"

This tactic works just as well in private conversations. Take Mika, a manager in our study, who effectively motivated an underperforming subordinate by asking, "So, where do you want to go from here? Will it be back to your office feeling sorry for yourself? Or do you want to show what you are capable of achieving?" Here's another question (also employing metaphor) used by Frank, an IT executive who needed to push back at the unrealistic goals being set for him: "How can you expect me to change an engine in a plane midflight?"

Three-part lists are another old trick of effective persuasion because they distill any message into key takeaways. Why three? Because most people can remember three things, three is sufficient to provide proof of a pattern, and three gives an impression of completeness. Three-part lists can be announced—as in "There are three things we need to do to get our bottom line back into the black"—or they can be under the radar, as in the sentence before this one.

Here's a list that Serge, a midlevel manager, used at a team meeting: "We have the best product on the market. We have the best team. Yet we did not make the sales target." And here's one that Karin, division head of a manufacturing company, employed in a speech to her staff: "We can turn this around with a three-point strategy: First, we need to look back and see what we did right. Next, we need to see where we went wrong. Then, we need to come up with a plan that will convince the board to give us the resources to get it right the next time."

Show integrity, authority, and passion

Expressions of moral conviction and *statements that reflect the sentiments of the group*—even when the sentiments are negative—establish your credibility by revealing the quality of your character to your listeners and making them identify and align themselves with you. On Victory Day at the end of the Second World War, Winston Churchill brilliantly captured the feelings of the British people and also conveyed a spirit of honor, courage, and compassion. He said: "This is your hour. This is not victory of a party or of any class. It's a victory of the great British nation as a whole. We were the first, in this ancient island, to draw the sword against tyranny. . . . There we stood, alone. The lights went out and the bombs came down. But every man, woman, and child in the country had no thought of quitting the struggle. . . . Now we have emerged from one deadly struggle—a terrible foe has been cast on the ground and awaits our judgment and our mercy."

Another nice example of moral conviction (plus a number of other CLTs) comes from Tina, a manager in an NGO pushing for a needed supply-chain change: "Who do you think will pay for the logistical mess we've created? It is not our donors who'll feel it but the children we're supposed to be feeding that will go to bed one more time with an empty belly and who may not make it through the night. Apart from wasting money, this is not right, especially because the fix is so simple." And here's Rami, a senior IT director trained in the CLTs, expertly reflecting the sentiments of his disheartened team: "I know what is going through your minds, because the same thing is going through mine. We all feel disappointed and demotivated. Some of you have told me you have had sleepless nights; others, that there are tensions in the team, even at home because of this. Personally, life to me has become dull and tasteless. I know how hard we have all worked and the bitterness we feel because success just slipped out of our reach. But it's not going to be like this for much longer. I have a plan."

Another CLT, which helps charismatic leaders demonstrate passion—and inspire it in their followers—is *setting high goals*. Gandhi set the almost impossible (and moral) goal of liberating India from British rule without using violence, as laid out in his famous "quit India" speech. An example from the business world that we often cite is the former CEO of Sharp, Katsuhiko Machida. In 1998, at a time when Sharp faced collapse, cathode-ray tubes dominated the TV market, and the idea of using LCD technology was commercially unviable, he energized his employees by stating the unthinkable: "By 2005, all TVs we sell in Japan will be LCD models."

But one must also *convey confidence that the goals can be achieved.* Gandhi noted: "I know the British Government will not be able to withhold freedom from us, when we have made enough self-sacrifice." In a later speech he expressed his conviction more forcefully: "Even if all the United Nations opposes me, even if the whole of India forsakes me, I will say, 'You are wrong. India will wrench with nonviolence her liberty from unwilling hands.' I will go ahead not for India's sake alone but for the sake of the world. Even if my eyes close before there is freedom, nonviolence will not end." Machida personally took his vision to Sharp's engineers to convince them that they could realize his risky goal. He made it the company's

74

most important project, brought together cross-functional teams from LCD and TV development to work on it, and told them plainly that it was crucial to Sharp's survival. Or take Ray, an engineer we know, addressing his team after a setback: "The deadline the CEO gave us is daunting. Other teams would be right to tremble at the knees, but we are not just another team. I know you can rise to the challenge. I believe in each one of you, which means that I believe that we can get the prototype to manufacturing in three months. Let's commit to do what it takes to get the job done: We have the smarts. We have the experience. All we need is the will, and that's something only great teams have." Passion cannot emerge unless the leader truly believes that the vision and strategic goal can be reached.

The three nonverbal cues—*expressions of voice, body, and face*—are also key to charisma. They don't come naturally to everyone, however, and they are the most culturally sensitive tactics: What's perceived as too much passion in certain Asian contexts might be perceived as too muted in southern European ones. But they are nonetheless important to learn and practice because they are easier for your followers to process than the verbal CLTs, and they help you hold people's attention by punctuating your speech. (For more on these, see the sidebar "Charisma in Voice and Body.")

Putting it all into practice

Now that you've learned the CLTs, how do you start using them? Simple: preparation and practice. When you're mapping out a speech or a presentation, you should certainly plan to incorporate the tactics and rehearse them. We also encourage leaders to think about them before one-on-one conversations or team meetings in which they need to be persuasive. The idea is to arm yourself with a few key CLTs that feel comfortable to you and therefore will come out spontaneously—or at least look as if they did. The leaders we've trained worked on improving their charisma in groups and got feedback from one another. You could ask your spouse or a friendly colleague to do the same or videotape yourself and do a self-critique.

The goal isn't to employ all the tactics in every conversation but to use a balanced combination. With time and practice, they will start to come out on the fly. One manager we know, who met his wife after being trained in the CLTs, showed her his "before" videos and told us she couldn't believe it was him. The charismatic guy in the "after" videos—the one whose CLT use had more than doubled—was the person she had married. Another manager, who learned the tactics six years ago and has since become the chief operating officer of his company, says he now uses them every day—personally and professionally—such as in a recent talk to his team about a relocation, which went "much better than expected" as a result.

CHARISMA IN VOICE AND BODY

Three tactics for showing passion—and winning over listeners.

Animated voice

People who are passionate vary the volume with which they speak, whispering at appropriate points or rising to a crescendo to hammer home a point. Emotion—sadness, happiness, excitement, surprise—must come through in the voice. Pauses are also important because they convey control.

Facial expressions

These help reinforce your message. Listeners need to see as well as hear your passion—especially when you're telling a story or reflecting their sentiments. So be sure to make eye contact (one of the givens of charisma), and get comfortable smiling, frowning, and laughing at work.

Gestures

These are signals for your listeners. A fist can reinforce confidence, power, and certitude. Waving a hand, pointing, or pounding a desk can help draw attention.

If you think you can't improve because you're just not naturally charismatic, you're wrong. The managers with the lowest initial charisma ratings in our studies were able to significantly narrow the gap between themselves and their peers to whom the tactics came naturally. It's true that no amount of training or practice will turn you into Churchill or Martin Luther King Jr. But the CLTs can make you more charismatic in the eyes of your followers, and that will invariably make you a more effective leader.

JOHN ANTONAKIS is a professor of business and economics at the University of Lausanne in Switzerland and consults for companies on leadership development. MARIKA FENLEY has a PhD in management focusing on gender and leadership from the Faculty of Business and Economics at the University of Lausanne. SUE LIECHTI holds a master's degree in psychology from the University of Lausanne and is an organizational development consultant.

Reprinted from *Harvard Business Review,*
June 2012 (product #R1206K).

5

To Win People Over, Speak to Their Wants and Needs

By Nancy Duarte

P racticing empathy can be difficult, because you have to step outside your comfort zone to understand someone else's point of view. But it's essential to exercising influence.

It's how method actors move us to feel, think, or act differently—they deeply immerse themselves in their characters, trying on new ways of being and behaving. Sometimes their identity experiments are even part of the story line, as in *Being John Malkovich*, *Avatar*, and *Tootsie*.

During *Tootsie*, walking in the shoes of a woman had such a profound impact on Dustin Hoffman that, 30 years later, recalling his decision to make the film brought tears to his eyes in an interview with the American Film Institute.

Before agreeing to work on the movie, Hoffman did some makeup tests to see if he would be believable as a woman. When he discovered that he could pass, but he wouldn't be *beautiful*, he realized he had to do this project. As he explained to his wife: "I think I'm an interesting woman [as Dorothy Michaels]. And I know that if I met myself at a party, I wouldn't talk to that character because she doesn't fulfill physically the demands that we're brought up to think women have to have in order for us to ask them out . . . There's too many interesting women I have not had the experience to know in this life because I've been brainwashed." Empathy made Hoffman's performance—and the film's message—more convincing and powerful.

The same thing happens in business all the time. Whether you're trying to get your team on board with a new way of working, asking investors to fund you, persuading customers to buy your product, or imploring the public to donate to your cause, your success depends on your ability to grasp the wants and needs of the people around you. We've seen this over and over again at my firm as we've created presentations for clients and coached them on effective delivery. If people feel listened to, they become more receptive to your message. And by doing the listening, you become more informed about what they really need—not just what you think they need—which will fuel your relationships with stakeholders over the long run.

How do you build your capacity for empathy? Exercises can help, and they're used in many fields. Secret shoppers pose as retail customers and record their observations. Product developers brainstorm use cases and interview consumers to envision how they'll interact with a product. Negotiators do role-playing to imagine opposing points of view before they get to the table.

Once you've started to develop empathy as a skill, you can make it integral to the work you do. You might try visualizing stakeholders' various perspectives the way Airbnb CEO Brian Chesky and his team did. As described in a *Fast Company* post, they storyboarded the guest, host, and hiring processes—inspired by Disney's filmmaking. They created a list of the key moments in these three experiences and then developed the most important and most emotionally charged ones into fuller narratives. Cofounder Nathan Blecharczyk says they learned a lot: "What the storyboards made clear is that we were missing a big part of the picture. . . . There were a lot of important moments where we weren't doing anything." The storyboards ended up helping the company define its mobile strategy and even inspired new features, which allowed Airbnb to connect with traveling customers wherever the customers were.[1]

It's also essential to listen carefully to your stakeholders and check your understanding of what's being said. Arbitrators do this to get a handle on what both sides need in a dispute, before trying to carve out a solution. Executives who are new to a company often embark on listening tours with employees and customers to get their perspective on issues and opportunities.

That's what Lou Gerstner did in the 1990s, when the board at IBM brought him in to turn around the almost bankrupt company. Gerstner called his listening tour Operation Bear Hug. He gave managers three months to meet with customers and ask about issues they were grappling with and how IBM could help. Managers then had to recap the conversations in memos. Gerstner also called customers on his own every day. And he "bear-hugged" employees by touring IBM's various sites and hosting gatherings to share updates, test ideas, and tackle concerns. He held 90-minute unscripted Q&A sessions with the staff, during which he would talk to 20,000 workers directly.

"I listened, and I tried very hard not to draw conclusions," Gerstner said.

It was an important step in the strategy-making process, one that enabled the executive team to build plans to make IBM relevant and competitive again. But it led to an even larger shift in IBM's culture that transformed the company from an inwardly focused bureaucracy to a market-driven innovator.

Empathize with the people you need to persuade to purchase your product or services or to work hard on your behalf. It gives you better ideas, and it makes you worth listening to. And if your stakeholders can empathize with you in return, you're on your way to building real, lasting relationships with them.

NANCY DUARTE is CEO of Duarte Design and the author of the *HBR Guide to Persuasive Presentations* (Harvard Business Review Press, 2012), as well as two books on the art of presenting, *Slide:ology: The Art and Science of Creating Great Presentations* (O'Reilly Media, 2008) and *Resonate: Present Visual Stories That Transform Audiences* (Wiley, 2010). She is a coauthor with Patti Sanchez of *Illuminate: Ignite Change Through Speeches, Stories, Ceremonies, and Symbols* (Portfolio, 2016).

Note

1. S. Kessler, "How Snow White Helped Airbnb's Mobile Mission," *Fast Company*, November 8, 2012, http://www.fast cocreate.com/1681924/how-snow-white-helped-airbnbs -mobile-mission; N. Blecharczyk, "Visualizing the Customer Experience," Sequoia Capital, https://www.sequoia cap.com/article/visualizing-customer-experience/; A. Carr, "Inside Airbnb's Grand Hotel Plans," *Fast Company*, March 17, 2014, http://www.fastcompany.com/3027107/ punk-meet-rock-airbnb-brian-chesky-chip-conley.

Reprinted from hbr.org, originally published
May 12, 2015 (product #H0228V).

6

Storytelling That Moves People

An interview with Robert McKee by Bronwyn Fryer

Persuasion is the centerpiece of business activity. Customers must be convinced to buy your company's products or services, employees and colleagues to go along with a new strategic plan or reorganization, investors to buy (or not to sell) your stock, and partners to sign the next deal. But despite the critical importance of persuasion, most executives struggle to communicate, let alone inspire. Too often, they get lost in the accoutrements of company-speak: PowerPoint slides, dry memos, and hyperbolic missives from the corporate communications department. Even the most carefully researched and considered efforts are routinely greeted with cynicism, lassitude, or outright dismissal.

Why is persuasion so difficult, and what can you do to set people on fire? In search of answers to those questions, HBR senior editor Bronwyn Fryer paid a visit to Robert McKee, the world's best known and most respected screenwriting lecturer, at his home in Los Angeles. An award-winning writer and director, McKee moved to California after studying for his PhD in cinema arts at the University of Michigan. He then taught at the University of Southern California's School of Cinema and Television before forming his own company, Two Arts, to take his lectures on the art of storytelling worldwide to an audience of writers, directors, producers, actors, and entertainment executives.

McKee's students have written, directed, and produced hundreds of hit films, including *Forrest Gump*, *Erin Brockovich*, *The Color Purple*, *Gandhi*, *Monty Python and the Holy Grail*, *Sleepless in Se-*

attle, Toy Story, and *Nixon.* They have won 18 Academy Awards, 109 Emmy Awards, 19 Writers Guild Awards, and 16 Directors Guild of America Awards. Emmy Award winner Brian Cox portrays McKee in the 2002 film *Adaptation,* which follows the life of a screenwriter trying to adapt the book *The Orchid Thief.* McKee also serves as a project consultant to film and television production companies such as Disney, Pixar, and Paramount as well as major corporations (including Microsoft) that regularly send their entire creative staffs to his lectures.

McKee believes that executives can engage listeners on a whole new level if they toss their PowerPoint slides and learn to tell good stories instead. In his best-selling book *Story: Substance, Structure, Style, and the Principles of Screenwriting,* published in 1997 by HarperCollins, McKee argues that stories "fulfill a profound human need to grasp the patterns of living—not merely as an intellectual exercise, but within a very personal, emotional experience."

What follows is an edited and abridged transcript of McKee's conversation with HBR.

Why should a CEO or a manager pay attention to a screenwriter?

A big part of a CEO's job is to motivate people to reach certain goals. To do that, he or she must engage their emotions, and the key to their hearts is story. There are two ways to persuade people. The first is by using conventional rhetoric, which is what most executives are trained in. It's an intellectual process, and in the business world it usually consists of a PowerPoint slide presentation in which you say, "Here is our company's biggest challenge, and here is what we need to do to prosper." And you build your case by giving statistics and facts and quotes from authorities. But there are two problems with rhetoric. First, the people you're talking to have their own set of authorities, statistics, and experiences. While you're trying to persuade them, they are arguing with you in their heads. Second, if you do succeed in persuading them, you've done so only on an intellectual basis. That's not good enough, because people are not inspired to act by reason alone.

The other way to persuade people—and ultimately a much more powerful way—is by uniting an idea with an emotion. The best way to do that is by telling a compelling story. In a story, you not only weave a lot of information into the telling but you also arouse your listener's emotions and energy. Persuading with a story is hard. Any intelligent person can sit down and make lists. It takes rationality but little creativity to design an argument using conventional rhetoric. But it demands vivid insight and storytelling skill to present an idea that packs enough emotional power to be memorable. If you can harness imagination and the principles of a well-told story, then you get people rising to their feet amid thunderous applause instead of yawning and ignoring you.

So, what is a story?

Essentially, a story expresses how and why life changes. It begins with a situation in which life is relatively in balance: You come to work day after day, week after week, and everything's fine. You expect it will go on that way. But then there's an event—in screenwriting, we call it the "inciting incident"—that throws life out of balance. You get a new job, or the boss dies of a heart attack, or a big customer threatens to leave. The story goes on to describe how, in an effort to restore balance, the protagonist's subjective expectations crash into an uncooperative objective reality. A good storyteller describes what it's like to deal with these opposing forces, calling on the protagonist to dig deeper, work with scarce resources, make difficult decisions, take action despite risks, and ultimately discover the truth. All great storytellers since the dawn of time—from the ancient Greeks through Shakespeare and up to the present day—have dealt with this fundamental conflict between subjective expectation and cruel reality.

How would an executive learn to tell stories?

Stories have been implanted in you thousands of times since your mother took you on her knee. You've read good books, seen movies, attended plays. What's more, human beings naturally *want* to work through stories. Cognitive psychologists describe how the human mind, in its attempt to understand and remember, assembles the bits and pieces of experience into a story, beginning with a personal desire, a life objective, and then portraying the struggle against the forces that block that desire. Stories are how we remember; we tend to forget lists and bullet points.

Businesspeople not only have to understand their companies' past, but then they must project the future. And how do you imagine the future? As a story. You create scenarios in your head of possible future events to try to anticipate the life of your company or your own personal life. So, if a businessperson understands that his or her own mind naturally wants to frame experience in a story, the key to moving an audience is not to resist this impulse but to embrace it by telling a good story.

What makes a good story?

You emphatically do not want to tell a beginning-to-end tale describing how results meet expectations. This is boring and banal. Instead, you want to display the struggle between expectation and reality in all its nastiness.

For example, let's imagine the story of a biotech startup we'll call Chemcorp, whose CEO has to persuade some Wall Street bankers to invest in the company. He could tell them that Chemcorp has discovered a chemical compound that prevents heart attacks and offer up a lot of slides showing them the size of the market, the business plan, the organizational chart, and so on. The bankers would nod politely and stifle yawns while thinking of all the other companies better positioned in Chemcorp's market.

Alternatively, the CEO could turn his pitch into a story, beginning with someone close to him—say, his father—who died of a heart attack. So nature itself is the first antagonist that the CEO-as-protagonist must overcome. The story might unfold like this: In his grief, he realizes that if there had been some chemical indication of heart disease, his father's death could have been prevented. His company discovers a protein that's present in the blood just before heart attacks and develops an easy-to-administer, low-cost test.

But now it faces a new antagonist: the FDA. The approval process is fraught with risks and dangers. The FDA turns down the first application, but new research reveals that the test performs even better than anyone had expected, so the agency approves a second application. Meanwhile, Chemcorp is running out of money, and a key partner drops out and goes off to start his own company. Now Chemcorp is in a fight-to-the-finish patent race.

This accumulation of antagonists creates great suspense. The protagonist has raised the idea in the bankers' heads that the story might not have a happy ending. By now, he has them on the edge of their seats, and he says, "We won the race, we got the patent, we're poised to go public and save a quarter-million lives a year." And the bankers just throw money at him.

Aren't you really talking about exaggeration and manipulation?

No. Although businesspeople are often suspicious of stories for the reasons you suggest, the fact is that statistics are used to tell lies and damn lies, while accounting reports are often BS in a ball gown—witness Enron and WorldCom.

When people ask me to help them turn their presentations into stories, I begin by asking questions. I kind of psychoanalyze their companies, and amazing dramas pour out. But most companies and executives sweep the dirty laundry, the difficulties, the antagonists, and the struggle under the carpet. They prefer to present a rosy—and boring—picture to the world. But as a storyteller, you want to position the problems in the foreground and then show how you've overcome them. When you tell the story of your struggles against real antagonists, your audience sees you as an exciting, dynamic person. And I know that the storytelling method works, because after I consulted with a dozen corporations whose principals told exciting stories to Wall Street, they all got their money.

What's wrong with painting a positive picture?

It doesn't ring true. You can send out a press release talking about increased sales and a bright future, but your audience knows it's never that easy. They know you're not spotless; they know your competitor doesn't wear a black hat. They know you've slanted your statement to make your company look good. Positive, hypothetical pictures and boilerplate press releases actually work against you because they foment distrust among the people you're trying to convince. I suspect that most CEOs do not believe their own spin doctors— and if they don't believe the hype, why should the public?

The great irony of existence is that what makes life worth living does not come from the rosy side.

We would all rather be lotus-eaters, but life will not allow it. The energy to live comes from the dark side. It comes from everything that makes us suffer. As we struggle against these negative powers, we're forced to live more deeply, more fully.

So acknowledging this dark side makes you more convincing?

Of course. Because you're more truthful. One of the principles of good storytelling is the understanding that we all live in dread. Fear is when you don't know what's going to happen. Dread is when you know what's going to happen and there's nothing you can do to stop it. Death is the great dread; we all live in an ever-shrinking shadow of time, and between now and then all kinds of bad things could happen.

Most of us repress this dread. We get rid of it by inflicting it on other people through sarcasm, cheating, abuse, indifference—cruelties great and small. We all commit those little evils that relieve the pressure and make us feel better. Then we rationalize our bad behavior and convince ourselves we're good people. Institutions do the same thing: They deny the existence of the negative while inflicting their dread on other institutions or their employees.

If you're a realist, you know that this is human nature; in fact, you realize that this behavior is the foundation of all nature. The imperative in nature is to follow the golden rule of survival: Do unto others what they do unto you. In nature, if you offer cooperation and get cooperation back, you get along. But if you offer cooperation and get antagonism back, then you give antagonism in return—in spades.

Ever since human beings sat around the fire in caves, we've told stories to help us deal with the dread of life and the struggle to survive. All great stories illuminate the dark side. I'm not talking about so-called "pure" evil, because there is no such thing. We are all evil and good, and these sides do continual battle. Kenneth Lay says wiping out people's jobs and life savings was unintentional. Hannibal Lecter is witty, charming, and brilliant, and he eats people's livers. Audiences appreciate the truthfulness of a storyteller who acknowledges the dark side of human beings and deals honestly with antagonistic events. The story engenders a positive but realistic energy in the people who hear it.

Does this mean you have to be a pessimist?

It's not a question of whether you're optimistic or pessimistic. It seems to me that the civilized human being is a skeptic—someone who believes nothing at face value. Skepticism is another principle of the storyteller. The skeptic understands the difference between text and subtext and always seeks what's really going on. The skeptic hunts for the truth beneath the surface of life, knowing that the real thoughts and feelings of institutions or individuals are unconscious and unexpressed. The skeptic is always looking behind the mask. Street kids, for example, with their tattoos, piercings, chains, and leather, wear amazing masks, but the skeptic knows the mask is only a persona. Inside anyone working that hard to look fierce is a marshmallow. Genuinely hard people make no effort.

So, a story that embraces darkness produces a positive energy in listeners?

Absolutely. We follow people in whom we believe. The best leaders I've dealt with—producers and directors—have come to terms with dark reality. Instead of communicating via spin doctors, they lead their actors and crews through the antagonism of a world in which the odds of getting the film made, distributed, and sold to millions of moviegoers are a thousand to one. They appreciate that the people who work for them love the work and live for the small triumphs that contribute to the final triumph.

CEOs, likewise, have to sit at the head of the table or in front of the microphone and navigate their companies through the storms of bad economies and tough competition. If you look your audience in the eye, lay out your really scary challenges, and say, "We'll be lucky as hell if we get through this, but here's what I think we should do," they will listen to you.

To get people behind you, you can tell a truthful story. The story of General Electric is wonderful and has nothing to do with Jack Welch's cult of celebrity. If you have a grand view of life, you can see it on all its complex levels and celebrate it in a story. A great CEO is someone who has come to terms with his or her own mortality and, as a result, has compassion for others. This compassion is expressed in stories.

Take the love of work, for example. Years ago, when I was in graduate school, I worked as an insurance fraud investigator. The claimant in one case was an immigrant who'd suffered a terrible head injury on a carmaker's assembly line. He'd been the fastest window assembler on the line and took great pride in his work. When I spoke to him, he was waiting to have a titanium plate inserted into his head.

The man had been grievously injured, but the company thought he was a fraud. In spite of that, he remained incredibly dedicated. All he wanted was to get back to work. He knew the value of work, no matter how repetitive. He took pride in it and even in the company that had falsely accused him. How wonderful it would have been for the CEO of that car company to tell the tale of how his managers recognized the falseness of their accusation and then rewarded the employee for his dedication. The company, in turn, would have been rewarded with redoubled effort from all the employees who heard that story.

How do storytellers discover and unearth the stories that want to be told?

The storyteller discovers a story by asking certain key questions. First, what does my protagonist want in order to restore balance in his or her life? Desire is the blood of a story. Desire is not a shopping list but a core need that, if satisfied, would stop the story in its tracks. Next, what is keeping my protagonist from achieving his or her desire? Forces within? Doubt? Fear? Confusion? Personal conflicts with friends, family, lovers? Social conflicts arising in the various institutions in society? Physical conflicts? The forces of Mother Nature? Lethal diseases in the air? Not enough time to get things done? The damned automobile that won't start? Antagonists come from people, society, time, space, and every object in it, or any combination of these forces at once. Then, how would my protagonist decide to act in order to achieve his or her desire in the face of these antagonistic forces? It's in the answer to that question that storytellers discover the truth of their characters, because the heart of a human being is revealed in the choices he or she makes under pressure. Finally, the storyteller leans back from the design of events he or she has created and asks, "Do I believe this? Is it neither an exaggeration nor a soft-soaping of the struggle? Is this an honest telling, though heaven may fall?"

Does being a good storyteller make you a good leader?

Not necessarily, but if you understand the principles of storytelling, you probably have a good understanding of yourself and of human nature, and that tilts the odds in your favor. I can teach the formal principles of stories, but not to a person who hasn't really lived. The art of storytelling takes intelligence, but it also demands a life experience that I've noted in gifted film directors: the pain of childhood. Childhood trauma forces you into a kind of mild schizophrenia that makes you see life simultaneously in two ways: First, it's direct, real-time experience, but at the same moment, your brain records it as material—material out of which you will create business ideas, science, or art. Like a double-edged knife, the creative mind cuts to the truth of self and the humanity of others.

Self-knowledge is the root of all great storytelling. A storyteller creates all characters from the self by asking the question, "If I were this character in these circumstances, what would I do?" The more you understand your own humanity, the more you can appreciate the humanity of others in all their good-versus-evil struggles. I would argue that the great leaders Jim Collins describes are people with enormous self-knowledge. They have self-insight and self-respect balanced by skepticism. Great storytellers—and, I suspect, great leaders—are skeptics who understand their own masks as well as the masks of life, and this understanding makes them humble. They see the humanity in others and deal with them in a compassionate yet realistic way. That duality makes for a wonderful leader.

ROBERT MCKEE is a celebrated screenwriting instructor formerly at the University of Southern California's School of Cinema and Television. His firm, Two Arts, brings his seminars on the art of storytelling worldwide to a broad audience of screenwriters, novelists, playwrights, poets, documentary makers, producers, and directors. BRONWYN FRYER is a collaborative writer and former senior editor with the *Harvard Business Review*.

Reprinted from *Harvard Business Review*,
June 2003 (product #R0306B).

7

The Surprising Persuasiveness of a Sticky Note

By Kevin Hogan

magine that you really need to convince someone to do something, such as follow through on a task. You might be surprised to learn that one of the best ways to get someone to comply with your request is through a tiny nuance that adds a personal touch: attaching a sticky note.

A brilliant set of experiments by Randy Garner at Sam Houston State University in Huntsville, Texas, found that a) adding a personal touch, and b) making someone feel like you're asking a favor of them (and not just anyone) can bring about impressive results when done in tandem.[1]

The goal of Garner's experiments was to see what was necessary to generate compliance in completing surveys—which are often quite lengthy and tedious—by fellow professors at the university, using only interoffice mail as the conduit of communication. The wild card factor in these experiments was the use of sticky notes. In one experiment, he sent surveys to three separate groups of 50 professors (150 professors total). Three groups received three different requests, as follows:

> *Group 1* received a survey with a sticky note attached asking for the return of the completed survey.

> *Group 2* received a survey with the same handwritten message on the cover letter instead of an attached sticky note.

> *Group 3* received a survey with a cover letter but no handwritten message.

What happened?

> *Group 3*: 36% of the professors returned the survey.

> *Group 2*: 48% of the professors returned the survey.

> *Group 1*: 76% of the professors returned the survey.

Generalizing this experiment in other contexts simply requires understanding *why* the sticky note worked so well. It represents many powerful behavioral triggers all in one little object:

1. It doesn't match the environment: The sticky note takes up space and looks a bit cluttered. The brain, therefore, wants it gone.

2. It gets attention first because of #1. It's difficult to ignore.

3. It's personalized. (That's the difference between Group 2 and Group 3 in the experiment.)

4. Ultimately, the sticky note represents *one person* communicating with *another important person*—almost as if it is a favor or special request, which makes the recipient feel important.

Garner couldn't help but explore the sticky note factor further. He decided to do a second experiment where he sent a group of professors a *blank* sticky note attached to one of the surveys. Here's what happened:

> *Group 1* received a survey with a personalized sticky note message.

> *Group 2* received a survey with a blank sticky note attached.

Group 3 received a survey with no sticky note.

What happened in the second study?

Group 3: 34% returned the survey with no sticky note (similar to the first experiment).

Group 2: 43% returned the survey with the blank sticky note

Group 1: 69% returned the survey with the personalized sticky note (similar to the first experiment).

The real magic, it seems, is not the sticky note itself but the sense of connection, meaning, and identity that the sticky note represents. The person sending the survey is *personally* asking *me* in a special way (not just writing it on the survey) to help him or her out.

But there's more to compliance than just the result. There's also the speed of compliance and the quality of the effort. Garner experimented to see how quickly people would return a follow-up survey if there was a sticky note attached and also measured how much information the person being surveyed returned if there was a sticky note attached versus the group that received no sticky note. Here's what he found:

> *Group 1* (with sticky note) returned their self-addressed stamped envelopes (SASEs) and surveys within an average of about 4 days.

> *Group 2* (no sticky note) returned their SASEs and surveys in an average of about 5 1/2 days.

But the most notable difference is that Group 1 also sent significantly more comments and answered other open-ended questions with more words than Group 2 did.

Further experiments revealed that if a task is easy to perform or comply with, a simple sticky note request needs no further personalization. But when the task is more involved, a more highly personalized sticky note was significantly more effective than a simple standard sticky note request. What makes it truly personal? Writing a brief message is effective, but adding the person's first name at the top and your initials at the bottom causes significantly greater compliance.

I've used this personalization theory with businesspeople around the world to great success. For example, a mortgage broker I worked with tested this approach in mailings, effectively doubling the number of phone calls from people pursuing a loan with the broker. And it's not just effective at the office or with clients. The people you live with are going to respond to the sticky note model as well. (Try sticking one on the bathroom mirror and see what happens.)

Recently, the personalized sticky note has been put into digital form for use in email, with mixed results. It's most effective in email when the two people have met or know each other. It had only a modest effect in sales letters designed to make an immediate sale, when the reader didn't know the author of the sales letter. Using the notes in sales letters designed for current clients and customers needs further testing.

The next time you need colleagues to comply with a request, or the next time you're giving a potential client a portfolio to review, try leaving a sticky note. A small personal touch will go a long way toward getting the results you want.

KEVIN HOGAN is the author of 21 books, including *The Science of Influence: How to Get Anyone to Say Yes* (Wiley, 2010) and *The Psychology of Persuasion: How to Persuade Others to Your Way of Thinking* (Pelican Publishing, 1996).

Note

1. R. Garner, "Post-it Note Persuasion: A Sticky Influence," and "What's In a Name? Persuasion Perhaps," *Journal of Consumer Psychology*, 2005.

Reprinted from hbr.org, originally published May 26, 2015 (product #H023LE).

8

When to Sell with Facts and Figures, and When to Appeal to Emotions

By Michael D. Harris

When should salespeople sell with facts and figures, and when should they try to speak to the buyer's emotional subconscious instead? When do you talk to Mr. Intuitive and when to Mr. Rational?

I'd argue that too often, selling to Mr. Rational leads to analysis paralysis, especially for complex products or services. And yet many of us continue to market almost exclusively to Mr. Rational. The result is that we spend too much time chasing sales opportunities that eventually stall out. We need to improve our ability to sell to Mr. Intuitive.

We default to selling to Mr. Rational because when we think of ourselves, we identify with our conscious rational mind. We can't imagine that serious executives would make decisions based on emotion, because we view our emotional decisions as irrational and irresponsible.

But what if Mr. Intuitive has a logic of his own? In recent years, psychologists and behavioral economists have shown that our emotional decisions are neither irrational nor irresponsible. In fact, we now understand that our unconscious decisions do in fact follow a clear logic. They are based on a deeply empirical mental-processing system that is capable of effortlessly cycling through millions of bits of data without getting overwhelmed. Our conscious mind, on the other hand, has a strict bottleneck, because it can only process three or four new pieces of information at a time due to the limitations of our working memory.[1]

The Iowa Gambling Task study, for example, highlights how effective the emotional brain is at effortlessly figuring out the probability of success for maximum gain.[2] Subjects were given an imaginary budget and four stacks of cards. The objective of the game was to win as much money as possible, and to do so, subjects were instructed to draw cards from any of the four decks.

The subjects were not aware that the decks were carefully prepared. Drawing from two of the decks led to consistent wins, while the other two had high payouts but carried oversized punishments. The logical choice was to avoid the dangerous decks, and after about 50 cards, people did stop drawing from the risky decks. It wasn't until the 80th card, however, that people could explain why. Logic is slow.

But the researchers tracked the subjects' anxiety and found that people started to become nervous when reaching for the risky deck after drawing only 10 cards. Intuition is fast.

Harvard Business School professor Gerald Zaltman says that 95% of our purchase decisions take place unconsciously. But why, then, are we not able to look back through our decision history and find countless examples of emotional decisions? Because our conscious mind will always make up reasons to justify our unconscious decisions.

In a study of people who'd had the left and right hemisphere of their brains severed in order to prevent future epileptic seizures, scientists were able to deliver a message to the right side of the brain to "Go to the water fountain down the hall and get a drink."[3] After seeing the message, the subject would get up and start to leave the room, and that's when the scientist would deliver a message to the opposite, left side of the brain, asking, "Where are you going?" Now remember, the left side of the brain never saw the message about the fountain. But did the left brain admit it didn't know the answer? No. Instead it shamelessly fabricated a rational reason, something like, "It's cold in here. I'm going to get my jacket."

So if you can't reliably use your own decision-making history as a guide, when do you know you should be selling based on logic and when on emotion?

Here's the short rule of thumb: Sell to Mr. Rational for simple sales and to Mr. Intuitive for complex sales.

This conclusion is backed by a 2011 study based on subjects selecting the best used car from a selection of four cars. Each car was rated in four different categories (such as gas mileage). But one car clearly had the best attributes. In this "easy" situation with only four variables, the conscious deciders were 15% better at choosing the best car than the unconscious deciders. When the researchers made the decision more complex—ratcheting the number of variables up to 12—unconscious deciders were 42% better than conscious deciders at selecting the best car. Many other studies have shown how our conscious minds become overloaded by too much information.

If you want to influence how a customer feels about your product, provide an experience that creates the desired emotion. One of the best ways for a customer to experience your complex product is by sharing a vivid customer story. Research has shown that stories can activate the region of the brain that processes sights, sounds, tastes, and movement.[4] Contrast this approach with that of a salesperson delivering a data dump in the form of an 85-slide PowerPoint presentation.

Rather than thinking of the emotional mind as irrational, think of it this way: An emotion is simply the way the unconscious communicates its decision to the conscious mind.

MICHAEL D. HARRIS is the CEO of Insight Demand and the author of *Insight Selling: Surprising Research on What Sales Winners Do Differently* (Wiley, 2014).

Notes

1. N. Cowan, "The Magical Number 4 in Short-Term Memory: A Reconsideration of Mental Storage Capacity," *Behavioral Brain Science* 24, no. 1 (February 2001): 87–114.
2. A. Bechara et al., "Insensitivity to Future Consequences Following Damage to Human Prefrontal Cortex," *Cognition* 50, no. 1–3 (April–June 1995): 7–15.

3. M. S. Gazzaniga, "The Split Brain Revisited," *Scientific American*, July 1, 1998.
4. G. Everding, "Readers Build Vivid Mental Simulations of Narrative Situations, Brain Scans Suggest," Medical Xpress, January 26, 2009, https://medicalxpress .com/news/2009-01-readers-vivid-mental-simulations -narrative.html.

Reprinted from hbr.org, originally published
January 26, 2015 (product #H01U9Y).

Index

How to be human at work.

HBR's Emotional Intelligence Series features smart, essential reading on the human side of professional life from the pages of *Harvard Business Review*. Each book in the series offers uplifting stories, practical advice, and research from leading experts on how to tend to our emotional well-being at work.

Harvard Business Review Emotional Intelligence Series

Available in paperback or ebook format. The specially priced six-volume set includes:

- Mindfulness
- Resilience
- Influence and Persuasion
- Authentic Leadership
- Happiness
- Empathy

HBR.ORG

Buy for your team, clients, or event.
Visit hbr.org/bulksales for quantity discount rates.

The most important management ideas all in one place.

We hope you enjoyed this book from *Harvard Business Review*. For the best ideas HBR has to offer turn to HBR's 10 Must Reads Boxed Set. From books on leadership and strategy to managing yourself and others, this 6-book collection delivers articles on the most essential business topics to help you succeed.

HBR's 10 Must Reads Series

The definitive collection of ideas and best practices on our most sought-after topics from the best minds in business.

- Change Management
- Collaboration
- Communication
- Emotional Intelligence
- Innovation
- Leadership
- Making Smart Decisions

- Managing Across Cultures
- Managing People
- Managing Yourself
- Strategic Marketing
- Strategy
- Teams
- The Essentials

hbr.org/mustreads

Resilience

HBR EMOTIONAL INTELLIGENCE SERIES

HBR Emotional Intelligence Series

How to be human at work

The HBR Emotional Intelligence Series features smart, essential reading on the human side of professional life from the pages of *Harvard Business Review*.

Empathy

Happiness

Mindfulness

Resilience

Other books on emotional intelligence from *Harvard Business Review*:

HBR's 10 Must Reads on Emotional Intelligence

HBR Guide to Emotional Intelligence

Resilience

HBR EMOTIONAL INTELLIGENCE SERIES

Harvard Business Review Press

Boston, Massachusetts

Library of Congress Cataloging-in-Publication Data

Title: Resilience.
Other titles: HBR emotional intelligence series.
Description: Boston, Massachusetts : Harvard Business Review Press, [2017] | Series: HBR emotional intelligence series
Identifiers: LCCN 2016056296 | ISBN 9781633693234 (pbk. : alk. paper)
Subjects: LCSH: Resilience (Personality trait) | Management.
Classification: LCC BF698.35.R47 R462 2017 | DDC 155.2/4—dc23 LC record available at https://lccn.loc.gov/2016056296

ISBN: 978-1-63369-234-4
eISBN: 978-1-63369-324-1

The paper used in this publication meets the requirements of the American National Standard for Permanence of Paper for Publications and Documents in Libraries and Archives Z39.48-1992.

Contents

Contents

Resilience

HBR EMOTIONAL INTELLIGENCE SERIES

1

How Resilience Works

By Diane Coutu

When I began my career in journalism—I was a reporter at a national magazine in those days—there was a man I'll call Claus Schmidt. He was in his mid-fifties, and to my impressionable eyes, he was the quintessential newsman: cynical at times, but unrelentingly curious and full of life, and often hilariously funny in a sandpaper-dry kind of way. He churned out hard-hitting cover stories and features with a speed and elegance I could only dream of. It always astounded me that he was never promoted to managing editor.

But people who knew Claus better than I did thought of him not just as a great newsman but as a quintessential survivor, someone who had endured in an environment often hostile to talent. He had lived through at least three major changes in the magazine's leadership, losing most of his best friends and colleagues on the way. At home, two of his children succumbed to incurable illnesses, and a third was killed in a traffic accident. Despite all this—or maybe because of it—he milled around the newsroom day after day, mentoring the cub reporters, talking about the novels he was writing—always looking forward to what the future held for him.

Why do some people suffer real hardships and not falter? Claus Schmidt could have reacted very differently. We've all seen that happen: One person cannot seem to get the confidence back after a layoff; another, persistently depressed, takes a few years off from life after her divorce. The question we would all like answered is, Why? What exactly is that quality of resilience that carries people through life?

It's a question that has fascinated me ever since I first learned of the Holocaust survivors in elementary school. In college, and later in my studies as an affiliate scholar at the Boston Psychoanalytic Society and Institute, I returned to the subject. For the past several months, however, I have looked on it with a new urgency, for it seems to me that the terrorism, war, and recession of recent months have made understanding resilience more important than ever. I have considered both the nature of individual resilience and what makes some organizations as a whole more resilient than others. Why do some people and some companies buckle under pressure? And what makes others bend and ultimately bounce back?

My exploration has taught me much about resilience, although it's a subject none of us will ever understand fully. Indeed, resilience is one of the great puzzles of human nature, like creativity or the religious instinct. But in sifting through psychological research and in reflecting on the many stories of resilience I've heard, I have seen a little more deeply into the hearts and minds of people like

Claus Schmidt and, in doing so, looked more deeply into the human psyche as well.

The buzz about resilience

Resilience is a hot topic in business these days. Not long ago, I was talking to a senior partner at a respected consulting firm about how to land the very best MBAs—the name of the game in that particular industry. The partner, Daniel Savageau (not his real name), ticked off a long list of qualities his firm sought in its hires: intelligence, ambition, integrity, analytic ability, and so on. "What about resilience?" I asked. "Well, that's very popular right now," he said. "It's the new buzzword. Candidates even tell us they're resilient; they volunteer the information. But frankly, they're just too young to know that about themselves. Resilience is something you realize you have *after* the fact."

"But if you could, would you test for it?" I asked. "Does it matter in business?"

Savageau paused. He's a man in his late forties and a success personally and professionally. Yet it hadn't been a smooth ride to the top. He'd started his life as a poor French Canadian in Woonsocket, Rhode Island, and had lost his father at six. He lucked into a football scholarship but was kicked out of Boston University twice for drinking. He turned his life around in his twenties, married, divorced, remarried, and raised five children. Along the way, he made and lost two fortunes before helping to found the consulting firm he now runs. "Yes, it does matter," he said at last. "In fact, it probably matters more than any of the usual things we look for." In the course of reporting this article, I heard the same assertion time and again. As Dean Becker, the president and CEO of Adaptiv Learning Systems, a four-year-old company in King of Prussia, Pennsylvania, that develops and delivers programs about resilience training, puts it: "More than education, more than experience, more than training, a person's level of resilience will determine who succeeds and who fails. That's true in the cancer ward, it's true in the Olympics, and it's true in the boardroom."

Academic research into resilience started about 40 years ago with pioneering studies by Norman Garmezy, now a professor emeritus at the University of Minnesota in Minneapolis. After studying why many children of schizophrenic parents did not suffer psychological illness as a result of growing up with them, he concluded that a certain quality of resilience played a greater role in mental health than anyone had previously suspected.

Today, theories abound about what makes resilience. Looking at Holocaust victims, Maurice Vanderpol, a former president of the Boston Psychoanalytic Society and Institute, found that many of the healthy survivors of concentration camps had what he calls a "plastic shield." The shield was comprised of several factors, including a sense of humor. Often the humor was black, but nonetheless it provided a critical sense of perspective. Other core characteristics that helped included the ability to form attachments to others and the possession of an inner psychological space that protected the survivors from the intrusions of abusive others. Research about other groups uncovered different qualities associated with resilience. The Search Institute, a Minneapolis-based nonprofit organization that focuses on resilience and youth, found that the more resilient kids have an uncanny ability to get adults to help them out. Still other research showed that resilient inner-city youth often have talents such as athletic abilities that attract others to them.

Many of the early theories about resilience stressed the role of genetics. Some people are just born resilient, so the arguments went. There's some truth to that, of course, but an increasing body of empirical evidence shows that resilience—whether in children, survivors of concentration camps, or businesses back from the brink—can be learned. For example, George Vaillant, the director of the Study of Adult Development at Harvard Medical School in Boston, observes that within various groups studied during a 60-year period, some people became markedly more resilient over their lifetimes. Other psychologists claim that unresilient people more easily develop resiliency skills than those with head starts.

Most of the resilience theories I encountered in my research make good common sense. But I also observed that almost all the theories overlap in three ways. Resilient people, they posit, possess three characteristics: a staunch acceptance of reality; a deep belief, often buttressed by strongly held values, that life is meaningful; and an uncanny ability to improvise. You can bounce back from hardship with just one or two of these qualities, but you will only be truly resilient with all three. These three characteristics hold true for resilient organizations as well. Let's take a look at each of them in turn.

Facing down reality

A common belief about resilience is that it stems from an optimistic nature. That's true but only as long as such optimism doesn't distort your sense of reality. In extremely adverse situations, rose-colored thinking can actually spell disaster. This point was made poignantly to me by management researcher and writer Jim Collins, who happened upon this concept while researching *Good to Great*, his book on how companies transform themselves out of mediocrity. Collins had a hunch (an exactly wrong hunch) that resilient companies were filled with optimistic people. He tried out that idea on Admiral Jim Stockdale, who was held prisoner and tortured by the Vietcong for eight years.

Collins recalls: "I asked Stockdale: 'Who didn't make it out of the camps?' And he said, 'Oh, that's easy. It was the optimists. They were the ones who said we were going to be out by Christmas. And then they said we'd be out by Easter and then out by Fourth of July and out by Thanksgiving, and then it was Christmas again.' Then Stockdale turned to me and said, 'You know, I think they all died of broken hearts.'"

In the business world, Collins found the same unblinking attitude shared by executives at all the most successful companies he studied. Like Stockdale, resilient people have very sober and down-to-earth views of those parts of reality that matter for survival. That's not to say that optimism doesn't have its place: In turning around a demoralized sales force, for instance, conjuring a sense of possibility can be a very powerful tool. But for bigger challenges, a cool, almost pessimistic, sense of reality is far more important.

Perhaps you're asking yourself, "Do I truly understand—and accept—the reality of my situation? Does my organization?" Those are good questions, particularly because research suggests most people slip into denial as a coping mechanism. Facing reality, really facing it, is grueling work. Indeed, it can be unpleasant and often emotionally wrenching. Consider the following story of organizational resilience, and see what it means to confront reality.

Prior to September 11, 2001, Morgan Stanley, the famous investment bank, was the largest tenant in the World Trade Center. The company had some 2,700 employees working in the south tower on 22 floors between the 43rd and the 74th. On that horrible day, the first plane hit the north tower at 8:46 a.m. and Morgan Stanley started evacuating just one minute later, at 8:47 a.m. When the second plane crashed into the south tower 15 minutes after that, Morgan Stanley's offices were largely empty. All told, the company lost only seven employees despite receiving an almost direct hit.

Of course, the organization was just plain lucky to be in the second tower. Cantor Fitzgerald, whose offices were hit in the first attack, couldn't have done anything to save its employees. Still, it was Morgan Stanley's hard-nosed realism that enabled the company to benefit from its luck. Soon after the 1993 attack on the World Trade Center, senior management recognized that working in such a symbolic center of U.S. commercial power made the company vulnerable to attention from terrorists and possible attack.

With this grim realization, Morgan Stanley launched a program of preparedness at the micro level. Few companies take their fire drills seriously. Not so Morgan Stanley, whose VP of security for the Individual Investor Group, Rick Rescorla, brought a military discipline to the job. Rescorla, himself a highly resilient, decorated Vietnam vet, made sure that people were fully drilled about what to do in a catastrophe. When disaster struck on September 11, Rescorla was on a bullhorn telling Morgan Stanley employees to stay calm and follow their well-practiced drill, even though some building supervisors were telling occupants that all was well. Sadly, Rescorla himself, whose life story has been widely covered in recent months, was one of the seven who didn't make it out.

"When you're in financial services where so much depends on technology, contingency planning is a major part of your business," says President and COO Robert G. Scott. But Morgan Stanley was prepared for the very toughest reality. It had not just one but three recovery sites where employees could congregate and business could take place if work locales were ever disrupted. "Multiple backup sites seemed like an incredible extravagance on September 10," concedes Scott. "But on September 12, they seemed like genius."

Maybe it was genius; it was undoubtedly resilience at work. The fact is, when we truly stare down reality, we prepare ourselves to act in ways that allow us to endure and survive extraordinary hardship. We train ourselves how to survive before the fact.

The search for meaning

The ability to see reality is closely linked to the second building block of resilience, the propensity to make meaning of terrible times. We all know people who, under duress, throw up their hands and cry, "How can this be happening to me?" Such people see themselves as victims, and living through hardship carries no lessons for them. But resilient people devise constructs about their suffering to create some sort of meaning for themselves and others.

I have a friend I'll call Jackie Oiseaux who suffered repeated psychoses over a 10-year period due to an undiagnosed bipolar disorder. Today, she holds down a big job in one of the top publishing companies in the country, has a family, and is a prominent member of her church community. When people ask her how she bounced back from her crises, she runs her hands through her hair. "People sometimes say, 'Why me?' But I've always said, 'Why *not* me?' True, I lost many things during my illness," she says, "but I found many more—incredible friends who saw me through the bleakest times and who will give meaning to my life forever."

This dynamic of meaning making is, most researchers agree, the way resilient people build bridges from present-day hardships to a fuller, better-constructed future. Those bridges make the present manageable, for lack of a better word, removing the sense that the present is overwhelming. This concept was beautifully articulated by Viktor E. Frankl, an Austrian psychiatrist and an Auschwitz survivor. In the midst of staggering suffering, Frankl invented "meaning therapy," a humanistic therapy technique that helps individuals make the kinds of decisions that will create significance in their lives.

In his book *Man's Search for Meaning*, Frankl described the pivotal moment in the camp when he developed meaning therapy. He was on his way to work one day, worrying whether he should trade his last cigarette for a bowl of soup. He wondered how he was going to work with a new foreman whom he knew to be particularly sadistic. Suddenly, he was disgusted by just how trivial and meaningless his life had become. He realized that to survive, he had to find some purpose. Frankl did so by imagining himself giving a lecture after the war on the psychology of the concentration camp, to help outsiders understand what he had been through. Although he wasn't even sure he would survive, Frankl created some concrete goals for himself. In doing so, he succeeded in rising above the sufferings of the moment. As he put it in his book: "We must never forget that we may also find meaning in life even when confronted with a hopeless situation, when facing a fate that cannot be changed."

Frankl's theory underlies most resilience coaching in business. Indeed, I was struck by how often businesspeople referred to his work. "Resilience training—what we call hardiness—is a way for us to help people construct meaning in their everyday lives," explains Salvatore R. Maddi, a University of California, Irvine psychology professor and the director of the Hardiness Institute in Newport Beach, California. "When people realize the power of resilience training, they often say, 'Doc, is this what psychotherapy is?' But psychotherapy is for people whose lives have fallen apart badly and need repair. We see our work as showing people life skills and attitudes. Maybe those things should be taught at home, maybe they should be taught in schools, but they're not. So we end up doing it in business."

Yet the challenge confronting resilience trainers is often more difficult than we might imagine. Meaning can be elusive, and just because you found it once doesn't mean you'll keep it or find it again. Consider Aleksandr Solzhenitsyn, who survived the war against the Nazis, imprisonment in the gulag, and cancer. Yet when he moved to a farm in peaceful, safe Vermont, he could not cope with the "infantile West." He was unable to discern any real meaning in what he felt to be the destructive and irresponsible freedom of the West. Upset by his critics, he withdrew into his farmhouse, behind a locked fence, seldom to be seen in public. In 1994, a bitter man, Solzhenitsyn moved back to Russia.

Since finding meaning in one's environment is such an important aspect of resilience, it should come as no surprise that the most successful organizations and people possess strong value systems. Strong values infuse an environment with meaning because they offer ways to interpret and shape events. While it's popular these days to ridicule values, it's surely no coincidence that the most resilient organization in the world has been the Catholic Church, which has survived wars, corruption, and schism for more than 2,000 years, thanks largely to its immutable set of values. Businesses that survive also have their creeds, which give them purposes beyond just making money. Strikingly, many companies describe their value systems in religious terms. Pharmaceutical giant Johnson & Johnson, for instance, calls its value system, set out in a document given to every new employee at orientation, the Credo. Parcel company UPS talks constantly about its Noble Purpose.

Value systems at resilient companies change very little over the years and are used as scaffolding in times of trouble. UPS Chairman and CEO Mike Eskew believes that the Noble Purpose helped the company to rally after the agonizing strike in 1997. Says Eskew: "It was a hugely difficult time, like a family feud. Everyone had close friends on both sides of the fence, and it was tough for us to pick sides. But what saved us was our Noble Purpose. Whatever side people were on, they all shared a common set of values. Those values are core to us and never change; they frame most of our important decisions. Our strategy and our mission may change, but our values never do."

The religious connotations of words like "credo," "values," and "noble purpose," however, should not be confused with the actual content of the values. Companies can hold ethically questionable values and still be very resilient. Consider Phillip Morris, which has demonstrated impressive resilience in the face of increasing unpopularity. As Jim Collins points out, Phillip Morris has very strong values, although we might not agree with them—for instance, the value of "adult choice." But there's no doubt that Phillip Morris executives believe strongly in its values, and the strength of their beliefs sets the company apart from most of the other tobacco companies. In this context, it is worth noting that resilience is neither ethically good nor bad. It is merely the skill and the capacity to be robust under conditions of enormous stress and change. As Viktor Frankl wrote: "On the average, only those prisoners could keep alive who, after years of trekking from camp to camp, had lost all scruples in their fight for existence; they were prepared to use every means, honest and otherwise, even brutal . . . in order to save themselves. We who have come back . . . we know: The best of us did not return."

Values, positive or negative, are actually more important for organizational resilience than having resilient people on the payroll. If resilient employees are all interpreting reality in different ways, their decisions and actions may well conflict, calling into doubt the survival of their organization. And as the weakness of an organization becomes apparent, highly resilient individuals are more likely to jettison the organization than to imperil their own survival.

Ritualized ingenuity

The third building block of resilience is the ability to make do with whatever is at hand. Psychologists follow the lead of French anthropologist Claude Levi-Strauss in calling this skill bricolage.[1] Intriguingly, the roots of that word are closely tied to the concept of resilience, which literally means "bouncing back." Says Levi-Strauss: "In its old sense, the verb *bricoler* . . . was always used with reference to some extraneous movement: a ball rebounding, a dog straying, or a horse swerving from its direct course to avoid an obstacle."

Bricolage in the modern sense can be defined as a kind of inventiveness, an ability to improvise a solution to a problem without proper or obvious tools or materials. Bricoleurs are always tinkering—building radios from household effects or fixing their own cars. They make the most of what they have, putting objects to unfamiliar uses. In the concentration camps, for example, resilient inmates knew to pocket pieces of string or wire whenever they found them. The string or wire might later become useful—to fix a pair of shoes, perhaps, which in freezing conditions might make the difference between life and death.

When situations unravel, bricoleurs muddle through, imagining possibilities where others are confounded. I have two friends, whom I'll call Paul Shields and Mike Andrews, who were roommates throughout their college years. To no one's surprise, when they graduated, they set up a business together selling educational materials to schools, businesses, and consulting firms. At first, the company was a great success, making both founders paper millionaires. But the recession of the early 1990s hit the company hard, and many core clients fell away. At the same time, Paul experienced a bitter divorce and a depression that made it impossible for him to work. Mike offered to buy Paul out but was instead slapped with a lawsuit claiming that Mike was trying to steal the business. At this point, a less resilient person might have just walked away from the mess. Not Mike. As the case wound through the courts, he kept the company going any way he could—constantly morphing the business until he found a model that worked: going into joint ventures to sell English-language training materials to Russian and Chinese companies. Later, he branched off into publishing newsletters for clients. At one point, he was even writing video scripts for his competitors. Thanks to all this bricolage, by the time the lawsuit was settled in his favor, Mike had an entirely different, and much more solid, business than the one he had started with.

Bricolage can be practiced on a higher level as well. Richard Feynman, winner of the 1965 Nobel Prize in physics, exemplified what I like to think of as intellectual bricolage. Out of pure curiosity, Feynman made himself an expert on cracking safes, not only looking at the mechanics of safecracking but also cobbling together psychological insights about people who used safes and set the locks. He cracked many of the safes at Los Alamos, for instance, because he guessed that theoretical physicists would not set the locks with random code numbers they might forget but would instead use a sequence with mathematical significance. It turned out that the three safes containing all the secrets to the atomic bomb were set to the same mathematical constant, e, whose first six digits are 2.71828.

Resilient organizations are stuffed with bricoleurs, though not all of them, of course, are Richard Feynmans. Indeed, companies that survive regard improvisation as a core skill. Consider UPS, which empowers its drivers to do whatever it takes to deliver packages on time. Says CEO Eskew: "We tell our employees to get the job done. If that means they need to improvise, they improvise. Otherwise we just couldn't do what we do every day. Just think what can go wrong: a busted traffic light, a flat tire, a bridge washed out. If a snowstorm hits Louisville tonight, a group of people will sit together and discuss how to handle the problem. Nobody tells them to do that. They come together because it's our tradition to do so."

That tradition meant that the company was delivering parcels in southeast Florida just one day after Hurricane Andrew devastated the region in 1992, causing billions of dollars in damage. Many people were living in their cars because their homes had been destroyed, yet UPS drivers and managers sorted packages at a diversion site and made deliveries even to those who were stranded in their cars. It was largely UPS's improvisational skills that enabled it to keep functioning after the catastrophic hit. And the fact that the company continued on gave others a sense of purpose or meaning amid the chaos.

Improvisation of the sort practiced by UPS, however, is a far cry from unbridled creativity. Indeed, much like the military, UPS lives on rules and regulations. As Eskew says: "Drivers always put their keys in the same place. They close the doors the same way. They wear their uniforms the same way. We are a company of precision." He believes that although they may seem stifling, UPS's rules were what allowed the company to bounce back immediately after Hurricane Andrew, for they enabled people to focus on the one or two fixes they needed to make in order to keep going.

Eskew's opinion is echoed by Karl E. Weick, a professor of organizational behavior at the University of Michigan Business School in Ann Arbor and one of the most respected thinkers on organizational psychology. "There is good evidence that when people are put under pressure, they regress to their most habituated ways of responding," Weick has written. "What we do not expect under life-threatening pressure is creativity." In other words, the rules and regulations that make some companies appear less creative may actually make them more resilient in times of real turbulence.

Claus Schmidt, the newsman I mentioned earlier, died about five years ago, but I'm not sure I could have interviewed him about his own resilience even if he were alive. It would have felt strange, I think, to ask him, "Claus, did you really face down reality? Did you make meaning out of your hardships? Did you improvise your recovery after each professional and personal disaster?" He may not have been able to answer. In my experience, resilient people don't often describe themselves that way. They shrug off their survival stories and very often assign them to luck.

Obviously, luck does have a lot to do with surviving. It was luck that Morgan Stanley was situated in the south tower and could put its preparedness training to work. But being lucky is not the same as being resilient. Resilience is a reflex—a way of facing and understanding the world—that is deeply etched into a person's mind and soul. Resilient people and companies face reality with staunchness, make meaning of hardship instead of crying out in despair, and improvise solutions from thin air. Others do not. This is the nature of resilience, and we will never completely understand it.

DIANE L. COUTU is a former senior editor at HBR specializing in psychology and business.

Note

1. See, e.g., Karl E. Weick, "The Collapse of Sense-making in Organizations: The Mann Gulch Disaster," *Administrative Science Quarterly*, December 1993.

Reprinted from *Harvard Business Review*,
May 2002 (product #R0205B).

2

Resilience for the Rest of Us

By Daniel Goleman

There are two ways to become more resilient: one by talking to yourself, the other by retraining your brain.

If you've suffered a major failure, take the sage advice given by psychologist Martin Seligman in the HBR article "Building Resilience" (April 2011). Talk to yourself. Give yourself a cognitive intervention, and counter defeatist thinking with an optimistic attitude. Challenge your downbeat thinking, and replace it with a positive outlook.

Fortunately, major failures come along rarely in life.

But what about bouncing back from the more frequent annoying screwups, minor setbacks, and irritating upsets that are routine in any leader's life? Resilience is, again, the answer—but with a different flavor. You need to retrain your brain.

The brain has a very different mechanism for bouncing back from the cumulative toll of daily hassles. And with a little effort, you can upgrade its ability to snap back from life's downers.

Whenever we get so upset that we say or do something we later regret (and who doesn't now and then?), that's a sure sign that our amygdala—the brain's radar for danger and the trigger for the fight-or-flight response—has hijacked the brain's executive centers in the prefrontal cortex. The neural key to resilience lies in how quickly we recover from that hijacked state.

The circuitry that brings us back to full energy and focus after an amygdala hijack concentrates in the left side of our prefrontal area, says Richard Davidson, a neuroscientist at the University of Wisconsin. He's also found that when we're distressed, there's heightened activity on the right side of the prefrontal area. Each of us has a characteristic level of left/right activity that predicts our daily mood range—if we're tilted to the right, more upsets; if to the left, we're quicker to recover from distress of all kinds.

To tackle this in the workplace, Davidson teamed with the CEO of a high-pressure, 24/7, biotech startup and meditation expert Jon Kabat-Zinn of the University of Massachusetts Medical School. Kabat-Zinn offered the employees at the biotech outfit instruction in mindfulness, an attention-training method that teaches the brain to register anything happening in the present moment with full focus—but without reacting.

The instructions are simple:

1. Find a quiet, private place where you can be undistracted for a few minutes. For instance, close your office door and mute your phone.

2. Sit comfortably, with your back straight but relaxed.

3. Focus your awareness on your breath, staying attentive to the sensations of the inhalation and exhalation, and start again on the next breath.

4. Do not judge your breathing or try to change it in any way.

5. See anything else that comes to mind as a distraction—thoughts, sounds, whatever. Let them go and return your attention to your breath.

After eight weeks and an average of 30 minutes a day practicing mindfulness, the employees had shifted their ratio from tilted toward the stressed-out right side to leaning toward the resilient left side. What's more, they said they remembered what they loved about their work: They got in touch with what had brought them energy in the first place.

To get the full benefit of mindfulness, a daily practice of 20 to 30 minutes works best. Think of it like a mental exercise routine. It can be very helpful to have guided instructions, but the key is to find a slot for the practice in your daily routine. (There are even instructions for using a long drive as your practice session.)

Mindfulness has steadily been gaining credence among hard-nosed executives. There are centers where mindfulness instruction has been tailored to businesspeople, from tony resorts like Miraval Resort in Arizona to programs in mindful leadership at the University of Massachusetts Medical School. Google University has been offering a course in mindfulness to employees for years.

Might you benefit from tuning up your brain's resilience circuitry by learning to practice mindfulness? Among high-performing executives, the effects of stress can be subtle. My colleagues Richard Boyatzis and Annie McKee suggest as a rough diagnostic of leadership stress asking yourself, "Do I have a vague sense of unease, restlessness, or the feeling that life is not great (a higher standard than 'good enough')?" A bit of mindfulness might put your mind at ease.

DANIEL GOLEMAN is a codirector of the Consortium for Research on Emotional Intelligence in Organizations at Rutgers University, coauthor of *Primal Leadership: Leading with Emotional Intelligence* (Harvard Business Review Press, 2013), and author of *The Brain and Emotional Intelligence: New Insights.*

Adapted from content posted on hbr.org
on March 4, 2016.

3

How to Evaluate, Manage, and Strengthen Your Resilience

By David Kopans

Think back to your last off-site meeting. You and the rest of your team likely poured over reports and spreadsheets, facts and figures. Strewn about the table were probably the tools of your trade: reams of data, balance sheets, and P&Ls. Managers understand that clear-eyed analysis—both quantitative and qualitative—is the key to building a resilient business. And yet when it comes to measuring and strengthening our own ability to adapt, grow, and prosper, rarely do we apply the same methodical approach.

But we should. Based on my own experience starting, building, and growing companies, as well as upon decades of research showing the underlying components of personal resilience, I've discovered a few fundamental things you can do to actually evaluate, manage, and strengthen your own resilience in the same way that you would increase the resiliency of your company:

Build up your positivity currency. We can't just print resilience the way countries print money. Individuals must use what I call a "positivity currency" approach that is grounded in actual positive interactions, events, and memories—factors that are known to boost resilience. This currency is only "printed" and stored as assets when we focus on positive things and express gratitude for them. Why? Because maintaining a positive outlook and regularly expressing gratitude are the bullion bars that have real value in backstopping and building resilience.

Research by Robert Emmons of UC Davis, Michael McCullough of the University of Miami, and others clearly shows that they are among the most reliable methods for increasing personal happiness and life satisfaction.[1] Creating such positivity currency can decrease anxiety, reduce symptoms of illness, and improve the quality of your sleep. All of which, of course, lead to greater personal resilience.

Keep records. None of the tools we use to evaluate companies work very well without good record keeping. That's also true when it comes to building individual resilience. When you commit positive interactions, events, and memories to the written word, they register higher value than other non-written forms of positivity currency-based activity, according to research by positive psychology expert Martin Seligman of the University of Pennsylvania.[2] Record your positive currency transactions (by jotting them down in a leather bound journal or a digital equivalent). The data points you record could be as simple as keeping a written tally by category (such as family, friends, or work) in a paper notebook, entering the information into a spreadsheet, or assigning hashtags to items in a digital gratitude journal.

Create a bull market. Financial markets boom when increasing numbers of investors want in. Likewise, our own resilience grows when we encourage positivity buyers to enter the market. It's not a difficult task; positivity is socially contagious. In the research behind their book *Connected: The Surprising Power of Our Social Networks and How They Shape Our Lives*, Harvard's Nicholas Christakis and the University of California, San Diego's James Fowler detail how happiness depends not just on our own choices and actions, but also on those of people who are two or even three degrees removed from us. What this means is by being more positive ourselves, we encourage others to do the same, and this in turn creates a virtuous "reverse run on the bank" positive feedback loop, and our own resilience is increased and strengthened by the actions of others.

Take a portfolio approach. Resilient businesses diversify risk. Accordingly, resilient individuals diversify their positivity currency. They look to increase their overall resilience by evaluating what it is that provides the highest returns across their entire "life portfolio" and then investing more in those areas. Most frequently, these high-return assets come from our lives outside of the office. Indeed, while we may spend the majority of waking hours at work, our job should not be central to our overall positive outlook. In a 2015 report entitled "The Happiness Study" from Blackhawk Engagement Solutions, respondents ranked their jobs eighth out of a list of 12 contributors to overall happiness. Ranking in the top spots were family, friends, health, hobbies, and community.[3] It follows that by generating more positivity currency in those areas, you will increase the ability to bring your best self to work.

Report regularly. Finally, just as regular review of a company's financials is important to building a resilient business, building individual resilience requires regular review of positivity currency data. This review not only enables you to glean insights and take corrective actions, but also to boost your resilience by simply increasing your exposure to positive interactions and expressions of gratitude. As suggested in a famous 2014 experiment conducted by Facebook's data scientists and published in the Proceedings of the National Academy of Sciences of the United States of America, if your news feed skews positive, so will you.[4]

Even if you don't analyze your positivity currency data deeply like a Wall Street quant, just exposing yourself to it on a regular basis will make you more resilient. So find a regular time to celebrate and reflect on your positivity currency (I do it while I wait for my morning coffee). Make it a habit, and your level of resilience—and that of your friends, family, and coworkers—will rise.

DAVID KOPANS is the founder and CEO of PF Loop, a company that aims to make positive change in the world through software applications and digital services grounded in positive psychology research.

Notes

1. R. Emmons, "Why Gratitude Is Good," *Greater Good*, November 16, 2010, http://greatergood.berkeley.edu/article/item/why_gratitude_is_good; and "Why Practice Gratitude," *Greater Good*, October 31, 2016, http://greatergood.berkeley.edu/topic/gratitude/definition#why_practice.
2. M. E. Seligman et al., "Positive Psychology Progress: Empirical Validation of Interventions," *American Psychologist* 60, no. 5 (July–August 2005): 410–421.
3. "The Happiness Study: An Employee Rewards and Recognition Study," Blackhawk Engagement Solutions,

June 2, 2105, www.bhengagement.com/report/
employee-happiness-study/.
4. A. D. I. Kramer et al., "Experimental Evidence of Massive-
Scale Emotional Contagion Through Social Networks,"
*Proceedings of the National Academy of Sciences of the
United States of America* 111, no. 24 (2014): 8788–8790.

Adapted from content posted on hbr.org on
June 14, 2016 (product # H02XDP).

4

Find the Coaching in Criticism

By Sheila Heen and Douglas Stone

F eedback is crucial. That's obvious: It improves performance, develops talent, aligns expectations, solves problems, guides promotion and pay, and boosts the bottom line.

But it's equally obvious that in many organizations, feedback doesn't work. A glance at the stats tells the story: Only 36% of managers complete appraisals thoroughly and on time. In one recent survey, 55% of employees said their most recent performance review had been unfair or inaccurate, and one in four said they dread such evaluations more than anything else in their working lives. When senior HR executives were asked about their biggest performance management challenge, 63% cited managers' inability or unwillingness to have difficult feedback discussions. Coaching and mentoring? Uneven at best.

Most companies try to address these problems by training leaders to give feedback more effectively and more often. That's fine as far as it goes; everyone benefits when managers are better communicators. But improving the skills of the feedback giver won't accomplish much if the receiver isn't able to absorb what is said. It is the receiver who controls whether feedback is let in or kept out, who has to make sense of what he or she is hearing, and who decides whether or not to change. People need to stop treating feedback only as something that must be pushed and instead improve their ability to pull.

For the past 20 years we've coached executives on difficult conversations, and we've found that almost everyone, from new hires to C-suite veterans, struggles with receiving feedback. A critical performance review, a well-intended suggestion, or an oblique comment that may or may not even be feedback

("Well, your presentation was certainly interesting") can spark an emotional reaction, inject tension into the relationship, and bring communication to a halt. But there's good news, too: The skills needed to receive feedback well are distinct and learnable. They include being able to identify and manage the emotions triggered by the feedback and extract value from criticism even when it's poorly delivered.

Why feedback doesn't register

What makes receiving feedback so hard? The process strikes at the tension between two core human needs—the need to learn and grow, and the need to be accepted just the way you are. As a result, even a seemingly benign suggestion can leave you feeling angry, anxious, badly treated, or profoundly threatened. A hedge such as "Don't take this personally" does nothing to soften the blow.

Getting better at receiving feedback starts with understanding and managing those feelings. You might think there are a thousand ways in which feedback can push your buttons, but in fact there are only three.

Truth triggers are set off by the content of the feedback. When assessments or advice seem off base, unhelpful, or simply untrue, you feel indignant, wronged, and exasperated.

Relationship triggers are tripped by the person providing the feedback. Exchanges are often colored by what you believe about the giver (He's got no credibility on this topic!) and how you feel about your previous interactions (After all I've done for you, I get this petty criticism?). So you might reject coaching that you would accept on its merits if it came from someone else.

Identity triggers are all about your relationship with yourself. Whether the feedback is right or wrong, wise or witless, it can be devastating if it causes your sense of who you are to come undone. In such moments you'll struggle with feeling overwhelmed, defensive, or off balance.

All these responses are natural and reasonable; in some cases they are unavoidable. The solution isn't to pretend you don't have them. It's to recognize what's happening and learn how to derive benefit from feedback even when it sets off one or more of your triggers.

Six steps to becoming a better receiver

Taking feedback well is a process of sorting and filtering. You need to understand the other person's point of view, try on ideas that may at first seem a poor fit, and experiment with different ways of doing things. You also need to discard or shelve critiques that are genuinely misdirected or are not helpful right away.

But it's nearly impossible to do any of those things from inside a triggered response. Instead of ushering you into a nuanced conversation that will help you learn, your triggers prime you to reject, counterattack, or withdraw.

The six steps below will keep you from throwing valuable feedback onto the discard pile or—just as damaging—accepting and acting on comments that you would be better off disregarding. They are presented as advice to the receiver. But, of course, understanding the challenges of receiving feedback helps the giver be more effective, too.

1. Know your tendencies

You've been getting feedback all your life, so there are no doubt patterns in how you respond. Do you defend yourself on the facts ("This is plain wrong"), argue about the method of delivery ("You're really doing this by email?"), or strike back ("You, of all people?")? Do you smile on the outside but seethe on the inside? Do you get teary or filled with righteous indignation? And what role does the passage of time play? Do you tend to reject feedback in the moment and then step back and consider it over time? Do you accept it all immediately but later decide it's not valid? Do you agree with it intellectually but have trouble changing your behavior?

When Michael, an advertising executive, hears his boss make an offhand joke about his lack of professionalism, it hits him like a sledgehammer. "I'm flooded with shame," he told us, "and all my failings rush to mind, as if I'm Googling 'things wrong with me' and getting 1.2 million hits, with sponsored ads from my father and my ex. In this state it's hard to see the feedback at 'actual size.'" But now that Michael understands his standard operating procedure, he's able to make better choices about where to go from there: "I can reassure myself that I'm exaggerating, and usually after I sleep on it, I'm in a better place to figure out whether there's something I can learn."

2. Disentangle the "what" from the "who"

If the feedback is on target and the advice is wise, it shouldn't matter who delivers it. But it does. When a relationship trigger is activated, entwining the content of comments with your feelings about the giver (or about how, when, or where she delivered the comments), learning is short-circuited. To keep that from happening, you have to work to separate the message from the messenger, and then consider both.

Janet, a chemist and a team leader at a pharmaceutical company, received glowing comments from her peers and superiors during her 360-degree review but was surprised by the negative feedback she got from her direct reports. She immediately concluded that the problem was theirs: "I have high standards, and some of them can't handle that," she remembers thinking. "They aren't used to someone holding their feet to the fire." In this way, she changed the subject from her management style to her subordinates' competence, preventing her from learning something important about the impact she had on others.

Eventually the penny dropped, Janet says. "I came to see that whether it was their performance problem or my leadership problem, those were not mutually exclusive issues, and both were worth solving." She was able to disentangle the issues and talk to her team about both. Wisely, she began the conversation with their feedback to her, asking, "What am I doing that's making things tough? What would improve the situation?"

3. Sort toward coaching

Some feedback is evaluative ("Your rating is a 4"); some is coaching ("Here's how you can improve").

Everyone needs both. Evaluations tell you where you stand, what to expect, and what is expected of you. Coaching allows you to learn and improve and helps you play at a higher level.

It's not always easy to distinguish one from the other. When a board member phoned James to suggest that he start the next quarter's CFO presentation with analyst predictions rather than internal projections, was that intended as a helpful suggestion, or was it a veiled criticism of his usual approach? When in doubt, people tend to assume the worst and to put even well-intentioned coaching into the evaluation bin. Feeling judged is likely to set off your identity triggers, and the resulting anxiety can drown out the opportunity to learn. So whenever possible, sort toward coaching. Work to hear feedback as potentially valuable advice from a fresh perspective rather than as an indictment of how you've done things in the past. When James took that approach, "the suggestion became less emotionally loaded," he says. "I decided to hear it as simply an indication of how that board member might more easily digest quarterly information."

4. Unpack the feedback

Often it's not immediately clear whether feedback is valid and useful. So before you accept or reject it, do some analysis to better understand it.

Here's a hypothetical example. Kara, who's in sales, is told by Johann, an experienced colleague, that she needs to "be more assertive." Her reaction might be to reject his advice ("I think I'm pretty assertive already"). Or she might acquiesce ("I really do need to step it up"). But before she decides what to do, she needs to understand what he really means. Does he think she should speak up more often, or just with greater conviction? Should she smile more or less? Have the confidence to admit she doesn't know something or the confidence to pretend she does?

Even the simple advice to "be more assertive" comes from a complex set of observations and judgments that Johann has made while watching Kara in meetings and with customers. Kara needs to dig into the general suggestion and find out what in particular prompted it. What did Johann see her do or fail to do? What did he expect, and what is he worried about? In other words, where is the feedback coming from?

Kara also needs to know where the feedback is going—exactly what Johann wants her to do differently and why. After a clarifying discussion, she might agree that she is less assertive than others on the sales floor but disagree with the idea that she should change. If all her sales heroes are quiet, humble, and deeply curious about customers' needs, Kara's view of what it means to be good at sales might look and sound very different from Johann's *Glengarry Glen Ross* ideal.

When you set aside snap judgments and take time to explore where feedback is coming from and where it's going, you can enter into a rich, informative conversation about perceived best practices—whether you decide to take the advice or not.

5. Ask for just one thing

Feedback is less likely to set off your emotional triggers if you request it and direct it. So don't wait until your annual performance review. Find opportunities to get bite-size pieces of coaching from a variety of people throughout the year. Don't invite criticism with a big, unfocused question like "Do you have any feedback for me?" Make the process more manageable by asking a colleague, a boss, or a direct report, "What's one thing you see me doing (or failing to do) that holds me back?" That person may name the first behavior that comes to mind or the most important one on his or her list. Either way, you'll get concrete information and can tease out more specifics at your own pace.

Roberto, a fund manager at a financial services firm, found his 360-degree review process overwhelming and confusing. "Eighteen pages of charts and graphs and no ability to have follow-up conversations to clarify the feedback was frustrating," he says, adding that it also left him feeling awkward around his colleagues.

Now Roberto taps two or three people each quarter to ask for one thing he might work on. "They don't offer the same things, but over time I hear themes, and that gives me a good sense of where my growth edge lies," he says. "And I have really good conversations—with my boss, with my team, even with peers where there's some friction in the relationship. They're happy to tell me one thing to change, and often they're right. It does help us work more smoothly together."

Research has shown that those who explicitly seek critical feedback (that is, who are not just fishing for praise) tend to get higher performance ratings. Why?

Mainly, we think, because someone who's asking for coaching is more likely to take what is said to heart and genuinely improve. But also because when you ask for feedback, you not only find out how others see you, you also *influence* how they see you. Soliciting constructive criticism communicates humility, respect, passion for excellence, and confidence, all in one go.

6. Engage in small experiments

After you've worked to solicit and understand feedback, it may still be hard to discern which bits of advice will help you and which ones won't. We suggest designing small experiments to find out. Even though you may doubt that a suggestion will be useful, if the downside risk is small and the upside potential is large, it's worth a try. James, the CFO we discussed earlier, decided to take the board member's advice for the next presentation and see what happened. Some directors were pleased with the change, but the shift in format prompted others to offer suggestions of their own. Today James reverse-engineers his presentations to meet board members' current top-of-mind concerns. He sends out an email a week beforehand asking for any burning questions and either front-loads his talk with answers to them or signals at the start that he will get to them later on. "It's a little more challenging to prepare for but actually much easier to give," he says. "I spend less time fielding unexpected questions, which was the hardest part of the job."

That's an example worth following. When someone gives you advice, test it out. If it works, great. If it doesn't, you can try again, tweak your approach, or decide to end the experiment. Criticism is never easy to take. Even when you know that it's essential to your development and you trust that the person delivering it wants you to succeed, it can activate psychological triggers. You might feel misjudged, ill-used, and sometimes threatened to your very core.

Your growth depends on your ability to pull value from criticism in spite of your natural responses and on your willingness to seek out even more advice and coaching from bosses, peers, and subordinates. They may be good or bad at providing it, or they may have little time for it—but you are the most important factor in your own development. If you're determined to learn from whatever feedback you get, no one can stop you.

SHEILA HEEN and DOUGLAS STONE are cofounders of Triad Consulting Group and teach negotiation at Harvard Law School. They are coauthors of *Thanks for the Feedback: The Science and Art of Receiving Feedback Well,* from which this article is adapted.

Reprinted from *Harvard Business Review,*
January–February 2014 (product #R1401K).

5

Firing Back

*How Great Leaders Rebound
After Career Disasters*

By Jeffrey A. Sonnenfeld and Andrew J. Ward

Among the tests of a leader, few are more challenging—and more painful—than recovering from a career catastrophe, whether it is caused by natural disaster, illness, misconduct, slipups, or unjust conspiratorial overthrow. But real leaders don't cave in. Defeat energizes them to rejoin the fray with greater determination and vigor.

Take the case of Jamie Dimon, who was fired as president of Citigroup but now is CEO of JPMorgan Chase. Or look at Vanguard founder Jack Bogle, who was removed from his position as president of Wellington Management but then went on to create the index fund and become a leading voice for governance reform. Similarly, there's former Coca-Cola president Steve Heyer, who was surprisingly passed over for the CEO position at Coke but then was quickly named head of Starwood Hotels. Most colorful, perhaps, is Donald Trump, who recovered from two rounds of financial distress in his casino business and is admired today both as a hugely successful estate developer and as a producer and star of popular reality TV shows—and of course ran successfully for President of the United States.

These stories are still the exception rather than the rule. F. Scott Fitzgerald's famous observation that there are no second acts in American lives casts an especially dark shadow over the derailed careers of business leaders. In our research—analyzing more than 450 CEO successions between 1988 and 1992 at large, publicly traded companies—we found that only 35% of ousted CEOs returned to an active executive role within two years of departure; 22% stepped back and took only advisory roles, generally counseling smaller organizations or sitting on boards.

But 43% effectively ended their careers and went into retirement.

What prevents a deposed leader from coming back? Leaders who cannot recover have a tendency to blame themselves and are often tempted to dwell on the past rather than look to the future. They secretly hold themselves responsible for their career setback, whether they were or not, and get caught in a psychological web of their own making, unable to move beyond the position they no longer hold. This dynamic is usually reinforced by well-meaning colleagues and even by family and friends, who may try to lay blame in an attempt to make sense of the chaos surrounding the disaster. Sadly, their advice can often be more damaging than helpful.

In every culture, the ability to transcend life's adversity is an essential feature of becoming a great leader. In his influential 1949 book, *The Hero with a Thousand Faces*, anthropologist Joseph Campbell showed us that the various stories of great leaders around the world, in every culture and every era, are all essentially the same story—the "hero myth." This myth is embodied in the life stages of such universal archetypes as Moses, Jesus, Muhammad, Buddha, Aeneas, Odysseus, and the Aztecs' Tezcatlipoca. Transformational leaders follow a path that entails a call to greatness, early successes (involving tough choices), ongoing trials, profound setbacks, and, ultimately, triumph as they reintegrate into society. If Campbell were writing today, he might want to include business leaders in his study, as they must confront similar trials on their way to greatness.

This article is intended to help leaders—or anyone suffering from an unexpected setback—examine their often abrupt fall from grace and to give them a process through which they can recover, and even exceed their past accomplishments. From our 22 years of interviews with 300 fired CEOs and other derailed professionals, our scholarly study of leadership, our consulting assignments, and our own searing personal experiences, we are convinced that leaders can triumph over tragedy, provided they take conscious steps to do so. For a start, they must carefully *decide how to fight back*. Once this crucial decision has been taken, they must *recruit others into battle*. They must then *take steps to recover their heroic status*, in the process proving to themselves and others that they have the *mettle* necessary to *rediscover their heroic mission*.

Few people exemplify this journey better than President Jimmy Carter. After his devastating 1980 reelection loss to Ronald Reagan, Carter was emotionally fatigued. As he told us sometime later, "I returned to Plains, Georgia, completely exhausted, slept for almost 24 hours, and then awoke to an altogether new, unwanted, and potentially empty life." While proud of his achievements—his success in deregulating energy, for example, his efforts to promote global human rights, and his ability to broker peace between Israel and Egypt through the Camp David Accords—post election, Carter needed to move past his sense of frustration and rejection, particularly his failure to secure the timely release of the American hostages in Iran.

Despite his pain and humiliation, Carter did not retreat into anger or self-pity. He realized that his global prominence gave him a forum to fight to restore his influential role in world events. Accordingly, he recruited others into battle by enlisting the enthusiastic support of his wife, Rosalynn, several members of his administration, academic researchers in the sciences and social sciences, world leaders, and financial backers to build the Carter Center. He proved his mettle by refusing to remove himself from the fray. Indeed, he continued to involve himself in international conflict mediation in Ethiopia and Eritrea, Liberia, Haiti, Bosnia, and Venezuela, demonstrating in the process that he was not a has-been. He regained his heroic stature when he was awarded the Nobel Peace Prize in 2002 "for his decades of untiring effort to find peaceful solutions to international conflicts, to advance democracy and human rights, and to promote economic and social development." And he has rediscovered his heroic mission by using the Carter Center to continue his drive to advance human rights and alleviate needless suffering.

Let us look now at how some great business leaders have followed the same path to recover from their own disastrous career setbacks.

Decide how to fight back

The first decision you will face in responding to a career disaster is the question of whether to confront the situation that brought you down—with an exhausting, expensive, and perhaps embarrassing battle—or to try to put it behind you as quickly as possible, in the hope that no one will notice or remember for long. In some cases, it's best to avoid direct and immediate confrontation. Home Depot cofounder Bernie Marcus, for example, decided to sidestep the quicksand of litigation against Sandy Sigoloff, the conglomerateur who fired Marcus from Handy Dan

Home Improvement. Marcus made his battleground the marketplace rather than the courtroom. Thanks to this strategy, he was free to set the historic course for the Home Depot, which now under his successor is approaching $100 billion in sales, with several hundred thousand employees.

Other comeback kids also began with a graceful retreat. Jamie Dimon was sacked as president of Citigroup by then chairman Sandy Weill following 16 years of partnership in building the institution. When he spoke to us and to others, he did not dwell on his disappointment or sense of injustice. Monica Langley in her 2003 book *Tearing Down the Walls* describes what happened when Weill asked Dimon to resign. Dimon was shocked but replied, "You've obviously thought this through, and there's nothing I can do." As he scanned the already-prepared press release, Dimon saw that the board agreed with Weill. The firm offered Dimon a generous, nonrestrictive severance package, so a battle with Weill seemed pointless. While he was unemployed, Dimon read biographies of great national leaders who had truly suffered. He also took up boxing—another way, perhaps, of dealing with the stress and pain. After a year of this, Dimon decided he needed closure, so he invited Weill to lunch at the Four Seasons to thank him. As Dimon recounts in Harvey Mackay's 2004 book, *We Got Fired!*: "I had mellowed by then. Sandy wasn't going to call me. . . . I knew I was ready to say thank you for what he did for me. I also knew he and I should talk about what happened. I wanted to get this event behind me so I could move on. Part of me said I had spent sixteen years with him. Twelve or thirteen were pretty good. You can't just look at one side and not the other. I made my own mistakes; I acknowledged I was partly to blame. Whether I was 40 percent or 60 percent to blame really didn't matter. I felt very good about my meeting with him." In this way, Dimon was able to turn his ouster into an event that yielded both helpful perspective and reassuring resolution. (See the sidebar "Getting Beyond Rage and Denial.")

GETTING BEYOND RAGE AND DENIAL

One of the most important steps on the route to re-covery is to confront and acknowledge failure. This can be as simple as understanding the Machiavellian politics of others. So as you set about rebuilding your career, make sure you:

- *Remember that failure is a beginning, not an end.* Comeback is always possible.

- *Look to the future.* Preemptive actions are often more effective than reactive ones—even if they only take the form of standing back and reflecting on what to do next.

About six months after that lunch, in March 2000, Dimon became CEO of Bank One, a huge Chicago bank that survived the merger of First Chicago and the original Banc One. That year, Bank One posted a loss of $511 million. Three years later, under Dimon's

- *Help people deal with your failure.* Even close friends may avoid you because they don't know what to say or do. Let them know that you are ready for assistance and what kind of aid would be most useful.

- *Know your narrative.* Reputation building involves telling and retelling your story to get your account of events out there and to explain your downfall. Be consistent.

leadership, Bank One was earning record profits of $3.5 billion, and its stock price had soared 85%. Adding to the sweetness of vindication, the following year Bank One merged with JPMorgan Chase, an institution with which Weill had long wanted Citigroup to merge. Dimon became CEO of the new company and is now widely regarded as one of the most influential financial executives in the world.

Of course, it's not always a good decision to sit on the sidelines and presume that justice will prevail. The highly respected Nick Nicholas, outmaneuvered as CEO of Time Warner by his skilled rival Gerald Levin, never challenged his old firm. He went off to Vail to ski at the time, awaiting a call back to service, soon becoming a very successful investor in new businesses, a professor, and a board director. But he never regained his role as the leader of a great public enterprise. Other deposed CEOs, such as Ford's Jacques Nasser, Hewlett-Packard's Carly Fiorina, IBM's John Akers, United Air Lines' Richard Ferris, and Apple's John Sculley have similarly failed to return to lead major public firms. They were considered brilliant leaders by many and were never accused of plundering the shareholders' wealth, like some rogue CEOs of recent years. But they never fought back, and they disappeared from the corner office.

The key determinant in the fight-or-flight question is the damage (or potential damage) incurred to the leader's reputation—the most important resource of all leaders. While departed CEOs and other leaders may have enough other resources and experience to rebound, it is their reputation that will make the difference between successful career recovery and failure.

Fights that will result only in a Pyrrhic victory are best avoided. Battles of pure revenge can resemble Shakespearean tragedies, where all parties lose. Hewlett-Packard board member Tom Perkins, for example, in trying to defend his friend and fellow director George Keyworth from allegations of leaking confidential board discussions, not only brought down HP chairman Patricia Dunn but also caused his friend far greater humiliation, forcing him off the board as well. A leader must consider whether fighting the allegations will exacerbate the damage by making the accusations more public.

When, however, the allegations are not only sufficient to cause a catastrophic career setback but would also block a career comeback, then leaders need to fight back. Consider former Israeli prime minister Ariel Sharon. He was a triumphant commander on the Egyptian front in the Six Day War of 1967. Fifteen years later, as minister of defense, Sharon initiated an attack on the Palestine Liberation Organization in Lebanon. Christian militias seized the opportunity to massacre hundreds of Palestinians in acts of revenge against the PLO in the Israeli-controlled Sabra and Shatila refugee camps.

In a February 21, 1983, cover story, *Time* magazine reported that these massacres were the result of a plot between Sharon and the militias to avenge the killing of Lebanon's Christian president Bashir Gemayel. Sharon sued *Time* in Israel and in New York in lengthy litigation. In both places, juries found *Time*'s accusations to be false and defamatory. The magazine settled and apologized. "It was a very long and hard struggle and was worth it," Sharon said publically at the time. "I came here to prove that *Time* magazine lied: We were able to prove that *Time* did lie."

A ferocious warrior, Sharon took on this carefully calculated battle for his reputation and executed it with focus and determination. He knew that if he did not vigorously defend himself, no one else would be able to help him. Sharon could not have regained his honor and returned to public office if he had not challenged these false charges and then moved on with his life.

Recruit others into battle

Whether you fight or tactically retreat for a while, it is essential to engage others right from the start to join your battle to put your career back on track. Friends and acquaintances play an instrumental role in providing support and advice in the process of recovery.

Those who really care for you can help you gain perspective on the good and bad choices you have made. You are also more likely to make yourself vulnerable with those you trust. Without such vulnerability, you cannot hope to achieve the candid, self-critical perspective you will need to learn from your experience. Still, although family and friends can provide invaluable personal support, they may be less effective when it comes to practical career assistance. Research has shown that slight acquaintances are actually more helpful than close friends in steering you toward opportunities for new positions in other organizations.

In an acclaimed study, Stanford University's Mark Granovetter discovered that of those individuals who landed jobs through personal contacts, only 16.7% found them through people they saw at least twice a week; 55.6% found positions through acquaintances seen at least once a year. But 27.8% of job candidates found work through distant acquaintances, whom they saw less than once a year—old college friends, former workmates, or people known through professional associations. In other words, more job contacts will come to you through people you see less than once a year than from people you see twice or more a week. That's because close friends share the same networks as you do, whereas acquaintances are more likely to introduce you to new people and contacts. Indeed, through the power of acquaintance networks, you can reach almost anyone within a few steps. Thus, distant acquaintances that don't appear to have any connection to you may prove key to your recovery when you are trying to get back on your feet.

But it's not enough to have a wide network of acquaintances. The quality of the connections, even the more distant ones, matters as well. That was the case for Home Depot's Bernie Marcus. Marcus was devastated when he was fired as CEO of Handy Dan on what he felt were trumped-up charges made by Sandy Sigoloff, the threatened boss of the parent company, Daylin. "There was a lot of self-pity on my part," Marcus told us. "I was drowning in my sorrow, going several nights at a time without sleeping. For the first time in my adult life, instead of building, I was more concerned with surviving."

Marcus, however, had an unexpected resource. Whether they were close friends and colleagues with whom he worked or acquaintances he dealt with on a casual basis, Marcus treated others with uncommon honesty, respect, and trust. This consideration was reciprocated by people in his network when he needed help; it was one of his less frequent acquaintances, Rip Fleming at Security Pacific National Bank, who made it possible for Marcus to launch Home Depot.

Marcus had raised $2 million in seed money for the Home Depot venture, but that was not enough to get his new company off the ground. He applied to several banks for a line of credit but was turned down every time. Eventually, he knocked at Fleming's door at Security Pacific National. Both Marcus and Fleming believed that the relationship between banker and client should amount to more than just the business transactions they conducted. Consequently, Fleming had become an adviser to Marcus at Handy Dan. Despite these strong professional ties, though, Fleming was initially reluctant to issue a line of credit until Marcus flew out to Los Angeles and sold Fleming on the idea. In the end, Security Pacific National provided a $3.5 million line of credit, which enabled Home Depot to get up and running. Unbeknownst to Marcus, the proposal was repeatedly turned down by the bank's loan committee and was approved only when Fleming marched into the president's office with his resignation letter in hand.

How you build relationships has a huge impact on your prospects for career recovery. Marcus had a way of building relatively strong relationships even in circumstances when most people would settle for weak acquaintanceships. This capacity for affiliation is a litmus test of a leader's ability to bounce back. People who can create connections are much more likely to engender the kind of help they need when fate turns against them.

Recover your heroic status

It's not enough for you to recruit others to advance your career. To launch your comeback, you must actually *do* things to win back the support of a wider audience. To manage this, you must regain what we call your heroic status.

The great leader has a heroic persona that confers a larger-than-life presence. You can achieve this status by developing a personal dream that you offer as a public possession. If your dream is accepted, you achieve renown. If for whatever reason your public vision is ultimately discarded, you suffer the loss of both your private dream and your public identity. After a career disaster, you can rebound only if you are able to rebuild your heroic stature—that is, the public reputation with which you were previously perceived. An intrinsic part of recovering this heroic status involves getting your story out. This calls for a public campaign to educate and inform.

When a CEO is fired, the true causes for the dismissal are often deliberately hidden, as the board seeks to protect the reputation of the firm and itself. The organization often engages in elaborate face-saving activities to disguise the real nature of the exit. Euphemistically, the press reports that the CEO resigned "for personal reasons" or "to spend more time with family." In our interviews with dismissed CEOs, we found that their greatest frustration stemmed from not being able to rebuild their heroic stature by telling their side of the story. We have interviewed several people who had seven-figure separation agreements that were contingent on their toeing the party line when they left. That's a problem when CEOs are publicly sacrificed even though they are not guilty of the accusations that led to their ouster. In such cases, CEOs' inability to challenge and set the record straight can lead to destructive speculation in the press, which can damage their reputations so much that it becomes all but impossible to recover.

Popular wisdom holds that a deposed leader should sign the nondisparagement agreement, accept the noncompete clause, take the money, and run. Our strong belief is that such agreements are a mistake. In the end, your cash will disappear, and you won't be able to get your story out. If you agree not to speak out, be prepared to be unemployed for a number of years.

A lesser-known player in the Enron saga, Daniel Scotto, comes to mind. Scotto was the financial analyst who headed up the research department for the large global investment bank Paribas. Early on, Scotto said that Enron was losing money in all its mainstream businesses and that it was only through offshore finagling that the company was creating the image of profitability. Paribas, which was underwriting a large part of the debt, asked Scotto to recant. When he wouldn't, Paribas put him on an imposed medical leave for three weeks and then fired him. He was forced to sign a nondisparagement agreement that hurt his ability to get his story out. Scotto has been unemployed for five years.

Martha Stewart is the best reminder that it doesn't have to be that way. As the most public example in recent times of a CEO who got her story out, Stewart is a model for how to regain your heroic status. She did it by carefully orchestrating a multitiered campaign to restore her reputation.

The day after she was indicted for obstruction of justice in the federal government's insider-trading investigation of ImClone stock, Stewart took out a full-page advertisement in *USA Today* and the *New York Times* and launched a new website, marthatalks. com. In an open letter to her public, Stewart clearly proclaimed her innocence and her intention to clear her name. She understood intuitively that when a hero stumbles, constituents have to reconcile two conflicting images of the person—the larger-than-life presence the hero once commanded and the hero's new fallen state. In her letter, Stewart managed to eliminate the confusion by making sure that people knew her side of the story. She openly denied any charges of insider trading and hammered home the unreliability of the three witnesses upon which the government based its case. Stewart very proactively helped others continue to believe in her heroic status.

Stewart's open letter was supported by a statement on her website by her attorneys, Robert G. Morvillo and John J. Tigue Jr., who challenged the media to investigate why the government waited nearly a year and a half to file the charges. "Is it because she is a woman who has successfully competed in a man's business world by virtue of her talent, hard work, and demanding standards?" they asked.

With the aid of her attorneys, Stewart ingeniously—and successfully—portrayed herself as a David struggling in a just and valiant quest against the Goliath of government. Her fans, far from abandoning a fallen star, rallied around her. The astounding strength of this sentiment is measured in the stock price of Martha Stewart Living Omnimedia. Even at the midpoint of Stewart's prison sentence, the stock had not merely rebounded—it was 50% higher than before anybody had heard of ImClone and the ill-fated stock transaction. Upon her release from prison, the share price neared an all-time high, ad revenue at her magazines picked up, and she launched two national network TV shows. The more Stewart got her story out, the more loyal her public became.

Stewart managed to provide a reassuring account of what really happened in her case. But what if you can't? What if you have truly stumbled? If you cannot refute the facts of your dismissal because they are so condemning, show authentic remorse. The public is often enormously forgiving of genuine contrition and atonement.

Prove your mettle

Protecting your reputation by knowing how to fight unjust accusations and bringing others on board are both essential precursors to relaunching a career in the aftermath of catastrophe. Ultimately, however, you will recover fully only when you take on that next role or start a new organization. When you show that you can still perform at a credible or superior level, others will begin to think of you as having the mettle to triumph over your career calamity. (See the sidebar "How to Come Back.")

Showing mettle is not easy. Fallen leaders face many barriers on the path to recovery, not least of which are doubts in their own ability to get back to the top. As one fired CEO told us, "I'd never sit here and say, 'Geez, all I have to do is just replicate and do it again.' The chances of doing it again are pretty small." Yet leaders who rebound are unfailingly those who get over this doubt about their ability to do it

HOW TO COME BACK

Our interviews with some 300 derailed CEOs and other professionals, as well as our scholarly leadership research, consulting assignments, and personal experiences, have brought to light five key steps for rebounding from career disaster. Anyone trying to recover from a catastrophic setback can use these steps to match, or even exceed, their past accomplishments.

- *Decide how to fight back.* Pyrrhic victories will hurt you by calling attention to the accusations leveled against you. But when your reputation is unfairly damaged, you must take quick action.

- *Recruit others into battle.* Friends and family can provide comfort and, perhaps, some perspective in your hour of need. But acquaintances may be more important in landing that next job.

(Continued)

- *Recover your heroic status.* Deposed leaders are often advised to sign nondisparagement agreements. Don't do it. Engage instead in a multitiered campaign to clear your reputation and restore your stature.

- *Prove your mettle.* After suffering career disaster, you will probably have doubts about your ability to get back to the top. You must overcome that insecurity and in the process find the courage to prove to others—and yourself—that you have not lost your magic touch.

- *Rediscover your heroic mission.* It is the single-minded pursuit of a lasting legacy that sets great leaders apart. To recover from a disastrous setback, find a new heroic mission that renews your passion and creates new meaning in your life.

again. Even when forced from familiar arenas into totally new fields, some leaders remain unafraid of trying new ventures. This capacity to bounce back from adversity—to prove your inner strength once more by overcoming your shattered confidence—is critical to earning lasting greatness.

Take Mickey Drexler. When Gap founder Donald Fisher poached Drexler away from Ann Taylor in 1983, the Gap was struggling to compete, since it sold the same brands of clothing as everyone else and was caught in a pricing game. Drexler expanded the retailer beyond the core Gap stores to brand extension such as GapKids, babyGap, and GapBody, as well as introducing other complementary brands, including Banana Republic and Old Navy. Between the time he arrived in 1983 and 2000, Gap's sales increased from $480 million to $13.7 billion, and its stock rose 169-fold.

Then things began to go awry. Drexler was accused of having lost his touch as a prescient merchant; suspicion arose in the minds of analysts and in the media that the goods had become too trendy. Although some people have suggested that the real problem was that Fisher's brother had built too many stores too close to one another, Drexler was blamed for the slump, as same-store sales dropped every quarter for two years, and the stock plummeted 75%. On May 21, 2002, Drexler presented the upcoming season's merchandise to the board, confident that he had a great selling line for the fall. It wasn't enough for the directors, and the next morning Fisher fired him, believing that the company was now too large for Drexler's hands-on management style.

Drexler was by this time independently wealthy, but he was nonetheless determined to prove that the failures of the previous two years were not primarily his fault and did not reflect his abilities. He knew that the only way to restore his belief in himself, as well as other people's confidence in him, was to return to a role in which he could once again demonstrate his expertise. He turned down a multimillion-dollar severance package from Gap because it contained a noncompete clause. After he explored a few other avenues, opportunity came knocking in the guise of struggling fashion retailer J.Crew.

With only about 200 stores, J.Crew was a small fraction of the Gap's size and consequently much more amenable to Drexler's hands-on style, giving him a greater opportunity to make an impact. Drexler invested $10 million of his own money to buy a 22% stake in the company from the retailer's private owner, the investment firm Texas Pacific. He took a salary that was less than a tenth of what he had earned at his former employer. "You've no idea how much it's costing me to run this company," he joked in a *New York* magazine article shortly after taking over.

The results more than proved that Drexler still had the right stuff. J.Crew rebounded from a $30 million operating loss in 2003 to an operating profit of over $37 million in 2004. Same-store sales per square foot, one of the key metrics in retailing, rose 18% from $338 to $400, while at his old employer, sales per square foot dropped 3%. By the summer of 2006,

Drexler had increased both sales and profits by 20% and launched a wildly embraced IPO to take J.Crew public. The media celebrated his recovery and acknowledged his obvious talent.

For Drexler, as for others, the comeback required him to prove his worth in a situation that was perceived to be enormously difficult. Start-ups or turnarounds are common contexts in which fallen leaders can recover grace. It is in these demanding situations that leaders find the mettle to prove to themselves and to others that they have not lost their magic touch and that no obstacle is too great to overcome in their quest for return.

Rediscover your heroic mission

Most great leaders want to build a legacy that will last beyond their lifetime. This does not mean having their names etched on an ivy-clad university ediface but rather advancing society by building and leading an organization. This is what we call the leader's heroic mission.

Most of the leaders we have profiled in this article were deeply engaged in building a lasting legacy even before they suffered their career setbacks. It is the loss of this mission that really raises a derailment to catastrophic proportions in the leader's own mind, since it puts at risk a lifetime of achievement. On the day Steve Jobs was fired from Apple in 1985, for example, his friend Mike Murray was so concerned about Jobs's reaction that he went over to Jobs's house and sat with him for hours until Murray was convinced that Jobs would not commit suicide.

Jobs did not wallow in despair for long. A week after his ouster from Apple, he flew to Europe and, after a few days in Paris, headed for the Tuscan hills of northern Italy, where he bought a bicycle and a sleeping bag and camped out under the stars, contemplating what he would do next. From Italy, he went to Sweden and then to Russia before returning home. Once back in California, with his passion and ambition renewed, Jobs set about re-creating himself as a force in the IT world. He went on to found another computer company, NeXT, which Apple purchased in 1996 for $400 million, at which point Jobs returned to Apple and at the same time became the driving force behind the hugely successful computer-graphics studio Pixar. Once back at Apple, Jobs revived and reenergized the company with breakthrough, high-design products, such as the iMac, iBook, and iPod, and took the company into emerging businesses, such as iTunes.

Like Martha Stewart, Steve Jobs was able to recapture his original heroic mission. Other deposed leaders, however, must truly start again because the door to their familiar field is firmly closed, and they must seek new opportunities and create a totally new heroic mission.

That's what Drexel Burnham Lambert financier Michael Milken, the imaginative "king of the junk bonds," had to do. Milken's life was almost the incarnation of the American dream. Born on the Fourth of July, Milken had become a billionaire by his mid-forties and one of the most influential financiers in the world. Then it all came tumbling down. He was charged with a 98-count criminal indictment, and a massive civil case was brought against him by the SEC for insider trading, stock parking, price manipulation, racketeering, and defrauding customers, among other crimes. He ended up pleading guilty to six relatively minor counts. In November 1990, he was sentenced to 10 years in prison, agreed to pay $600 million at the time, and ended up paying a further $42 million over a probation violation. After serving 22 months, Milken was released early for cooperating with other inquiries. But he was barred from the securities industry for life.

A week later, Milken was diagnosed with prostate cancer and was told he had 12 to 18 months to live. He immediately turned his maniacal zeal into a new heroic mission to conquer this disease. Through aggressive treatment and his own dietary research, he survived to build a huge foundation supporting research to battle prostate cancer. He also created an economic research institute that attracts the world's top scientific, political, religious, and business leaders. Milken still argues that he was wrongly accused. Others may disagree, but few would doubt that he has earned restitution. The public has come to accept that he has paid for his crimes, and there has even been some reconsideration of their actual severity.

It is the single-minded, passionate pursuit of a heroic mission that sets leaders like Steve Jobs and Michael Milken and Jimmy Carter apart from the general population, and it is what attracts and motivates followers to join them. In the worst of cases, to have that life purpose ripped from you and to be prohibited from its further pursuit can leave an unbearable void and doubts as to your reason for being. Finding a new mission to replace your lifelong purpose can be a great struggle, but one that is necessary if you are to recover.

The tragedies and triumphant comebacks of the leaders we have profiled in this article can seem remote, bordering on the mythological, perhaps. But their stories point to important lessons about recovering from career catastrophe. Stunning comeback is possible in all industries, though the challenges vary according to the leadership norms of each field's culture. For example, clergy ensnarled in publicized sex scandals will probably see their careers dissolve, whereas entertainment figures may not only recover but actually benefit from notoriety. Where one profession values trust, another values celebrity. Thus, recovery plans must be adapted to the cultures of different industries.

Whatever the arena in which your recovery takes shape, the important thing to remember is that we all have choices in life, even in defeat. We can lose our health, our loved ones, our jobs, but much can be saved. No one can truly define success and failure for us—only we can define that for ourselves. No one can take away our dignity unless we surrender it. No one can take away our hope and pride unless we relinquish them. No one can steal our creativity, imagination, and skills unless we stop thinking. No one can stop us from rebounding unless we give up.

JEFFREY A. SONNENFELD is the senior associate dean for executive programs, the Lester Crown Professor of Management Practice at the Yale School of Management, and the president of the Executive Leadership Institute at Yale University in New Haven, Connecticut. ANDREW J. WARD is an assistant professor of management at the University of Georgia in Athens, Georgia. This article is drawn from their book of the same title (Harvard Business School Press, 2007).

Reprinted from *Harvard Business Review,*
February 2007 (product #R0701G).

6

Resilience Is About How You Recharge, Not How You Endure

By Shawn Achor and Michelle Gielan

As constant travelers and parents of a 2-year-old, we sometimes fantasize about how much work we can do when one of us gets on a plane, undistracted by phones, friends, and *Finding Nemo*. We race to get all our ground work done: packing, going through TSA, doing a last-minute work call, calling each other, boarding the plane. Then, when we try to have that amazing in-flight work session, we get nothing done. Even worse, after refreshing our email or reading the same studies over and over, we are too exhausted when we land to soldier on with the emails that have inevitably still piled up.

Why should flying deplete us? We're just sitting there doing nothing. Why can't we be tougher—more resilient and determined in our work—so we can accomplish all of the goals we set for ourselves? Through our current research, we have come to realize that the problem is not our hectic schedule or the plane travel itself; the problem comes from a misunderstanding of what it means to be resilient and the resulting impact of overworking.

We often take a militaristic, "tough" approach to resilience and grit. We imagine a marine slogging through the mud, a boxer going one more round, or a football player picking himself up off the turf for one more play. We believe that the longer we tough it out, the tougher we are, and therefore the more successful we will be. However, this entire conception is scientifically inaccurate.

The very lack of a recovery period is dramatically holding back our collective ability to be resilient and successful. Research has found that there is a direct correlation between lack of recovery and increased incidence of health and safety problems.[1] And lack of recovery—whether by disrupting sleep with thoughts of work or having continuous cognitive arousal by watching our phones—is costing our companies $62 billion a year (that's billion, not million) in lost productivity.[2]

And just because work stops, it doesn't mean we are recovering. We "stop" work sometimes at 5 p.m., but then we spend the night wrestling with solutions to work problems, talking about our work over dinner, and falling asleep thinking about how much work we'll do tomorrow. In a study released last month, researchers from Norway found that 7.8% of Norwegians have become workaholics.[3] The scientists cite a definition of "workaholism" as "being overly concerned about work, driven by an uncontrollable work motivation, and investing so much time and effort to work that it impairs other important life areas."[4]

We believe that this definition applies to the majority of American workers (including those who read HBR), and this prompted us to begin a study of

113

workaholism in the United States. Our study will use a large corporate data set from a major medical company to examine how technology extends our working hours and thus interferes with necessary cognitive recovery. We believe this is resulting in huge health care costs and high turnover rates for employers.

Misconceptions about resilience is often bred from an early age. Parents trying to teach their children resilience might celebrate a high school student staying up until 3 a.m. to finish a science fair project. What a distortion of resilience! A resilient child is a well-rested one. When an exhausted student goes to school, he risks hurting everyone on the road with his impaired driving, he doesn't have the cognitive resources to do well on his English test, he has lower self-control with his friends, and at home, he is moody with his parents. Overwork and exhaustion are the opposite of resilience. And the bad habits we learn when we're young only magnify when we hit the workforce.

In her excellent book *The Sleep Revolution*, Arianna Huffington wrote, "We sacrifice sleep in the name of productivity, but ironically our loss of sleep, despite the extra hours we spend at work, adds up to 11 days of lost productivity per year per worker, or about $2,280."

The key to resilience is trying really hard, then stopping, recovering, and then trying again. This conclusion is based on biology. Homeostasis is a fundamental biological concept describing the ability of the brain to continuously restore and sustain well-being.[5] Positive neuroscientist Brent Furl from Texas A&M University coined the term "homeostatic value" to describe the value that certain actions have for creating equilibrium, and thus well-being, in the body. When the body is out of alignment from overworking, we waste vast mental and physical resources trying to return to balance before we can move forward.

As *Power of Full Engagement* authors Jim Loehr and Tony Schwartz have written, if you have too much time in the performance zone, you need more time in the recovery zone; otherwise you risk burnout. Mustering your resources to "try hard" requires burning energy in order to overcome your currently low arousal level. This is called "upregulation." It also exacerbates exhaustion. Thus, the more imbalanced we become due to overworking, the more value there is in activities that allow us to return to a state of balance. The value of a recovery period rises in proportion to the amount of work required of us.

So how do we recover and build resilience? Most people assume that if you stop doing a task like answering emails or writing a paper that your brain will naturally recover, that when you start again later in the day or the next morning, you'll have your energy back. But surely everyone reading this has had times when they lie in bed for hours, unable to fall asleep because their brain is thinking about work. If you lie in bed for eight hours, you may have rested, but you can still feel exhausted the next day. That's because rest and recovery are not the same thing. Stopping does not equal recovering.

If you're trying to build resilience at work, you need adequate internal and external recovery periods. As researchers Fred R. H. Zijlstra, Mark Cropley, and Leif W. Rydstedt write in their 2014 paper: "Internal recovery refers to the shorter periods of relaxation that take place within the frames of the workday or the work setting in the form of short scheduled or unscheduled breaks, by shifting attention or changing to other work tasks when the mental or physical resources required for the initial task are temporarily depleted or exhausted. External recovery refers to actions that take place outside of work—e.g. in the free time between the workdays, and during weekends, holidays or vacations."[6] If after work you lie around on your bed and get riled up by political commentary on your phone or get stressed thinking about decisions about how to renovate your home, your brain has not received a break from high mental arousal states. Our brains need a rest as much as our bodies do.

If you really want to build resilience, you can start by strategically stopping. Give yourself the resources to be tough by creating internal and external recovery periods. In her upcoming book *The Future of Happiness*, based on her work at Yale Business School, Amy Blankson describes how to strategically stop during the day by using technology to control overworking.[7] She suggests downloading the Instant or Moment apps to see how many times you turn on your phone each day. The average person turns on their phone 150 times every day.[8] If every distraction took only one minute (which would be seriously optimistic), that would account for 2.5 hours of every day.

You can use apps like Offtime or Unplugged to create tech free zones by strategically scheduling automatic airplane modes. In addition, you can take a cognitive break every 90 minutes to recharge your batteries. Try to not have lunch at your desk, but instead spend time outside or with your friends—not talking about work. Take all of your paid time off, which not only gives you recovery periods but raises your productivity and the likelihood of promotion.[9]

As for us, we've started using our plane time as a work-free zone and thus as time to dip into the recovery phase. The results have been fantastic. We are usually tired already by the time we get on a plane, and the cramped space and spotty internet connection make work more challenging. Now, instead of swimming upstream, we relax, meditate, sleep, watch movies, journal, or listen to entertaining podcasts. And when we get off the plane, instead of being depleted, we feel rejuvenated and ready to return to the performance zone.

SHAWN ACHOR is the *New York Times* best-selling author of *The Happiness Advantage* and *Before Happiness*, and a popular TED talk, "The Happy Secret to Better Work." He has lectured or researched at over a third of the *Fortune* 100 companies and in 50 countries, as well as for the NFL, Pentagon, and White House. Shawn is leading a series of courses on "21 Days to Inspire Positive Change" with the Oprah Winfrey Network. MICHELLE GIELAN, a national CBS News anchor turned University of Pennsylvania positive psychology researcher, is now the best-selling author of *Broadcasting Happiness*. She is partnering with Arianna Huffington to research how transformative stories fuel success.

Notes

1. J. K. Sluiter, "The Influence of Work Characteristics on the Need for Recovery and Experienced Health: A Study on Coach Drivers," *Ergonomics* 42, no. 4 (1999): 573–583.
2. American Academy of Sleep Medicine, "Insomnia Costing U.S. Workforce $63.2 Billion a Year in Lost Productivity," *ScienceDaily*, September 2, 2011.
3. C. S. Andreassen et al., "The Relationships Between Workaholism and Symptoms of Psychiatric Disorders: A Large-Scale Cross-Sectional Study," *PLoS One* 11, no. 5 (2016).
4. C. S. Andreassen et al., "Psychometric Assessment of Workaholism Measures," *Journal of Managerial Psychology* 29, no. 1 (2014): 7–24.
5. "What Is Homeostasis?" *Scientific American*, January 3, 2000.

6. F. R. H. Zijlstra et al., "From Recovery to Regulation: An Attempt to Reconceptualize 'Recovery from Work'" (special issue paper, John Wily & Sons, 2014), 244.

7. A. Blankson, *The Future of Happiness* (Dallas, Texas: BenBella Books, forthcoming 2017).

8. J. Stern, "Cellphone Users Check Phones 150x/Day and Other Internet Fun Facts," *Good Morning America*, May 29, 2013.

9. S. Achor, "Are the People Who Take Vacations the Ones Who Get Promoted?" *Harvard Business Review* online, June 12, 2015.

Adapted from content posted on hbr.org,
June 24, 2016 (product #H02Z3O).

Index

How to be human at work.

HBR's Emotional Intelligence Series features smart, essential reading on the human side of professional life from the pages of *Harvard Business Review*. Each book in the series offers uplifting stories, practical advice, and research from leading experts on how to tend to our emotional well-being at work.

Harvard Business Review Emotional Intelligence Series

Available in paperback or ebook format. The specially priced six-volume set includes:

- Mindfulness
- Resilience
- Influence and Persuasion

- Authentic Leadership
- Happiness
- Empathy

The most important management ideas all in one place.

We hope you enjoyed this book from *Harvard Business Review*. For the best ideas HBR has to offer turn to HBR's 10 Must Reads Boxed Set. From books on leadership and strategy to managing yourself and others, this 6-book collection delivers articles on the most essential business topics to help you succeed.

HBR's 10 Must Reads Series

The definitive collection of ideas and best practices on our most sought-after topics from the best minds in business.

- Change Management
- Collaboration
- Communication
- Emotional Intelligence
- Innovation
- Leadership
- Making Smart Decisions

- Managing Across Cultures
- Managing People
- Managing Yourself
- Strategic Marketing
- Strategy
- Teams
- The Essentials

hbr.org/mustreads

Buy for your team, clients, or event.
Visit hbr.org/bulksales for quantity discount rates.

Authentic
Leadership

HBR Emotional Intelligence Series

How to be human at work

The HBR Emotional Intelligence Series features smart, essential reading on the human side of professional life from the pages of *Harvard Business Review*.

Authentic Leadership

Empathy

Happiness

Influence and Persuasion

Mindfulness

Resilience

Other books on emotional intelligence from *Harvard Business Review*:

HBR's 10 Must Reads on Emotional Intelligence

HBR Guide to Emotional Intelligence

Authentic Leadership

HBR EMOTIONAL INTELLIGENCE SERIES

Harvard Business Review Press

Boston, Massachusetts

Library of Congress Cataloging-in-Publication Data

Title: Authentic leadership.
Other titles: HBR emotional intelligence series.
Description: Boston, Massachusetts : Harvard Business Review
Press, [2017] | Series: HBR emotional intelligence series | Includes index.
Identifiers: LCCN 2017027307 | ISBN 9781633693913 (pbk. : alk. paper)
Subjects: LCSH: Leadership—Psychological aspects. | Self-consciousness (Awareness) | Authenticity (Philosophy) | Corporate culture.
Classification: LCC HD57.7 .A8496 2017 | DDC 658.4/092—dc23 LC record available at https://lccn.loc.gov/2017027307

The paper used in this publication meets the requirements of the American National Standard for Permanence of Paper for Publications and Documents in Libraries and Archives Z39.48-1992.

ISBN: 978-1-63369-391-3
eISBN: 978-1-63369-329-0

Contents

Contents

Authentic
Leadership

HBR EMOTIONAL INTELLIGENCE SERIES

1

Discovering Your Authentic Leadership

By Bill George, Peter Sims, Andrew N. McLean, and Diana Mayer

During the past 50 years, leadership scholars have conducted more than 1,000 studies in an attempt to determine the definitive styles, characteristics, or personality traits of great leaders. None of these studies has produced a clear profile of the ideal leader. Thank goodness. If scholars had produced a cookie-cutter leadership style, individuals would be forever trying to imitate it. They would make themselves into personae, not people, and others would see through them immediately.

No one can be authentic by trying to imitate someone else. You can learn from others' experiences, but there is no way you can be successful when you are trying to be like them. People trust you when you are genuine and authentic, not a replica of someone else. Amgen CEO and president Kevin Sharer, who gained priceless experience working as Jack Welch's assistant in the 1980s, saw the downside of GE's cult of personality in those days. "Everyone wanted to be like Jack," he explains. "Leadership has many voices. You need to be who you are, not try to emulate somebody else."

Over the past five years, people have developed a deep distrust of leaders. It is increasingly evident that we need a new kind of business leader in the 21st century. In 2003, Bill George's book, *Authentic Leadership: Rediscovering the Secrets to Creating Lasting Value*, challenged a new generation to lead authentically. Authentic leaders demonstrate a passion for their purpose, practice their values consistently, and lead with their hearts as well as their heads. They establish long-term, meaningful relationships and have the self-discipline to get results. They know who they are.

Many readers of *Authentic Leadership*, including several CEOs, indicated that they had a tremendous desire to become authentic leaders and wanted to know how. As a result, our research team set out to answer the question, "How can people become and remain authentic leaders?" We interviewed 125 leaders to learn how they developed their leadership abilities. These interviews constitute the largest in-depth study of leadership development ever undertaken. Our interviewees discussed openly and honestly how they realized their potential and candidly shared their life stories, personal struggles, failures, and triumphs.

The people we talked with ranged in age from 23 to 93, with no fewer than 15 per decade. They were chosen based on their reputations for authenticity and effectiveness as leaders, as well as our personal knowledge of them. We also solicited recommendations from other leaders and academics. The resulting group includes women and men from a diverse array of racial, religious, and socioeconomic backgrounds and nationalities. Half of them are CEOs, and the other half comprises a range of profit and nonprofit leaders, midcareer leaders, and young leaders just starting on their journeys.

After interviewing these individuals, we believe we understand why more than 1,000 studies have not produced a profile of an ideal leader. Analyzing 3,000 pages of transcripts, our team was startled to see that these people did not identify any universal characteristics, traits, skills, or styles that led to their success. Rather, their leadership emerged from their life stories. Consciously and subconsciously, they were constantly testing themselves through real-world experiences and reframing their life stories to understand who they were at their core. In doing so, they discovered the purpose of their leadership and learned that being authentic made them more effective.

These findings are extremely encouraging: You do not have to be born with specific characteristics or traits of a leader. You do not have to wait for a tap on the shoulder. You do not have to be at the top of your organization. Instead, you can discover your potential right now. As one of our interviewees, Young & Rubicam chairman and CEO Ann Fudge, said, "All of us have the spark of leadership in us, whether it is in business, in government, or as a nonprofit volunteer. The challenge is to understand ourselves well enough to discover where we can use our leadership gifts to serve others."

Discovering your authentic leadership requires a commitment to developing yourself. Like musicians and athletes, you must devote yourself to a lifetime of realizing your potential. Most people Kroger CEO David Dillon has seen become good leaders were self-taught. Dillon said, "The advice I give to individuals in our company is not to expect the company to hand you a development plan. You need to take responsibility for developing yourself."

In the following pages, we draw upon lessons from our interviews to describe how people become authentic leaders. First and most important, they frame their life stories in ways that allow them to see themselves not as passive observers of their lives but rather as individuals who can develop self-awareness from their experiences. Authentic leaders act on that awareness by practicing their values and principles, sometimes at substantial risk to themselves. They are careful to balance their motivations so that they are driven by these inner values as much as by a desire for external rewards or recognition. Authentic leaders also keep a strong support team around them, ensuring that they live integrated, grounded lives.

Learning from your life story

The journey to authentic leadership begins with understanding the story of your life. Your life story provides the context for your experiences, and through it, you can find the inspiration to make an impact in the world. As the novelist John Barth once wrote, "The story of your life is not your life. It is your story." In other words, it is your personal narrative that matters, not the mere facts of your life. Your life narrative is like a permanent recording playing in your head. Over and over, you replay the events and personal interactions that are important to your life, attempting to make sense of them to find your place in the world.

While the life stories of authentic leaders cover the full spectrum of experiences—including the positive impact of parents, athletic coaches, teachers, and mentors—many leaders reported that their motivation came from a difficult experience in their lives. They described the transformative effects of the loss of a job; personal illness; the untimely death of a close friend or relative; and feelings of being excluded, discriminated against, and rejected by peers. Rather than seeing themselves as victims, though, authentic leaders used these formative experiences to give meaning to their lives. They reframed these events to rise above their challenges and to discover their passion to lead.

Let's focus now on one leader in particular, Novartis chairman and CEO Daniel Vasella, whose life story was one of the most difficult of all the people we interviewed. He emerged from extreme challenges in his youth to reach the pinnacle of the global pharmaceutical industry, a trajectory that illustrates the trials many leaders have to go through on their journeys to authentic leadership.

Vasella was born in 1953 to a modest family in Fribourg, Switzerland. His early years were filled with medical problems that stoked his passion to become a physician. His first recollections were of a hospital where he was admitted at age four when he suffered from food poisoning. Falling ill with asthma at age five, he was sent alone to the mountains of eastern Switzerland for two summers. He found the four-month separations from his parents especially difficult because his caretaker had an alcohol problem and was unresponsive to his needs.

At age eight, Vasella had tuberculosis, followed by meningitis, and was sent to a sanatorium for a year. Lonely and homesick, he suffered a great deal that year, as his parents rarely visited him. He still remembers the pain and fear when the nurses held him down during the lumbar punctures so that he would not move. One day, a new physician arrived and took time to explain each step of the procedure. Vasella asked the doctor if he could hold a nurse's hand rather than being held down. "The amazing thing is that this time the procedure didn't hurt," Vasella recalls. "Afterward, the doctor asked me, 'How was that?' I reached up and gave him a big hug. These human gestures of forgiveness, caring, and compassion made a deep impression on me and on the kind of person I wanted to become."

Throughout his early years, Vasella's life continued to be unsettled. When he was 10, his 18-year-old sister passed away after suffering from cancer for two years. Three years later, his father died in surgery. To support the family, his mother went to work in a distant town and came home only once every three weeks. Left to himself, he and his friends held beer parties and got into frequent fights. This lasted for three years until he met his first girlfriend, whose affection changed his life.

At 20, Vasella entered medical school, later graduating with honors. During medical school, he sought out psychotherapy so he could come to terms with his early experiences and not feel like a victim. Through analysis, he reframed his life story and realized that he wanted to help a wider range of people than he could as an individual practitioner. Upon completion of his residency, he applied to become chief physician at the University of Zurich; however, the search committee considered him too young for the position.

Disappointed but not surprised, Vasella decided to use his abilities to increase his impact on medicine. At that time, he had a growing fascination with finance and business. He talked with the head of the pharmaceutical division of Sandoz, who offered him the opportunity to join the company's US affiliate. In his five years in the United States, Vasella flourished in the stimulating environment, first as a sales representative and later as a product manager, and advanced rapidly through the Sandoz marketing organization.

When Sandoz merged with Ciba-Geigy in 1996, Vasella was named CEO of the combined companies, now called Novartis, despite his young age and limited experience. Once in the CEO's role, Vasella blossomed as a leader. He envisioned the opportunity to build a great global health care company that could help people through lifesaving new drugs, such as Gleevec, which has proved to be highly effective for patients with chronic myeloid leukemia. Drawing on the physician role models of his youth, he built an entirely new Novartis culture centered on compassion, competence, and competition. These moves established Novartis as a giant in the industry and Vasella as a compassionate leader.

Vasella's experience is just one of dozens provided by authentic leaders who traced their inspiration directly from their life stories. Asked what empowered them to lead, these leaders consistently replied that they found their strength through transformative experiences. Those experiences enabled them to understand the deeper purpose of their leadership.

Knowing your authentic self

When the 75 members of Stanford Graduate School of Business's Advisory Council were asked to recommend the most important capability for leaders to develop, their answer was nearly unanimous: self-awareness. Yet many leaders, especially those early in their careers, are trying so hard to establish themselves in the world that they leave little time for self-exploration. They strive to achieve success in tangible ways that are recognized in the external world—money, fame, power, status, or a rising stock price. Often their drive enables them to be professionally successful for a while, but they are unable to sustain that success. As they age, they may find something is missing in their lives and realize they are holding back from being the person they want to be. Knowing their authentic selves requires the courage and honesty to open up and examine their experiences. As they do so, leaders become more humane and willing to be vulnerable.

Of all the leaders we interviewed, David Pottruck, former CEO of Charles Schwab, had one of the most persistent journeys to self-awareness. An all-league football player in high school, Pottruck became MVP of his college team at the University of Pennsylvania. After completing his MBA at Wharton and a stint with Citigroup, he joined Charles Schwab as head of marketing, moving from New York to San Francisco. An extremely hard worker, Pottruck could not understand why his new colleagues resented the long hours he put in and his aggressiveness in pushing for results. "I thought my accomplishments would speak for themselves," he said. "It never occurred to me that my level of energy would intimidate and offend other people, because in my mind I was trying to help the company."

Pottruck was shocked when his boss told him, "Dave, your colleagues do not trust you." As he recalled, "That feedback was like a dagger to my heart. I was in denial, as I didn't see myself as others saw me. I became a lightning rod for friction, but I had no idea how self-serving I looked to other people. Still, somewhere in my inner core the feedback resonated as true." Pottruck realized that he could not succeed unless he identified and overcame his blind spots.

Denial can be the greatest hurdle that leaders face in becoming self-aware. They all have egos that need to be stroked, insecurities that need to be smoothed, fears that need to be allayed. Authentic leaders realize that they have to be willing to listen to feedback— especially the kind they don't want to hear. It was only after his second divorce that Pottruck finally was able to acknowledge that he still had large blind spots: "After my second marriage fell apart, I thought I had a wife-selection problem." Then he worked with a counselor who delivered some hard truths: "The good news is you do not have a wife-selection problem; the bad news is you have a husband-behavior problem." Pottruck then made a determined effort to change. As he described it, "I was like a guy who has had three heart attacks and finally realizes he has to quit smoking and lose some weight."

These days Pottruck is happily remarried and listens carefully when his wife offers constructive feedback. He acknowledges that he falls back on his old habits at times, particularly in high-stress situations, but now he has developed ways of coping with stress. "I have had enough success in life to have that foundation of self-respect, so I can take the criticism and not deny it. I have finally learned to tolerate my failures and disappointments and not beat myself up."

Practicing your values and principles

The values that form the basis for authentic leader-ship are derived from your beliefs and convictions, but you will not know what your true values are until they are tested under pressure. It is relatively easy to list your values and to live by them when things are going well. When your success, your career, or even your life hangs in the balance, you learn what is most important, what you are prepared to sacrifice, and what trade-offs you are willing to make.

Leadership principles are values translated into ac-tion. Having a solid base of values and testing them un-der fire enables you to develop the principles you will use in leading. For example, a value such as "concern for others" might be translated into a leadership prin-ciple such as "create a work environment where peo-ple are respected for their contributions, provided job security, and allowed to fulfill their potential."

Consider Jon Huntsman, the founder and chairman of Huntsman Corporation. His moral values were deeply challenged when he worked for the Nixon administration in 1972, shortly before Watergate. After a brief stint in the US Department of Health, Education, and Welfare (HEW), he took a job under H. R. Haldeman, President Nixon's powerful chief of staff. Huntsman said he found the experience of taking orders from Haldeman "very mixed. I wasn't geared to take orders, irrespective of whether they were ethically or morally right." He explained, "We had a few clashes, as plenty of things that Haldeman wanted to do were questionable. An amoral atmosphere permeated the White House."

One day, Haldeman directed Huntsman to help him entrap a California congressman who had been opposing a White House initiative. The congressman was part owner of a plant that reportedly employed undocumented workers. To gather information to embarrass the congressman, Haldeman told Huntsman to get the plant manager of a company Huntsman owned to place some undocumented workers at the congressman's plant in an undercover operation.

"There are times when we react too quickly and fail to realize immediately what is right and wrong," Huntsman recalled. "This was one of those times when I didn't think it through. I knew instinctively it was wrong, but it took a few minutes for the notion to percolate. After 15 minutes, my inner moral compass made itself noticed and enabled me to recognize this wasn't the right thing to do. Values that had accompanied me since childhood kicked in. Halfway through my conversation with our plant manager, I said to him, 'Let's not do this. I don't want to play this game. Forget that I called.'"

Huntsman told Haldeman that he would not use his employees in this way. "Here I was saying no to the second most powerful person in the country. He didn't appreciate responses like that, as he viewed

YOUR DEVELOPMENT AS AN AUTHENTIC LEADER

As you read this article, think about the basis for your leadership development and the path you need to follow to become an authentic leader. Then ask yourself these questions:

1. *Which people and experiences in your early life had the greatest impact on you?*

2. *What tools do you use to become self-aware?* What is your authentic self? What are the moments when you say to yourself, "This is the real me"?

3. *What are your most deeply held values?* Where did they come from? Have your values changed significantly since your childhood? How do your values inform your actions?

4. *What motivates you extrinsically?* What are your intrinsic motivations? How do you balance extrinsic and intrinsic motivation in your life?

(Continued)

YOUR DEVELOPMENT AS AN AUTHENTIC LEADER

5. *What kind of support team do you have?* How can your support team make you a more authentic leader? How should you diversify your team to broaden your perspective?

6. *Is your life integrated?* Are you able to be the same person in all aspects of your life—personal, work, family, and community? If not, what is holding you back?

7. *What does being authentic mean in your life?* Are you more effective as a leader when you behave authentically? Have you ever paid a price for your authenticity as a leader? Was it worth it?

8. *What steps can you take today, tomorrow, and over the next year to develop your authentic leadership?*

them as signs of disloyalty. I might as well have been saying farewell. So be it. I left within the next six months."

Balancing your extrinsic and intrinsic motivations

Because authentic leaders need to sustain high levels of motivation and keep their lives in balance, it is critically important for them to understand what drives them. There are two types of motivations—extrinsic and intrinsic. Although they are reluctant to admit it, many leaders are propelled to achieve by measuring their success against the outside world's parameters. They enjoy the recognition and status that come with promotions and financial rewards. Intrinsic motivations, on the other hand, are derived from their sense of the meaning of their life. They are closely linked to one's life story and the way one frames it. Examples include personal growth, helping other people develop, taking on social causes, and making a difference in the world. The key is to find a balance between your desires for external validation and the intrinsic motivations that provide fulfillment in your work.

Many interviewees advised aspiring leaders to be wary of getting caught up in social, peer, or parental expectations. Debra Dunn, who has worked in Silicon Valley for decades as a Hewlett-Packard executive, acknowledged the constant pressures from external sources: "The path of accumulating material possessions is clearly laid out. You know how to measure it. If you don't pursue that path, people wonder what is wrong with you. The only way to avoid getting caught up in materialism is to understand where you find happiness and fulfillment."

Moving away from the external validation of personal achievement is not always easy. Achievement-oriented leaders grow so accustomed to successive accomplishments throughout their early years that it takes courage to pursue their intrinsic motivations. But at some point, most leaders recognize that they need to address more difficult questions in order to pursue truly meaningful success. McKinsey's Alice Woodwark, who at 29 has already achieved notable success, reflected: "My version of achievement was pretty naive, born of things I learned early in life about praise and being valued. But if you're just chasing the rabbit around the course, you're not running toward anything meaningful."

Intrinsic motivations are congruent with your values and are more fulfilling than extrinsic motivations. John Thain, CEO of the New York Stock Exchange, said, "I am motivated by doing a really good job at whatever I am doing, but I prefer to multiply my impact on society through a group of people." Or as Ann Moore, chairman and CEO of Time, put it, "I came here 25 years ago solely because I loved magazines and the publishing world." Moore had a dozen job offers after business school but took the lowest-paying one with Time because of her passion for publishing.

Building your support team

Leaders cannot succeed on their own; even the most outwardly confident executives need support and advice. Without strong relationships to provide perspective, it is very easy to lose your way.

Authentic leaders build extraordinary support teams to help them stay on course. Those teams counsel them in times of uncertainty, help them in times of difficulty, and celebrate with them in times of success. After their hardest days, leaders find comfort in being with people on whom they can rely so they can be open and vulnerable. During the low points, they cherish the friends who appreciate them for who they are, not what they are. Authentic leaders find that their support teams provide affirmation, advice, perspective, and calls for course corrections when needed.

How do you go about building your support team? Most authentic leaders have a multifaceted support structure that includes their spouses or significant others, families, mentors, close friends, and colleagues. They build their networks over time, as the experiences, shared histories, and openness with people close to them create the trust and confidence they need in times of trial and uncertainty. Leaders must give as much to their supporters as they get from them so that mutually beneficial relationships can develop.

It starts with having at least one person in your life with whom you can be completely yourself, warts and all, and still be accepted unconditionally. Often that person is the only one who can tell you the honest truth. Most leaders have their closest relationships with their spouses, although some develop these bonds with another family member, a close friend, or a trusted mentor. When leaders can rely on unconditional support, they are more likely to accept themselves for who they really are.

Many relationships grow over time through an expression of shared values and a common purpose. Randy Komisar of venture capital firm Kleiner Perkins Caufield & Byers said his marriage to Hewlett-Packard's Debra Dunn is lasting because it is rooted in similar values. "Debra and I are very independent but extremely harmonious in terms of our personal aspirations, values, and principles. We have a strong resonance around questions like, 'What is your legacy in this world?' It is important to be in sync about what we do with our lives."

Many leaders have had a mentor who changed their lives. The best mentoring interactions spark mutual learning, exploration of similar values, and shared enjoyment. If people are only looking for a leg up from their mentors, instead of being interested in their mentors' lives as well, the relationships will not last for long. It is the two-way nature of the connection that sustains it.

Personal and professional support groups can take many forms. Piper Jaffray's Tad Piper is a member of an Alcoholics Anonymous group. He noted, "These are not CEOs. They are just a group of nice, hard-working people who are trying to stay sober, lead good lives, and work with each other about being open, honest, and vulnerable. We reinforce each other's behavior by talking about our chemical dependency in a disciplined way as we go through the 12 steps. I feel blessed to be surrounded by people who are thinking about those kinds of issues and actually doing something, not just talking about them."

Bill George's experiences echo Piper's: In 1974, he joined a men's group that formed after a weekend retreat. More than 30 years later, the group is still meeting every Wednesday morning. After an opening period of catching up on each other's lives and dealing with any particular difficulty someone may be facing, one of the group's eight members leads a discussion on a topic he has selected. These discussions are open, probing, and often profound. The key to their success is that people say what they really believe without fear of judgment, criticism, or reprisal. All the members consider the group to be one of the most important aspects of their lives, enabling them to clarify their beliefs, values, and understanding of vital issues, as well as serving as a source of honest feedback when they need it most.

Integrating your life by staying grounded

Integrating their lives is one of the greatest challenges leaders face. To lead a balanced life, you need to bring together all of its constituent elements—work, family, community, and friends—so that you can be the same person in each environment. Think of your life as a house, with a bedroom for your personal life, a study for your professional life, a family room for your family, and a living room to share with your friends. Can you knock down the walls between these rooms and be the same person in each of them?

As John Donahoe, president of eBay Marketplaces and former worldwide managing director of Bain, stressed, being authentic means maintaining a sense of self no matter where you are. He warned, "The world can shape you if you let it. To have a sense of yourself as you live, you must make conscious choices. Sometimes the choices are really hard, and you make a lot of mistakes."

Authentic leaders have a steady and confident presence. They do not show up as one person one day and another person the next. Integration takes discipline, particularly during stressful times when it is easy to become reactive and slip back into bad habits. Donahoe feels strongly that integrating his life has enabled him to become a more effective leader. "There is no nirvana," he said. "The struggle is constant, as the trade-offs don't get any easier as you get older." But for authentic leaders, personal and professional lives are not a zero-sum game. As Donahoe said, "I have no doubt today that my children have made me a far more effective leader in the workplace. Having a strong personal life has made the difference." Leading is high-stress work. There is no way to avoid stress when you are responsible for people, organizations, outcomes, and managing the constant uncertainties of the environment. The higher you go, the greater your freedom to control your destiny but also the higher the degree of stress. The question is not whether you can avoid stress but how you can control it to maintain your own sense of equilibrium.

Authentic leaders are constantly aware of the importance of staying grounded. Besides spending time with their families and close friends, authentic leaders get physical exercise, engage in spiritual practices, do community service, and return to the places where they grew up. All are essential to their effectiveness as leaders, enabling them to sustain their authenticity.

Empowering people to lead

Now that we have discussed the process of discovering your authentic leadership, let's look at how authentic leaders empower people in their organizations to achieve superior long-term results, which is the bottom line for all leaders.

Authentic leaders recognize that leadership is not about their success or about getting loyal subordinates to follow them. They know the key to a successful organization is having empowered leaders at all levels, including those who have no direct reports. They not only inspire those around them, they empower those individuals to step up and lead.

A reputation for building relationships and empowering people was instrumental in chairman and

CEO Anne Mulcahy's stunning turnaround of Xerox. When Mulcahy was asked to take the company's reins from her failed predecessor, Xerox had $18 billion in debt, and all credit lines were exhausted. With the share price in free fall, morale was at an all-time low. To make matters worse, the SEC was investigating the company's revenue recognition practices.

Mulcahy's appointment came as a surprise to everyone—including Mulcahy herself. A Xerox veteran, she had worked in field sales and on the corporate staff for 25 years, but not in finance, R&D, or manufacturing. How could Mulcahy cope with this crisis when she had had no financial experience? She brought to the CEO role the relationships she had built over 25 years, an impeccable understanding of the organization, and, above all, her credibility as an authentic leader. She bled for Xerox, and everyone knew it. Because of that, they were willing to go the extra mile for her.

After her appointment, Mulcahy met personally with the company's top 100 executives to ask them if they would stay with the company despite the challenges ahead. "I knew there were people who weren't supportive of me," she said. "So I confronted a couple of them and said, 'This is about the company.'"

The first two people Mulcahy talked with, both of whom ran big operating units, decided to leave, but the remaining 98 committed to stay. Throughout the crisis, people in Xerox were empowered by Mulcahy to step up and lead in order to restore the company to its former greatness. In the end, her leadership enabled Xerox to avoid bankruptcy as she paid back $10 billion in debt and restored revenue growth and profitability with a combination of cost savings and innovative new products. The stock price tripled as a result.

———————

Like Mulcahy, all leaders have to deliver bottom-line results. By creating a virtuous circle in which the results reinforce the effectiveness of their leadership, authentic leaders are able to sustain those results through good times and bad. Their success enables them to attract talented people and align employees' activities with shared goals, as they empower others on their team to lead by taking on greater challenges. Indeed, superior results over a sustained period of time is the ultimate mark of an authentic leader. It may be possible to drive short-term outcomes without being authentic, but authentic leadership is the only way we know to create sustainable long-term results.

For authentic leaders, there are special rewards. No individual achievement can equal the pleasure of leading a group of people to achieve a worthy goal. When you cross the finish line together, all the pain and suffering you may have experienced quickly vanishes. It is replaced by a deep inner satisfaction that you have empowered others and thus made the world a better place. That's the challenge and the fulfillment of authentic leadership.

BILL GEORGE is a professor of management practice at Harvard Business School and the former chair and CEO of Medtronic. PETER SIMS is a management writer and entrepreneur. He is the author of *Little Bets: How Breakthrough Ideas Emerge from Small Discoveries*. He is also the founder of the BLK SHP. ANDREW N. MCLEAN is a research associate at Harvard Business School. DIANA MAYER is a former Citigroup executive in New York. This article was adapted from *True North: Discover Your Authentic Leadership* by Bill George with Peter Sims.

Reprinted from *Harvard Business Review*,
February 2007 (product #R0702H).

2

The Authenticity Paradox

By Herminia Ibarra

Authenticity has become the gold standard for leadership. But a simplistic understanding of what it means can hinder your growth and limit your impact.

Consider Cynthia, a general manager in a health care organization. Her promotion into that role increased her direct reports tenfold and expanded the range of businesses she oversaw—and she felt a little shaky about making such a big leap. A strong believer in transparent, collaborative leadership, she bared her soul to her new employees: "I want to do this job," she said, "but it's scary, and I need your help." Her candor backfired; she lost credibility with people who wanted and needed a confident leader to take charge.

Or take George, a Malaysian executive in an auto parts company where people valued a clear chain of command and made decisions by consensus. When a Dutch multinational with a matrix structure acquired the company, George found himself working with peers who saw decision making as a freewheeling contest for the best-debated ideas. That style didn't come easily to him, and it contradicted everything he had learned about humility growing up in his country. In a 360-degree debrief, his boss told him that he needed to sell his ideas and accomplishments more aggressively. George felt he had to choose between being a failure and being a fake.

Because going against our natural inclinations can make us feel like impostors, we tend to latch on to authenticity as an excuse for sticking with what's comfortable. But few jobs allow us to do that for long. That's doubly true when we advance in our careers or when demands or expectations change, as Cynthia, George, and countless other executives have discovered.

In my research on leadership transitions, I have observed that career advances require all of us to move way beyond our comfort zones. At the same time, however, they trigger a strong countervailing impulse to protect our identities: When we are unsure of ourselves or our ability to perform well or measure up in a new setting, we often retreat to familiar behaviors and styles.

But my research also demonstrates that the moments that most challenge our sense of self are the ones that can teach us the most about leading effectively. By viewing ourselves as works in progress and evolving our professional identities through trial and error, we can develop a personal style that feels right to us and suits our organizations' changing needs.

That takes courage, because learning, by definition, starts with unnatural and often superficial behaviors that can make us feel calculating instead of genuine and spontaneous. But the only way to avoid being pigeonholed and ultimately become better leaders is to do the things that a rigidly authentic sense of self would keep us from doing.

Why leaders struggle with authenticity

The word "authentic" traditionally referred to any work of art that is an original, not a copy. When used to describe leadership, of course, it has other meanings—and they can be problematic. For example, the notion of adhering to one "true self" flies in the face of much research on how people evolve with experience, discovering facets of themselves they would never have unearthed through introspection alone. And being utterly transparent—disclosing every single thought and feeling—is both unrealistic and risky. (See figure 1, "What is authenticity?")

FIGURE 1

What is authenticity?

A too-rigid definition of authenticity can get in the way of effective leadership. Here are three examples and the problems they pose.

Being true to yourself.
Which self? We have many selves, depending on the different roles that we play in life. We evolve and even transform ourselves with experience in new roles. How can you be true to a future self that is still uncertain and unformed?

Maintaining strict coherence between what you feel and what you say or do.
You lose credibility and effectiveness as a leader if you disclose everything you think and feel, especially when you are unproven.

Making values-based choices.
When we move into bigger roles, values that were shaped by past experiences can lead us astray. For instance, "tight control over operating details" might produce authentic but wrong-headed behavior in the face of new challenges.

Leaders today struggle with authenticity for several reasons. First, we make more-frequent and more-radical changes in the kinds of work we do. As we strive to *improve* our game, a clear and firm sense of self is a compass that helps us navigate choices and progress toward our goals. But when we're looking to *change* our game, a too-rigid self-concept becomes an anchor that keeps us from sailing forth, as it did at first with Cynthia.

Second, in global business, many of us work with people who don't share our cultural norms and have different expectations for how we should behave. It can often seem as if we have to choose between what is expected—and therefore effective—and what feels authentic. George is a case in point.

Third, identities are always on display in today's world of ubiquitous connectivity and social media. How we present ourselves—not just as executives but as people, with quirks and broader interests—has become an important aspect of leadership. Having to carefully curate a persona that's out there for all to see can clash with our private sense of self.

In dozens of interviews with talented executives facing new expectations, I have found that they most often grapple with authenticity in the following situations.

Taking charge in an unfamiliar role

As everyone knows, the first 90 days are critical in a new leadership role. First impressions form quickly, and they matter. Depending on their personalities, leaders respond very differently to the increased visibility and performance pressure.

Psychologist Mark Snyder, of the University of Minnesota, identified two psychological profiles that inform how leaders develop their personal styles. "High self-monitors"—or chameleons, as I call them— are naturally able and willing to adapt to the demands of a situation without feeling fake. Chameleons care about managing their public image and often mask their vulnerability with bluster. They may not always get it right the first time, but they keep trying on different styles like new clothes until they find a good fit for themselves and their circumstances. Because of that flexibility, they often advance rapidly. But chameleons can run into problems when people perceive them as disingenuous or lacking a moral center— even though they're expressing their "true" chameleon nature.

By contrast, "true-to-selfers" (Snyder's "low self-monitors") tend to express what they really think and feel, even when it runs counter to situational demands. The danger with true-to-selfers like Cynthia and George is that they may stick too long with comfortable behavior that prevents them from meeting new requirements, instead of evolving their style as they gain insight and experience.

Cynthia (whom I interviewed after her story appeared in a *Wall Street Journal* article by Carol Hymowitz) hemmed herself in like this. She thought she was setting herself up for success by staying true to her highly personal, full-disclosure style of management. She asked her new team for support, openly acknowledging that she felt a bit at sea. As she scrambled to learn unfamiliar aspects of the business, she worked tirelessly to contribute to every decision and solve every problem. After a few months, she was on the verge of burnout. To make matters worse, sharing her vulnerability with her team members so early on had damaged her standing. Reflecting on her transition some years later, Cynthia told me: "Being authentic doesn't mean that you can be held up to the light and people can see right through you." But at the time, that was how she saw it—and instead of building trust, she made people question her ability to do the job.

Delegating and communicating appropriately are only part of the problem in a case like this. A deeper-seated issue is finding the right mix of distance and closeness in an unfamiliar situation. Stanford psychologist Deborah Gruenfeld describes this as managing the tension between authority and approachability. To be authoritative, you privilege your knowledge, experience, and expertise over the team's, maintaining a measure of distance. To be approachable, you emphasize your relationships with people, their input, and their perspective, and you lead with empathy and warmth. Getting the balance right presents an acute authenticity crisis for true-to-selfers, who typically have a strong preference for behaving one way or the other. Cynthia made herself too approachable and vulnerable, and it undermined and drained her. In her bigger role, she needed more distance from her employees to gain their confidence and get the job done.

Selling your ideas (and yourself)

Leadership growth usually involves a shift from having good ideas to pitching them to diverse stakeholders. Inexperienced leaders, especially true-to-selfers, often find the process of getting buy-in distasteful because it feels artificial and political; they believe that their work should stand on its own merits.

Here's an example: Anne, a senior manager at a transportation company, had doubled revenue and fundamentally redesigned core processes in her unit. Despite her obvious accomplishments, however, her boss didn't consider her an inspirational leader. Anne also knew she was not communicating effectively in her role as a board member of the parent company. The chairman, a broad-brush thinker, often became impatient with her detail orientation. His feedback to her was "step up, do the vision thing." But to Anne that seemed like valuing form over substance. "For me, it is manipulation," she told me in an interview. "I can do the storytelling too, but I refuse to play on people's emotions. If the string-pulling is too obvious, I can't make myself do it." Like many aspiring leaders, she resisted crafting emotional messages to influence and inspire others because that felt less authentic to her than relying on facts, figures, and spreadsheets. As a result, she worked at cross-purposes with the board chairman, pushing hard on the facts instead of pulling him in as a valued ally.

Many managers know deep down that their good ideas and strong potential will go unnoticed if they don't do a better job of selling themselves. Still, they can't bring themselves to do it. "I try to build a network based on professionalism and what I can deliver for the business, not who I know," one manager told me. "Maybe that's not smart from a career point of view. But I can't go against my beliefs . . . So I have been more limited in 'networking up.'"

Until we see career advancement as a way of extending our reach and increasing our impact in the organization—a collective win, not just a selfish pursuit—we have trouble feeling authentic when touting our strengths to influential people. True-to-selfers find it particularly hard to sell themselves to senior management when they most need to do so: when they are still unproven. Research shows, however, that this hesitancy disappears as people gain experience and become more certain of the value they bring.

Processing negative feedback

Many successful executives encounter serious negative feedback for the first time in their careers when they take on larger roles or responsibilities. Even when the criticisms aren't exactly new, they loom larger because the stakes are higher. But leaders often convince themselves that dysfunctional aspects of their "natural" style are the inevitable price of being effective.

Let's look at Jacob, a food company production manager whose direct reports gave him low marks in a 360 review on emotional intelligence, team building, and empowering others. One team member wrote that it was hard for Jacob to accept criticism.

Another remarked that after an angry outburst, he'd suddenly make a joke as if nothing had happened, not realizing the destabilizing effect of his mood changes on those around him. For someone who genuinely believed that he'd built trust among his people, all this was tough to swallow.

Once the initial shock had subsided, Jacob acknowledged that this was not the first time he'd received such criticism (some colleagues and subordinates had made similar comments a few years earlier). "I thought I'd changed my approach," he reflected, "but I haven't really changed so much since the last time." However, he quickly rationalized his behavior to his boss: "Sometimes you have to be tough in order to deliver results, and people don't like it," he said. "You have to accept that as part of the job description." Of course, he was missing the point. Because negative feedback given to leaders often centers on style rather than skills or expertise, it can feel like a threat to their identity—as if they're being

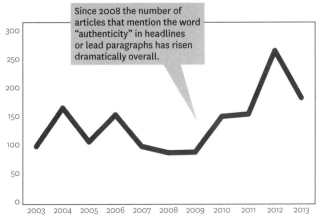

WHY COMPANIES ARE PUSHING AUTHENTICITY TRAINING

Since 2008 the number of articles that mention the word "authenticity" in headlines or lead paragraphs has risen dramatically overall.

Source: *New York Times, Financial Times, Washington Post, Economic Post, Forbes, Wall Street Journal,* and HBR

Managers can choose from countless books, articles, and executive workshops for advice on how to be more authentic at work. Two trends help explain the exploding popularity of the concept and the training industry it has fed.

(Continued)

WHY COMPANIES ARE PUSHING AUTHENTICITY TRAINING

First, trust in business leaders fell to an all-time low in 2012, according to the Edelman Trust Barometer. Even in 2013, when trust began to climb back up, only 18% of people reported that they trusted business leaders to tell the truth, and fewer than half trusted businesses to do the right thing.

Second, employee engagement is at a nadir. A 2013 Gallup poll found that only 13% of employees worldwide are engaged at work. Only one in eight workers—out of roughly 180 million employees studied—is psychologically committed to his or her job. In study after study, frustration, burnout, disillusionment, and misalignment with personal values are cited among the biggest reasons for career change.

At a time when public confidence and employee morale are so low, it's no surprise that companies are encouraging leaders to discover their "true" selves.

asked to give up their "secret sauce." That's how Jacob saw it. Yes, he could be explosive—but from his point of view, his "toughness" allowed him to deliver results year after year. In reality, though, he had succeeded up to this point *despite* his behavior. When his role expanded and he took on greater responsibility, his intense scrutiny of subordinates became an even bigger obstacle because it took up time he should have been devoting to more-strategic pursuits.

A great public example of this phenomenon is Margaret Thatcher. Those who worked with her knew she could be merciless if someone failed to prepare as thoroughly as she did. She was capable of humiliating a staff member in public, she was a notoriously bad listener, and she believed that compromise was cowardice. As she became known to the world as the "Iron Lady," Thatcher grew more and more convinced of the rightness of her ideas and the necessity of her coercive methods. She could beat anyone into submission with the power of her rhetoric and conviction, and she only got better at it. Eventually, though, it was her undoing—she was ousted by her own cabinet.

A playful frame of mind

Such a rigid self-concept can result from too much introspection. When we look only within for answers, we inadvertently reinforce old ways of seeing the world and outdated views of ourselves. Without the benefit of what I call outsight—the valuable external perspective we get from experimenting with new leadership behaviors—habitual patterns of thought and action fence us in. To begin thinking like leaders, we must first act: plunge ourselves into new projects and activities, interact with very different kinds of people, and experiment with new ways of getting things done. Especially in times of transition and uncertainty, thinking and introspection should follow experience—not vice versa. Action changes who we are and what we believe is worth doing.

Fortunately, there are ways of increasing outsight and evolving toward an "adaptively authentic" way of leading, but they require a playful frame of mind. Think of leadership development as trying on possible selves rather than working on yourself—which, let's face it, sounds like drudgery. When we adopt a playful attitude, we're more open to possibilities. It's OK to be inconsistent from one day to the next. That's not being a fake; it's how we experiment to figure out what's right for the new challenges and circumstances we face.

My research suggests three important ways to get started.

Learn from diverse role models

Most learning necessarily involves some form of imitation—and the understanding that nothing is "original." An important part of growing as a leader is viewing authenticity not as an intrinsic state but as the ability to take elements you have learned from others' styles and behaviors and make them your own.

But don't copy just one person's leadership style; tap many diverse role models. There is a big difference between imitating someone wholesale and borrowing selectively from various people to create your own collage, which you then modify and improve. As the playwright Wilson Mizner said, copying one author is plagiarism, but copying many is research.

I observed the importance of this approach in a study of investment bankers and consultants who were advancing from analytical and project work to roles advising clients and selling new business. Though most of them felt incompetent and insecure in their new positions, the chameleons among them consciously borrowed styles and tactics from successful senior leaders—learning through emulation how to use humor to break tension in meetings, for instance, and how to shape opinion without being overbearing. Essentially, the chameleons faked it until they found what worked for them. Noticing their efforts, their managers provided coaching and mentoring and shared tacit knowledge.

As a result, the chameleons arrived much faster at an authentic but more skillful style than the true-to-selfers in the study, who continued to focus solely on demonstrating technical mastery. Often the true-to-selfers concluded that their managers were "all talk and little content" and therefore not suitable role models. In the absence of a "perfect" model they had a harder time with imitation—it felt bogus. Unfortunately, their managers perceived their inability to adapt as a lack of effort or investment and thus didn't give them as much mentoring and coaching as they gave the chameleons.

Work on getting better

Setting goals for learning (not just for performance) helps us experiment with our identities without feeling like impostors, because we don't expect to get everything right from the start. We stop trying to protect our comfortable old selves from the threats that change can bring and start exploring what kinds of leaders we might become.

Of course, we all want to perform well in a new situation—get the right strategy in place, execute like crazy, deliver results the organization cares about. But focusing exclusively on those things makes us afraid to take risks in the service of learning. In a series of ingenious experiments, Stanford psychologist Carol Dweck has shown that concern about how we will appear to others inhibits learning on new or unfamiliar tasks. Performance goals motivate us to show others that we possess valued attributes, such as intelligence and social skill, and to prove to ourselves that we

THE CULTURAL FACTOR

Whatever the situation—taking charge in unfamiliar territory, selling your ideas and yourself, or processing negative feedback—finding authentic ways of being effective is even more difficult in a multicultural environment.

As my INSEAD colleague Erin Meyer finds in her research, styles of persuading others and the kinds of arguments that people find persuasive are far from universal; they are deeply rooted in a culture's philosophical, religious, and educational assumptions. That said, prescriptions for how leaders are supposed to look and sound are rarely as diverse as the leaders themselves. And despite corporate initiatives to build understanding of cultural differences and promote diversity, the fact is that leaders are still expected to express ideas assertively, to claim credit for them, and to use charisma to motivate and inspire people.

(Continued)

THE CULTURAL FACTOR

Authenticity is supposed to be an antidote to a single model of leadership. (After all, the message is to be yourself, not what someone else expects you to be.) But as the notion has gained currency, it has, ironically, come to mean something much more limiting and culturally specific. A closer look at how leaders are taught to discover and demonstrate authenticity—by telling a personal story about a hardship they have overcome, for example—reveals a model that is, in fact, very American, based on ideals such as self-disclosure, humility, and individualistic triumph over adversity.

This amounts to a catch-22 for managers from cultures with different norms for authority, communication, and collective endeavor because they must behave inauthentically in order to conform to the strictures of "authentic" leadership.

have them. By contrast, learning goals motivate us to develop valued attributes.

When we're in performance mode, leadership is about presenting ourselves in the most favorable light. In learning mode, we can reconcile our yearning for authenticity in how we work and lead with an equally powerful desire to grow. One leader I met was highly effective in small-group settings but struggled to convey openness to new ideas in larger meetings, where he often stuck to long-winded presentations for fear of getting derailed by others' comments. He set himself a "no PowerPoint" rule to develop a more relaxed, improvisational style. He surprised himself by how much he learned, not only about his own evolving preferences but also about the issues at hand.

Don't stick to "your story"

Most of us have personal narratives about defining moments that taught us important lessons. Consciously or not, we allow our stories, and the images of ourselves that they paint, to guide us in new situations. But the stories can become outdated as we grow, so sometimes it's necessary to alter them dramatically or even to throw them out and start from scratch.

That was true for Maria, a leader who saw herself as a "mother hen with her chicks all around." Her coach, former Ogilvy & Mather CEO Charlotte Beers, explains in *I'd Rather Be in Charge* that this self-image emerged from a time when Maria had to sacrifice her own goals and dreams to take care of her extended family. It eventually began to hold her back in her career: Though it had worked for her as a friendly and loyal team player and a peacekeeper, it wasn't helping her get the big leadership assignment she wanted. Together Maria and her coach looked for another defining moment to use as a touchstone— one that was more in keeping with Maria's desired future self, not who she had been in the past. They chose the time when Maria, as a young woman, had left her family to travel the world for 18 months. Acting from that bolder sense of self, she asked for—and got—a promotion that had previously been elusive.

Dan McAdams, a Northwestern psychology professor who has spent his career studying life stories, describes identity as "the internalized and evolving story that results from a person's selective appropriation of past, present, and future." This isn't just academic jargon. McAdams is saying that you have to believe your story—but also embrace how it changes over time, according to what you need it to do. Try out new stories about yourself, and keep editing them, much as you would your résumé.

Again, revising one's story is both an introspective and a social process. The narratives we choose should not only sum up our experiences and aspirations but also reflect the demands we face and resonate with the audience we're trying to win over.

Countless books and advisers tell you to start your leadership journey with a clear sense of who you are. But that can be a recipe for staying stuck in the past. Your leadership identity can and should change each time you move on to bigger and better things.

The only way we grow as leaders is by stretching the limits of who we are—doing new things that make us uncomfortable but that teach us through direct experience who we want to become. Such growth doesn't require a radical personality make-over. Small changes—in the way we carry ourselves, the way we communicate, the way we interact—often make a world of difference in how effectively we lead.

HERMINIA IBARRA is a professor of organizational behavior and the Cora Chaired Professor of Leadership and Learning at INSEAD. She is the author of *Act Like a Leader, Think Like a Leader* (Harvard Business Review Press, 2015) and *Working Identity: Unconventional Strategies for Reinventing*

Your Career (Harvard Business School Press, 2003). Follow her on Twitter @HerminiaIbarra and visit her website www.herminiaibarra.com.

Reprinted from *Harvard Business Review*, January–February 2015 (product #R1501C).

3

What Bosses Gain by Being Vulnerable

By Emma Seppala

One morning in Bangalore, South India, Archana Patchirajan, founder of a technology startup, called her entire staff in for a meeting. When everyone was seated, she announced that she had to let them go because the startup had run out of funds. She could no longer pay them. Shockingly, her staff of high-caliber engineers who had their pick of jobs in the booming Silicon Valley of India, refused to go. They said they would rather work for half their pay than leave her. They stayed and kept working so hard that, a few years later, Patchirajan's company—Hubbl, which provides internet advertising solutions—sold for $14 million.

Patchirajan continues to work on startups from the United States, and her staff, though thousands of miles away from her, continues to work for her.

What explains the connection and devotion that Patchirajan's staff had toward her?

Patchirajan's story is particularly extraordinary when you consider the alarming fact that according to a Gallup study, 70% of employees are "not engaged" or are "actively disengaged" at work.[1] As a consequence, they are "less emotionally connected" and also "less likely to be productive." What is it about Patchirajan that not only prevented this phenomenon in her staff but actually flipped it?

When I asked one of Patchirajan's longest-standing employees what drove him and the rest of the team to stay with her, these are some of the things he shared: "We all work as a family because she treats us as such." "She knows everyone in the office and has a personal relationship with each one of us." "She does not get upset when we make mistakes but gives us the time to learn how to analyze and fix the situation."

If you look at these comments, they suggest that Patchirajan's relationship with her employees runs deeper than that of the usual employer-employee relationship. Simply put, she is vulnerable and authentic with them. She shared her doubts honestly when the company was going downhill, she does not adhere to a strict hierarchy but treats her employees like family members, and she has a personal relationship with each one of them. Sound touchy-feely, daunting, or counterintuitive? Here's why it's not.

Brené Brown, an expert on social connection, conducted thousands of interviews to discover what lies at the root of social connections. A thorough analysis of the data revealed what it was: vulnerability. Vulnerability here does not mean being weak or submissive. To the contrary, it implies the courage to be oneself. It means replacing "professional distance and cool" with uncertainty, risk, and emotional exposure. Opportunities for vulnerability present themselves to us at work every day. Some examples Patchirajan gives of vulnerability include calling an employee or colleague whose child is not well, reaching out to someone who has just had a loss in their family, asking someone for help, taking responsibility for something that went wrong at work, or sitting by the bedside of a colleague or employee with a terminal illness.

More important, Brown describes vulnerability and authenticity as being at the root of human connection. And human connection is often dramatically absent from workplaces. Johann Berlin, CEO of Transformational Leadership for Excellence (TLEX), recounts an experience he had while teaching a workshop at a *Fortune* 100 company. The participants were all higher-level management. After an exercise in which pairs of participants shared an event from their life with each other, one of the top executive managers approached Berlin. Visibly moved by the experience, he said "I've worked with my colleague for more than 25 years and have never known about the difficult times in his life." In a short moment of authentic connection, this manager's understanding and connection with his colleague deepened in ways that hadn't happened in decades of working together.

Why is human connection missing at work? As leaders and employees, we are often taught to keep a distance and project a certain image—one of confidence, competence, and authority. We may disclose our vulnerability to a spouse or close friend behind closed doors at night, but we would never show it elsewhere during the day, let alone at work.

However, data suggests that we may want to revisit the idea of projecting an image. Research shows that people subconsciously register a lack of authenticity in others. Just by looking at someone, we download large amounts of information. "We are programmed to observe each other's states so we can more appropriately interact, empathize, or assert our boundaries—whatever the situation may require," says Paula Niedenthal, professor of psychology at the University of Wisconsin–Madison. We are wired to read each others' expressions in a very nuanced way. This process is called "resonance," and it is so automatic and rapid that it often happens below our awareness.

Like an acute sounding board, parts of our brain internally echo what others do and feel. Just by looking at someone, you experience them: You internally resonate with them. Ever seen someone trip and momentarily felt a twinge of pain for them? Observing them activates the "pain matrix" in your brain, research shows.[2] Ever been moved by the sight of a person helping someone? You vicariously experienced it and thereby felt elevation. Someone's smile activates the smile muscles in our face, while a frown activates our frown muscles, according to research by Ulf Dimberg at Uppsala University in Sweden.[3] We internally register what another person is feeling. As a consequence, if a smile is fake, we are more likely to feel uncomfortable than comfortable.

While we may try to appear perfect, strong, or intelligent to be respected by others, pretense often has the opposite effect intended. Paula Niedenthal's research shows that we resonate too deeply with one another to ignore inauthenticity.[4] Just think of how uncomfortable you feel around someone you perceive as "taking on airs" or "putting on a show." We tend to see right through them and feel less connected. Or think of how you respond when you know someone is upset, but they're trying to conceal it. "What's wrong?" you ask, only to be told, "Nothing!" Rarely does this answer satisfy—because we sense it's not true.

Our brains are wired to read cues so subtle that even when we don't consciously register the cues, our bodies respond. For example, when someone is angry but keeps their feelings bottled up, we may not realize that they are angry (they don't *look* angry) but still our blood pressure will increase, according to research by James Gross at Stanford University.[5]

Why do we feel more comfortable around someone who is authentic and vulnerable? Because we are particularly sensitive to signs of trustworthiness in our leaders.[6] Servant leadership, for example, which is characterized by authenticity and values-based leadership, yields more positive and constructive behavior in employees and greater feelings of hope and trust in both the leader and the organization.[7] In turn, trust in a leader improves employee performance.[8] You can even see this at the level of the brain. Employees who recall a boss who resonated with them show enhanced activation in parts of the brain related to positive emotion and social connection.[9] The reverse is true when they think of a boss who did not resonate.

One example of authenticity and vulnerability is forgiveness. Forgiveness doesn't mean tolerance of error but rather a patient encouragement of growth.

Forgiveness is what Archana Patchirajan's employee described as, "She does not get upset when we make mistakes but gives us the time to learn how to analyze and fix the situation." Forgiveness may be another soft-sounding term but, as University of Michigan researcher Kim Cameron points out in the book *Positive Organizational Behavior*, it has hard results: A culture of forgiveness in organizations can lead to increased employee productivity as well as less voluntary turnover.[10] Again, a culture that is forgiving breeds trust. As a consequence, an organization becomes more resilient in times of organizational stress or downsizing.

Why do we fear vulnerability or think it's inappropriate for the workplace? For one, we are afraid that if someone finds out who we really are or discovers a soft or vulnerable spot, they will take advantage of us. However, as I describe in my hbr.org article, "The Hard Data on Being a Nice Boss," kindness goes further than the old sink-or-swim paradigm.

Here's what may happen if you embrace an authentic and vulnerable stance: Your staff will see you as a human being; they may feel closer to you, they may be prompted to share advice, and—if you are attached to hierarchy—you may find that your team begins to feel more horizontal. While these types of changes might feel uncomfortable, you may see, as in Patchirajan's case, that the benefits are worth it.

There are additional benefits you may reap from a closer connection to employees, too. One study out of Stanford shows that CEOs are looking for more advice and counsel but that two thirds of them don't get it.[11] This isolation can skew perspectives and lead to potentially disadvantageous leadership choices. Who better to receive advice from than your own employees, who are intimately familiar with your product, your customers, and problems that might exist within the organization?

Rather than feeling like another peg in the system, your team members will feel respected and honored for their opinions and will consequently become more loyal. The research shows that the personal connection and happiness employees derive from their work fosters greater loyalty than the amount on their paycheck.[12]

EMMA SEPPALA, PH.D., is the science director of Stanford University's Center for Compassion and Altruism Research and Education and author of *The Happiness Track*. She is also founder of Fulfillment Daily. Follow her on Twitter @emmaseppala or her website www.emmaseppala.com.

Notes

1. "Report: State of the American Workplace," Gallup poll, September 22, 2014, http://www.gallup.com/services/176708/state-american-workplace.aspx.
2. C. Lamm et al., "What Are You Feeling? Using Functional Magnetic Resonance Imaging to Assess the Modulation of Sensory and Affective Responses During Empathy for Pain," *PLOS One* 2, no. 12 (2007): e1292.
3. U. Dimberg, M. Thunberg, K. Elmehed, "Unconscious Facial Reactions to Emotional Facial Expressions," *Psychological Science* 11, no. 1 (2000): 86–89.

4. S. Korb et al., "The Perception and Mimicry of Facial Movements Predict Judgments of Smile Authenticity," *PLOS One* 9, no. 6 (2014): e99194.

5. J. Gross and R. Levenson, "Emotional Suppression: Physiology, Self-Report, and Expressive Behavior," *Journal of Personality and Social Psychology* 64, no. 6 (1993): 970–986.

6. K. Dirks and D. Ferrin, "Trust in Leadership: Meta-Analytic Findings and Implications for Research and Practice," *Journal of Applied Psychology* 87, no. 4 (2002): 611–628.

7. E. Joseph and B. Winston, "A Correlation of Servant Leadership, Leader Trust, and Organizational Trust," *Leadership & Organization Development Journal* 26, no. 1 (2005): 6–22; T. Searle and J. Barbuto, "Servant Leadership, Hope, and Organizational Virtuousness: A Framework Exploring Positive Micro and Macro Behaviors and Performance Impact," *Journal of Leadership & Organizational Studies* 18, no. 1 (2011): 107–117.

8. T. Bartram and G. Casimir, "The Relationship Between Leadership and Follower In-Role Performance and Satisfaction with the Leader: The Mediating Effects of Empowerment and Trust in the Leader," *Leadership & Organization Development Journal* 28, no. 1 (2007): 4–19.

9. R. Boyatzis et al., "Examination of the Neural Substrates Activated in Memories of Experiences with Resonant and Dissonant Leaders," *The Leadership Quarterly* 23, no. 2 (2012): 259–272.

10. K. Cameron, "Forgiveness in Organizations," *Positive Organizational Behavior*, ed. D. L. Nelson and C. L. Cooper (London: Sage Publications, 2007), 129–142.

11. Stanford GSB staff, "David Larcker: 'Lonely at the Top' Resonates for Most CEOs," *Insights* by Stanford Graduate School of Business, July 31, 2013, https://www.gsb.stanford.edu/insights/david-larcker-lonely-top-resonates-most-ceos.

12. The Association of Accounting Technicians, "Britain's Workers Value Companionship and Recognition Over a Big Salary, a Recent Report Revealed," July 15, 2014, https://www.aat.org.uk/about-aat/press-releases/britains-workers-value-companionship-recognition-over-big-salary.

Adapted from content posted on hbr.org, December 11, 2014 (product #H01R7U).

4

Practice Tough Empathy

By Rob Goffee and Gareth Jones

There's altogether too much hype nowadays about the idea that leaders *must* show concern for their teams. There's nothing worse than seeing a manager return from the latest interpersonal-skills training program with "concern" for others. Real leaders don't need a training program to convince their employees that they care. Real leaders empathize fiercely with the people they lead. They also care intensely about the work their employees do.

Consider Alain Levy, the former CEO of Polygram. Although he often comes across as a rather aloof intellectual, Levy is well able to close the distance between himself and his followers. On one occasion, he helped some junior record executives in Australia choose singles off albums. Picking singles is a critical task in the music business: The selection of a song can make or break the album. Levy sat down with the young people and took on the work with passion. "You bloody idiots," he added his voice to the melee, "you don't know what the hell you're talking about; we always have a dance track first!" Within 24 hours, the story spread throughout the company; it was the best PR Levy ever got. "Levy really knows how to pick singles," people said. In fact, he knew how to identify with the work, and he knew how to enter his followers' world—one where strong, colorful language is the norm—to show them that he cared.

Clearly, as the above example illustrates, we do not believe that the empathy of inspirational leaders is the soft kind described in so much of the management literature. On the contrary, we feel that real leaders manage through a unique approach we call tough empathy. Tough empathy means giving people what they need, not what they want. Organizations like the Marine Corps and consulting firms specialize in tough empathy. Recruits are pushed to be the best that they can be; "grow or go" is the motto. Chris Satterwaite, the CEO of Bell Pottinger Communications and a former chief executive of several ad agencies, understands what tough empathy is all about. He adeptly handles the challenges of managing creative people while making tough decisions. "If I have to, I can be ruthless," he says. "But while they're with me, I promise my people that they'll learn."

At its best, tough empathy balances respect for the individual and for the task at hand. Attending to both, however, isn't easy, especially when the business is in survival mode. At such times, caring leaders have to give selflessly to the people around them and know when to pull back. Consider a situation at Unilever at a time when it was developing Persil Power, a detergent that eventually had to be removed from the market because it destroyed clothes that were laundered in it. Even though the product was showing early signs of trouble, CEO Niall FitzGerald stood by his troops. "That was the popular place to be, but I should not have been there," he says now. "I should have stood back, cool and detached, looked at the whole field, watched out for the customer." But caring with detachment is not easy, especially since, when done right, tough empathy is harder on you than on your employees. "Some theories of leadership make caring look effortless. It isn't," says Paulanne Mancuso, president and CEO of Calvin Klein Cosmetics. "You have to do things you don't want to do, and that's hard." It's tough to be tough.

Tough empathy also has the benefit of impelling leaders to take risks. When Greg Dyke took over at the BBC, his commercial competitors were able to spend substantially more on programs than the BBC could. Dyke quickly realized that in order to thrive in a digital world, the BBC needed to increase its expenditures. He explained this openly and directly to the staff. Once he had secured their buy-in, he began thoroughly restructuring the organization. Although many employees were let go, he was able to maintain people's commitment. Dyke attributed his success to his tough empathy with employees: "Once you have the people with you, you can make the difficult decisions that need to be made."

One final point about tough empathy: Those more apt to use it are people who really care about something. And when people care deeply about something—anything—they're more likely to show their true selves. They will not only communicate authenticity, which is the precondition for leadership, but they will show that they are doing more than just playing a role. People do not commit to executives who merely live up to the obligations of their jobs. They want more. They want someone who cares passionately about the people and the work—just as they do.

ROB GOFFEE is Emeritus Professor of Organisational Behaviour at London Business School, where he teaches in the world-renowned Senior Executive Programme. GARETH JONES is a Fellow of the Centre for Management Development at London Business School and a visiting professor at Spain's IE Business School in Madrid. Goffee and Jones consult to the boards of several global companies and are coauthors of *Why Should Anyone Be Led by You?*, *Clever*, and *Why Should Anyone Work Here?*, all published by Harvard Business Review Press.

Excerpted from "Why Should Anyone Be Led By You?" in *Harvard Business Review*, September–October 2000 (product #R00506).

5

Cracking the Code That Stalls People of Color

By Sylvia Ann Hewlett

I t's a topic that corporations once routinely ignored, then dismissed, and are only now beginning to discuss: the dearth of professionals of color in senior positions. Professionals of color hold only 11% of executive posts in corporate America.[1] Among *Fortune* 500 CEOs, only six are black, eight are Asian, and eight are Hispanic.[2]

Performance and hard work, along with sponsors, get top talent recognized and promoted, but leadership potential isn't enough to lever men and women into the executive suite. Top jobs are given to those who also look and act the part, who manifest "executive presence" (EP). According to research by the Center for Talent Innovation (CTI), EP constitutes 26% of what senior leaders say it takes to get the next promotion.[3] Yet because senior leaders are overwhelmingly Caucasian, professionals of color (African American, Asian, and Hispanic individuals) find themselves at an immediate disadvantage in trying to look, sound, and act like a leader. And the feedback that might help them do so is markedly absent at all levels of management.

Executive presence rests on three pillars: gravitas (the core characteristic, according to 67% of the 268 senior executives surveyed), an amalgam of behaviors that convey confidence, inspire trust, and bolster credibility; communication skills (according to 28%); and appearance, the filter through which communication skills and gravitas become more apparent. While they are aware of the importance of EP, men and women of color are nonetheless hard-pressed to interpret and embody aspects of a code written by and for white men.

Research from CTI finds that professionals of color, like their Caucasian counterparts, prioritize gravitas over communication and communication over appearance. Yet, "cracking the code" of executive presence presents unique challenges for professionals of color because standards of appropriate behavior, speech, and attire demand they suppress or sacrifice aspects of their cultural identity in order to conform. They overwhelmingly feel that EP at their firm is based on white male standards—African Americans, especially, were 97% more likely than their Caucasian counterparts to agree with this assessment—and that conforming to these standards requires altering their authenticity, a new version of "bleached-out professionalism" that contributes to feelings of resentment and disengagement. (See figures 2 and 3.) People of color already feel they have to work harder than their

FIGURE 2

Executive presence at my company is defined as conforming to traditionally white male standards

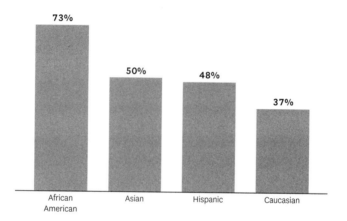

Source: Center for Talent Innovation

Caucasian counterparts just to be perceived as being on a par with them; more than half (56%) of minority professionals also feel they are held to a stricter code of EP standards.

FIGURE 3

I feel the need to compromise my authenticity to conform to executive presence standards at my company

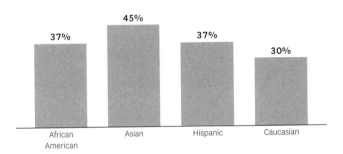

Source: Center for Talent Innovation

Executive presence further eludes professionals of color because they're not likely to get feedback on their "presentation of self." Qualitative findings affirm that their superiors, most of whom are white, hesitate to call attention to gravitas shortfalls or communication blunders for fear of coming across as racially insensitive or discriminatory. While sponsors might close this gap by specifically addressing EP issues with their high potentials, CTI's 2012 research shows that professionals of color are much less likely to have a sponsor than Caucasians (8% versus 13%).[4] When they do get feedback, they're unclear about how to act on it, particularly if they were born outside the United States. (See figure 4.) This is a serious problem for corporations that need local expertise to expand their influence in global markets.

In short, because feedback is either absent, overly vague, or contradictory, executive presence remains an inscrutable set of rules for professionals of color— rules they're judged by but cannot interpret and embody except at considerable cost to their authenticity. Consequently, in a workplace where unconscious bias continues to permeate the corridors of power and leadership is mostly white and male, professionals of color are measurably disadvantaged in their efforts to be perceived as leaders.

FIGURE 4

Unclear on how to correct issues raised by feedback

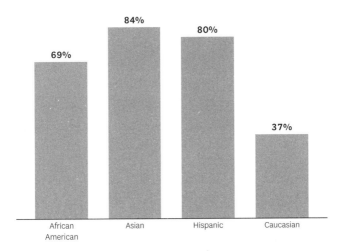

Source: Center for Talent Innovation

As America becomes more diverse at home and its companies are increasingly engaged in the global marketplace, winning in today's fiercely competitive economy requires a diverse workforce that "matches the market." Such individuals are better attuned to the unmet needs of consumers or clients like themselves. Research from CTI shows, however, that their insights need a key ingredient to reach full-scale implementation: a cadre of equally diverse leaders.[5] Yet the power of difference is missing at the top, just when it matters most.

SYLVIA ANN HEWLETT is the founder and CEO of the Center for Talent Innovation and the founder of Hewlett Consulting Partners LLC.

Notes

1. U.S. Equal Employment Opportunity Commission, *Job Patterns For Minorities And Women In Private Industry* (2009 EEO-1 National Aggregate Report), 2009.
2. DiversityInc. staff, "Where's the Diversity in *Fortune* 500 CEOs?" October 8, 2012, https://www.diversityinc.com/diversity-facts/wheres-the-diversity-in-fortune-500-ceos/.
3. S. Hewlett et al., "Cracking the Code: Executive Presence and Multicultural Professionals," Center for Talent Innovation, 2013.

4. S. Hewlett et al., "Vaulting the Color Bar: How Sponsorship Levers Multicultural Professionals into Leadership," Center for Talent Innovation, 2012.
5. S. Hewlett et al., "Innovation, Diversity, and Market Growth," Center for Talent Innovation, 2013.

Adapted from content posted on hbr.org,
January 22, 2014 (product #H00MV0).

6

For a Corporate Apology to Work, the CEO Should Look Sad

By Sarah Green Carmichael

S traight up, we made some mistakes," Whole Foods co-CEOs John Mackey and Walter Robb said in a video apology in response to an over-charging scandal.

"We weren't prepared for the crisis, and we dropped the ball," wrote Airbnb CEO Brian Chesky on the Airbnb blog in 2011, after a guest trashed a host's home.

"This should never have happened. It is simply unacceptable," said Mary Barra, CEO of GM, in one of several public apologies in the wake of safety scandals at the automaker.

The corporate apology, once a relative rarity, has become a normal part of business discourse. Stuff happens, and then we say we're sorry for it. But just because corporate apologies have become commonplace doesn't mean they're all created equal.

Two new studies shed light on what makes some apologies effective and what makes others backfire.

First, Leanne ten Brinke of the UC Berkeley Haas School of Business and Gabrielle S. Adams of the London Business School examine how expressions of emotion affect corporate apologies. Publishing in the journal *Organizational Behavior and Human Decision Processes*, they present the findings of two studies.[1]

In the first study, they looked at how investors reacted to real apologies from executives. They examined 29 online videos of apologies made between 2007 and 2011. Using an established system for distinguishing facial expressions (the Facial Action Coding System, or FACS), their researchers watched each video second by second, without sound, and tracked the expressions that flitted across the executives' faces. Were they frowning? Smiling? Looking sad? Then Brinke and Adams looked at what happened to the company's stock price after the apology. They found that for those leaders who had apologized with a smile, the stock price dropped—perhaps because the leader seemed insincere delivering his apology, or even seemed to be enjoying the suffering his company had caused. The more the person smiled, the worse his company performed.

For the leaders who appeared genuinely contrite, at first it seemed like there was no impact on stock price: The company neither performed worse nor performed better. "Normative emotions simply allow the company to move forward," they write.

But then the researchers took a closer look at CEO apologies, specifically—16 out of the 29 cases. They found that when an apology was delivered by a CEO who looked sad, the company's stock price actually rose post-apology. They determined that "a good apology can build investor confidence," especially in the long term.

To investigate this further, Brinke and Adams conducted an experiment in which they hired an actor to portray an airline CEO apologizing for a computer malfunction that canceled 140 flights, stranding thousands of passengers—a scenario based on a real Alaska Airlines snafu. They made sure his fictional apology contained all the verbal elements of a good apology: the components previous research has identified as being central to repairing relationships, including an explicit "I'm sorry," an offer of repair, an explanation, taking responsibility, and a promise of forbearance. They then recruited subjects to watch this fictional CEO apologize—either happily, sadly, or neutrally. When the CEO appeared sad, participants rated him as more sincere and were more likely to want to reconcile with him. When the CEO delivered his apology with a smile on his face—or, interestingly, a neutral expression—the study participants were less likely to trust him, and the apology even seemed to exacerbate their negative feelings.

Even seasoned leaders are likely to find delivering an apology to be an uncomfortable experience, and when we feel uncomfortable, a normal reaction is to grimace, laugh awkwardly, or even try to break the tension with a joke. Leaders (especially Americans) may also feel they can't show too much sadness or anguish but instead must present a positive front at all times. The research by Brinke and Adams reminds us how these understandable impulses can backfire.

Another paper that appeared in the *Journal of Corporate Finance* adds an interesting wrinkle to this subject.[2] Researchers Don Chance, James Cicon, and Stephen P. Ferris examined 150 press releases from 1993 to 2009 to examine how companies fared when they blamed themselves for poor performance as opposed to blaming external factors. They found that while companies are twice as likely to blame external factors when things go wrong, passing the buck results in continued financial decline. Conversely, companies that take responsibility for their missed earnings stabilize and eventually see an uptick in financial performance. (Interestingly, both groups were about equally likely to fire their CEOs.)

Why? After eliminating numerous factors, the researchers conclude that being honest and specific about the source of the problem—both characteristics of self-blaming statements—not only cheers up investors, it likely helps the company turn around the issue more quickly. Conversely, the companies that blamed external factors were often vague (blaming "economic forces" for instance) and seen as less honest (since many of their wounds had actually been self-inflicted).

The message is loud and clear: When you mess up, admit it. And look appropriately sad about it.

SARAH GREEN CARMICHAEL is a senior editor at *Harvard Business Review*. Follow her on Twitter @skgreen.

Notes

1. L. ten Brinke and G. Adams, "Saving Face? When Emotion Displays During Public Apologies Mitigate Damage to Organizational Performance," *Organizational Behavior and Human Decision Processes* 130 (2015): 1–12.
2. D. Chance, J. Cicon, and S. Ferris, "Poor Performance and the Value of Corporate Honesty," *Journal of Corporate Finance* 33 (2015): 1–18.

Adapted from "Research: For a Corporate Apology to Work, the CEO Should Look Sad," hbr.org, August 24, 2015 (product #H02AMD).

7

Are Leaders Getting Too Emotional?

An interview with Gautam Mukunda
and Gianpiero Petriglieri by Adi Ignatius
and Sarah Green Carmichael

There's a lot of crying and shouting both in politics and at the office. Gautam Mukunda of Harvard Business School and Gianpiero Petriglieri of INSEAD help us try to make sense of it all.

Sarah Green Carmichael: *It seems today, with leaders being in public more, there is an emphasis on our leaders always being authentic—that's the buzzword. And tears and shouting do seem to exude authenticity. Gianpiero, what do you make of that? Are our leaders crying and shouting to prove to us that they are real in some way?*

Gianpiero Petriglieri: I don't think people care about leaders being authentic. I think people care about leaders being consistent. Emotions are a great way to convey that you mean what you're saying.

I think we also need to make a distinction between people in positions of power, where emotional expression is always problematic because you expect a certain contained demeanor—although norms are changing, as Gautam has said—and leaders, where emotions are the whole thing. Emotions constitute the connection between people whom we follow and ourselves. So just because you happen to be in a position of visible power, that doesn't mean people regard you as a leader.

In fact, demonstrating emotion is a way of claiming, "Hey, I'm here. I think you should pay attention to this. And I am credibly voicing a concern that we should all care about." Emotions are a way in which people in power try to lead.

Adi Ignatius: *Gianpiero, let me follow up on that because you said that people don't care about their leaders being authentic, and that's basically challenging an entire industry—a sub-industry in the management business that says leaders do need to be authentic. Talk about that a little bit, particularly in the context of emotions. You almost sounded Machiavellian in what you were saying, that a leader can be whatever—they can be emotional—but the point is to be consistent and therefore effective. Can you talk more about that?*

GP: Now when you talk about authenticity, you're talking about two different things. One is spontaneity, which is to say, "I voice my feelings of the moment." Now that might—or much more likely might not—be appropriate for you as a leader.

Then, another part of authenticity means, "I voice credibly, consistently, and authentically the feelings that other people are also feeling. I am showing that we are, in a way, sharing the same concern. I am, in many ways, concerned and I care about the same things that you care about."

This is what you see leaders doing all the time. Sometimes in a Machiavellian way. But sometimes in a very genuine way. In fact, one of the very reasons why we end up following someone is because they seem to be genuinely concerned about things we care about. In politics you see it a lot. You see in political campaigns one candidate saying, "I am one of you guys. I am like you. I have your same background. I care about the same things. But this other guy, he or she is really out for themselves." And the other person is saying the same thing: "No, no, no. *I'm* actually talking about what we all care about. And this other person is out for themselves."

Whoever manages to define themselves as one of us and define the opponent as personally interested wins. So what I'm saying is we don't particularly care that our leader is expressing something that's authentic to them. What we really care about is that our leader is expressing emotions that are meaningful to us.

This is why emotional expression is a double-edged sword. Because sometimes people interpret an emotion as essentially an act of selfishness— that the emotion is really an expression of you being more preoccupied with yourself than with me.

But sometimes people interpret an emotion as an act of generosity: This really shows that you were feeling what I am also feeling. Remember Bill Clinton? In '92 there was a moment during his first campaign where he said in a rally, "I feel your pain." And that remained a legendary moment in his first election. Because he was doing what leaders always try to do, not always manipulatively or in a way that's Machiavellian, but often very genuinely to convey that the leader shares not just the same *understanding* of our situation but the same *experience* of our situation. This is what most of us have always wanted in the people that we then trust to lead, not just that they intellectually understand our circumstances, but that they feel what it's like to be in our circumstances—that they feel our pain, they feel our concerns, they aspire to our same aspirations, they desire our same desires.

That's ultimately what we care about when we say we want leaders to be authentic. We want them to have a lived understanding of our predicament. We don't just want them to express what happens to be true to them at that particular moment.

AI: *Gautam, do you agree with that? Because that seems to be a statement that empathy and emotional intelligence are really the key to leadership. I'm simplifying, but does that all make sense to you?*

Gautam Mukunda: I think empathy and emotional intelligence are extraordinarily powerful keys to leadership. You do often hear people saying—if you look at the Trump phenomenon here in the United States, for example—that they want leaders to tell them what they really think, as opposed to just telling them what the leader *thinks* they want to hear in order to gain power.

But of course it's worth noting that the same people who say this then support those who tell them what they want to hear, not in fact what they really think. So there is some level of doublethink, where, "Donald Trump says what I think, so that must be what he really thinks."

It's that ability to tell people what they want to hear in a way that they believe that you're being sincere that strikes me as being a pretty effective tool in getting power. And certainly, what I got from Gianpiero's comment is the extent to which we want our leaders to be not just self-interested but interested in the welfare of the group, of the people they lead, as much as themselves. And that, essentially, many of these contests for power involve people struggling to define their opponents as only being self-interested.

I think that's true across almost any organization. A leader who is self-interested is one whose followers will be much less likely to lead. But to me, then, you get this question: What are emotions?

Even a very skilled actor, for example, finds it difficult to fake tears on cue. That's something that even professional actors can struggle with. So when President Obama cries over children who are murdered in a school, there is a sense that he's revealing some deeply held emotion.

It is also striking, of course, that so much of the conservative response to that statement was to suggest that he had onions or something under the podium that were allowing him to fake it, both because I think the people saying this realize how powerful it was to see a president break down in tears and because it reveals something about themselves—that they felt that the murder of many innocent children was somehow something that wouldn't move a person to tears.

GP: You see, I don't think people just want to hear leaders tell them what they think. I think people want to see leaders show them what they themselves feel. They want to see their leaders express the feeling that they also sense to be true.

Of course, not everyone shares the same feelings. The example Gautam brings up—President Obama crying—it's an extremely powerful message. And it humanizes a leader. For people who share the same dismay, the same discomfort, that humanization actually enhances his leadership. And for people who oppose his understanding of the situation, for people who don't share his sentiments, that humanization diminishes his leadership. This is where emotional expression is always a double-edged sword. Because the people who share the sentiments you are expressing will actually feel closer to you and, therefore, feel that you are more of a leader. And the people who don't share those sentiments will suddenly feel more distant from you, and they will suspect that you are being manipulative, Machiavellian, and whatnot.

In that moment, you have a man who occupies one of the most powerful positions of leadership in the world facing, on his watch, a tragedy. A tragedy that, despite all his power, he cannot reverse. He is therefore expressing frustration at the limitation of that power—a frustration that's not just his own but is also expressed on behalf of a large group of people who probably feel that it is a tragedy that could easily have been prevented with political will, with political action. And it isn't prevented simply because there is not enough political will to implement the changes that you would need for gun control.

SGC: *In that moment, President Obama crying—would that moment have been different if he were a female president? Is there something different about when you see a man break down that way and a female leader of that stature break down that way?*

GM: I mean, surely, without a doubt. The criticism that someone is too emotional is one of the classic gendered tropes that are used to go after female leaders. It's worth noting that when Hillary Clinton cried a little bit in 2008 in New Hampshire it was highlighted as one of the high points of her campaign. This was one of the moments that turned it around and put her back into the race against Obama in 2008.

But it's illustrative that one of the criticisms of Hillary is that she's robotic. Right? So that was a breakthrough of that facade.

I think for most women leaders it's a much riskier proposition to cry than for a male leader to do so. It just plays into gendered stereotypes that opponents of that leader can use to weaken them very rapidly.

SGC: *We should also probably mention here that there may be racial stereotypes. There may be other emotions, like maybe anger, that Obama might get in trouble for expressing that Hillary would not.*

GM: Without a doubt. On those few occasions when Barack Obama has revealed how he thinks about the way he presents himself—and it's clear that he is someone who thinks deeply about this kind of thing and is very self-reflective on these issues—he has said that, above all else, the thing that he most strives to avoid is being perceived as the angry black man. That's the phrase that he used. And that this is a profound force that is shaping how he wants to be seen.

He essentially feels that visible expressions of anger are, because of racial dynamics in the United States, almost entirely off limits to him as a leader. And in fact, if you note, before he was reelected, anger was in fact entirely off limits to him as a leader. I can't think of any time that he expressed anger in those first four years. What we've started to see after he was reelected, and particularly in the past year, is that he essentially has more freedom to express these emotions. And he is taking advantage of it quite powerfully on some occasions.

AI: *So given what you said, would you advise female executives to hold their emotions in check? That it may not be fair, but society will still hold it against them if they cry in public in front of their teams?*

GM: First, I would advise any leader, male or female, to work pretty hard to do that. The power of these moments is at least in part precisely because they are rare.

John Boehner's tendency to break down in tears became a punch line in Washington. I don't think it was an asset to his leadership. When Barack Obama did it, it was striking because we had never seen a president do something like that, that I can recall.

So male or female, I would say, if you are extraordinarily emotional at all times, that is likely to be a handicap for you as a leader at least to some extent. I would tell female executives that it is deeply unfair, but they are being judged more harshly.

And they surely know that better than I ever could; I've never spoken with a woman leader who wasn't well aware of that fact and who hadn't thought through the fact that they were being judged by standards that their male counterparts were not.

But it is too easy to use gendered attacks—to argue that someone is overly emotional and not thinking things through—against a female leader, or any female leader in a contentious situation where there are people trying to undercut her, to not be extremely cautious of that concern.

SGC: *Gianpiero, do you have anything to add either about the anger issue or the weeping issue?*

GP: I generally think outrage is a lot easier to fake than sadness. And perhaps a lot easier to mistrust, frankly. See, I think we risk spending too much tension under the stereotypes about what you should or shouldn't do.

I would tend to agree that, especially for a senior or a visible leader in politics or business, it's a good rule of thumb to have a relatively contained demeanor. I also think that anyone who wants to really be a leader—not just call themselves one—

has to have some kind of relationship with their emotional life. They ought to be able to ask themselves not just, "Do I express emotions or not?" but to be a little bit more sophisticated with themselves and with others to ask, "How do I express emotions?"

If you are attentive to the undercurrent of organizational lives, emotions are constantly being expressed. When I work with senior management teams, my first question is never, "Do you openly express emotions or not?" My first question is, "How do you tend to express emotions?"

So, for example, one classic way to scream your divergence with a group's opinion is simply not to show up. Or to show up late to a meeting and say nothing when everyone else is very animated. That's a very overt, very visible expression of disappointment or even aggression. Now, whether that's discussed, whether that's decoded, whether that's verbalized is a different thing. Just because we aren't verbalizing our emotions or melting into tears doesn't mean we aren't expressing strong emotions or that we aren't expressing emotions appropriately. Too detached of an emotional response can very often be extremely inappropriate and extremely ineffective.

So I think, as a leader, the more important questions are: Do you know what you're feeling? And do you know whose feelings those are? Do you know why you're feeling that way? Are you interpreting those feelings just as an expression of your emotional state of the moment? Or are you able to think more deeply about what those feelings are telling you about what's happening around you—what's happening to the people that you're responsible for? And can you make sense of and then articulate them in a way that is useful, in a way that actually advances the task?

GAUTAM MUKUNDA is an assistant professor in the Organizational Behavior Unit of Harvard Business School. He received his Ph.D. from MIT in political science. His first book is *Indispensable: When Leaders Really Matter* (Harvard Business Review Press, 2012). GIANPIERO PETRIGLIERI is an associate professor of organizational behavior at INSEAD, where he directs the Management Acceleration Programme, the school's flagship executive program for emerging leaders. A medical doctor and psychiatrist by training, he researches and practices leadership development. Follow him on Twitter @gpetriglieri. ADI IGNATIUS is the editor in chief of *Harvard Business Review*. SARAH GREEN CARMICHAEL is a senior editor at *Harvard Business Review*. Follow her on Twitter @skgreen.

Adapted from "Are Leaders Getting Too Emotional?"
on *HBR IdeaCast* (podcast), March 17, 2016.

Index

How to be human at work.

HBR's Emotional Intelligence Series features smart, essential reading on the human side of professional life from the pages of *Harvard Business Review*. Each book in the series offers uplifting stories, practical advice, and research from leading experts on how to tend to our emotional well-being at work.

Harvard Business Review Emotional Intelligence Series

Available in paperback or ebook format. The specially priced six-volume set includes:

- Mindfulness
- Resilience
- Influence and Persuasion

- Authentic Leadership
- Happiness
- Empathy

The most important management ideas all in one place.

We hope you enjoyed this book from *Harvard Business Review*. For the best ideas HBR has to offer turn to HBR's 10 Must Reads Boxed Set. From books on leadership and strategy to managing yourself and others, this 6-book collection delivers articles on the most essential business topics to help you succeed.

HBR's 10 Must Reads Series

The definitive collection of ideas and best practices on our most sought-after topics from the best minds in business.

- Change Management
- Collaboration
- Communication
- Emotional Intelligence
- Innovation
- Leadership
- Making Smart Decisions

- Managing Across Cultures
- Managing People
- Managing Yourself
- Strategic Marketing
- Strategy
- Teams
- The Essentials

hbr.org/mustreads

Buy for your team, clients, or event.
Visit hbr.org/bulksales for quantity discount rates.